# EGO: Edging Golf Out

# EGO: Edging Golf Out

Chuck Thompson

© 2024 Chuck Thompson
All rights reserved.

ISBN: 978-1-7363185-3-9
Library of Congress Control Number: 2023913171
LCCN Imprint Name: Jacksonville, Florida

*I dedicate this book to my amazing wife, Zarita "Cherry" Thompson, and my four children, Chaz, Christian, Coley, and Azha. I am truly blessed with two angels and three champions. It is because of their sacrifices and support that I am able to realize my dream of making a difference in the world by helping others. Cherry has devoted her life to me and our children, giving us the joy of being members of a loving, happy family. She is just as proud of her titles of nurturer, wife, and mother as I am of mine as father, husband, and founder of MMC®. Together, we have found balance.*

*Cherry, I am not worthy of you, but I am eternally grateful for your love, and I am honored to be your husband; I know I married up. Thank you for everything, but most of all, thank you for saying yes. I love you, baby.*

# TABLE OF CONTENTS

| | Introduction | xi |
|---|---|---|
| 1 | Egos and Missed Opportunities | 1 |
| 2 | Career Development | 31 |
| 3 | Personal Development | 56 |
| 4 | Developing New Skill Sets | 103 |
| 5 | Developing Your Business | 132 |
| 6 | Developing Your Growth Tool Kit | 153 |
| 7 | Developing Leadership Skills | 181 |
| 8 | Sustainable Development | 203 |
| 9 | Healthy Egos and New Opportunities | 235 |

*"The greatest danger for most of us is not that our aim is too high and we miss it, but that it is too low and we reach it."*

—Michelangelo

# INTRODUCTION

*EGO: Edging Golf Out* is a follow-up to my first book, *Golf: The Untapped Market*. *Golf: The Untapped Market* was written to provide owners, operators, and golf professionals with the tools, techniques, and resources to grow their businesses. *EGO: Edging Golf Out* was written to provide owners, operators, golf professionals, touring professionals, associations, organizations, manufacturers, retailers, investors, advertisers, sponsors, donors, and golf enthusiasts in general with additional tools, techniques, and resources to help them grow their businesses with a strong emphasis on the shared objective of saving and growing the game and working collaboratively toward that goal.

After two decades in the golf industry, I have not witnessed any significant growth worth mentioning yet, but I constantly hear chatter about how the game is expanding. Every day, my team and I are in the trenches with facility owners and operators, working hard to attract new golfers, not recycled golfers from another facility, to develop their businesses. Since 2006, my team and I have partnered with more than 500 golf facilities, and since 1991, we have worked with over 1000 businesses. I launched Mulligan Marketing Concepts (MMC®) originally to acquire members from untapped markets for upscale health clubs. Between the two industries, we have acquired millions of members and have raised almost one billion US dollars between immediate cash and backend/operational revenue for our clients. Because of this achievement, and given the two industries I have worked in, health clubs and golf facilities, I am confident in saying, "I know a little about growing businesses and egos."

When I was in my late twenties, I founded MMC® to grow health clubs' membership. I chose this name because these businesses needed a second opportunity that would not cost them anything to try something new. At the time, I had never been on a golf course and had never imagined I would ever play the game. I was more of a full-contact athlete. The name was appropriate for a second chance at growing their business, and maybe even a more poignant reason was most health-club owners preferred the back nine over putting in the work to grow their business.

MMC® took off at a snail's pace because most thought it was too far outside the box. However, after a few years of fortitude, the company and our acquisition campaign swept the nation. I was already blessed, or should I say possibly cursed, with an ego, but when hundreds of owners, general managers, and their employees began praising me for turning around their business, my ego exploded. I was still young and full of myself as it was, and then all of a sudden, I started getting all of these platitudes, and I let them go to my head. As the old saying goes, "I was starting to believe my own press."

My friends and family noticed it at first, and then it started affecting my business. I remained oblivious to the new me, but the change in attitude and personality was evident to everyone else. I became cocky, arrogant, self-absorbed, and difficult to work with. Everything had to be my way or the highway.

I was still acquiring new clients as a result of the campaign's strength, but I wasn't engaging with my clients on the same level as I had in the past. Fortunately for me, my ego also makes me want to be the very best I can be, which means I am constantly analyzing anything and everything. My dad had told me when I was a kid, "Chuck, if everyone around you is a dummy, the dummy may be closer than you think." At that time, I began to believe that everyone around me was lazy and inept, so I knew I needed to focus on myself since I was becoming someone neither I nor anybody else liked. I figured it was a good place to start because so many people had told me I had become egotistical. Actually, when I heard that in the beginning, I was ecstatic since I had read that having a strong ego was beneficial. What I did not realize at the time was that the ego has two sides: a healthy side and a destructive side.

While I have made progress in taming my ego over the years, I must admit that there have been instances in recent times when it resurfaced unexpectedly. Personal development is an ongoing journey, akin to pursuing any worthwhile goal. It demands hard work and perseverance. I feel a sense of shame in acknowledging these vulnerabilities and imperfections openly because my ego urges me to conceal any flaws and minimize my destructive behavior. However, yielding to this internal voice would only nourish my ego, rather than managing it.

In this book, I delve into this sensitive subject, primarily laying the groundwork in chapter 1. It is important to emphasize that my intention is not to accuse, blame, or insinuate that others possess an inflated ego. Instead, I share my personal experiences and the knowledge I have gained through my exploration of the ego. If you discover something valuable within these pages, I encourage you to apply it to your own journey of personal development. At the very least, it will enhance your understanding of your customers and foster stronger customer relationships.

Understanding the profound impact of our ego is crucial, as it has the power to shape our lives, businesses, and industries. By recognizing the triggers that allow the ego to dominate our interactions and relationships, we can embark on a transformative journey. Throughout this book, I will share practical techniques I personally employ to manage my ego effectively. It is important to note that significant changes take time, as the ego is not constructed overnight. However, with awareness and consistent effort, you will witness tangible improvements in your conversations and relationships sooner than you might expect.

Prioritizing personal development is key, as it directly influences the success of our businesses. The book follows a natural progression, beginning with personal growth, extending to our careers, the businesses we represent, the growth of our organizations, and ultimately, the advancement of the entire industry. Each stage of development yields multiplied dividends, much like compound interest. Moreover, the tools and approaches presented can be applied at various levels within the industry pyramid.

Before you dismiss this book, I urge you to silence the voice in your head that discourages you; it is simply your ego attempting to resist change. Embrace the journey ahead, enjoy the read, and let the transformation unfold.

With this book, my ultimate objective is to provide valuable assistance by sharing the tools that have greatly benefited me throughout my career. These tried-and-tested tools are guaranteed to enhance your business, advance your professional journey, and elevate the game itself.

*Note: This book delves into sensitive subjects, and the nonfiction stories shared are intended solely as fables from which valuable lessons can be learned. As the saying goes, "Any fool can learn from experience, but it takes a wise person to learn from other people's experiences." To preserve the integrity of the lessons and avoid any unintended embarrassment, the names of individuals and facilities will not be disclosed throughout this book, except for my team and I. Anonymity will be maintained to ensure the focus remains on the insights and knowledge imparted.*

Disclaimer: I have been a dedicated student throughout my life, devoting at least two hours every day to learning. During my nearly twenty years on the road, I maximized my study time by listening to educational, inspirational, and motivational material for up to ten hours a day in my car. I have immersed myself in thousands of books, attended countless seminars and workshops, and continuously stayed updated on sales, marketing, and personal development. Approximately 90 percent of my learning comes from these three disciplines.

When I write a book, I draw upon a wealth of knowledge accumulated over the span of forty years through my memories, extensive note-taking, and personal experiences. Writing a book was never part of my original plan, let alone writing two. I have internalized and absorbed the knowledge I have acquired over the years. It would be both impractical and more likely impossible to list all the resources that have influenced me, as they are numerous and varied. Throughout the years, I have assimilated the wisdom shared by hundreds, if not thousands, of experts across various fields. These wise individuals, including authors, philosophers, sages, scholars, professors, psychologists, scientists, doctors, and motivational and inspirational teachers, have been sharing these timeless principles since as early as 1500 BC. Each of them has offered their own distinct perspective, yet they all converge on the same fundamental truths. Like me, they have dedicated themselves to illuminating these principles, each in their own remarkable manner.

This repetition and exposure to diverse perspectives have deeply ingrained these principles within me. I want to underscore the fact that the essence of personal development shared in this book predominantly draws from the vast well of wisdom crafted by others. I am humbly grateful and deeply appreciative for having the privilege of sharing with you the valuable insights I have gained from the work of others. The only credit I claim is for applying these principles to our unique circumstances within the golf industry.

# 1

## EGOS AND MISSED OPPORTUNITIES

The ego can be understood as the "I" within us, representing our self-perception. It encompasses our characteristics, beliefs, and behaviors, operating at a subconscious level. The ego serves as a protector of our identity, fiercely safeguarding established beliefs, attitudes, and behaviors.

Our ego also plays a role in how we present ourselves to others and how they perceive us. It forms our persona, the image we project to the world. The ego is an essential aspect of our nature, but it consists of both positive and negative aspects. The negative side of the ego manifests as a "me first" mentality, seeking attention and approval at all costs. It gives rise to greed and selfishness, leading us to prioritize our own interests above those of others. When we feel misunderstood, deceived, disregarded, or belittled, the ego responds with anger. It exhibits self-centered and immature thinking, focusing solely on its own desires without regard for others' feelings, thoughts, or needs.

People with large egos often have a fragile opinion of themselves, which is constantly under threat. Their egos frequently lead them to believe they are highly significant, solely based on their own convictions. However, in reality, nobody is inherently more significant than others. Your importance diminishes notably unless you provide value and service to others. It is crucial to control your pride and learn to regulate it; otherwise, people will not be inclined to spend time with you unless absolutely necessary. Arrogance arises from excessive pride, which leads one away from humility and further distances them from meaningful human connections. Such a way of living is not advisable.

Many times, when we are young, it is natural for us to be full of conceit and have a false sense of pride. If we do not address it through self-development, life will eventually correct us. It might be challenging to tolerate scrutiny and criticism while engaging in self-examination, but we must avoid being vain and overly obsessed with our image. Embarrassment and failure are perceived as more serious or destructive only by the ego; however, it is essential to remember that everyone faces failures and difficulties.

In our youth, we may often be triggered by words, such as being told we could not do something despite our belief and determination to prove otherwise. We may also face judgments about not fitting a certain type or mode, or being labeled with qualities we do not possess. In such instances, people make snap judgments about us without giving us an opportunity to try or respond. It is possible that you, too, have experienced incidents in your past that, at the time, might have seemed minor but were similar to those mentioned in the previous sentence. These incidents have influenced you and your ego, ultimately shaping you into the person you are today.

Our ego often causes us to believe that we are being ignored, that our thoughts are not respected, or that the other person is acting in this way due to stereotypes or prejudices. Frequently, one may not consider how the information they convey is being received or how it is perceived by the other person since they are preoccupied with their own tasks or concerns.

The positive side of our ego, on the other hand, is empowering and uplifting. It radiates good energy, instilling a belief in our ability to make a difference and help others. It exudes a joyful and loving energy that inspires trust in those around us. It embodies an attitude of "I can do it," encouraging us to strive for greatness in everything we undertake. A healthy sense of self-worth and confidence emerges, motivating us to value both people and things in our lives.

The ability to push oneself to achieve goals, even when faced with obstacles and skepticism, is indeed crucial for success. However, it is equally important to recognize when one's ego starts hindering progress and growth. While egos can have their benefits, it is essential to have a balanced perspective.

When seeking guidance from mentors with strong egos, it is worthwhile to observe how they conduct themselves in various situations. While they may not always exhibit compassion or understanding toward you, their behavior toward others, such as customers or individuals they admire, can provide valuable insights. It is important to strive for a broader understanding and learn from everyone, regardless of their ego.

In life, encountering varying personalities and egos is inevitable. Therefore, focusing on personal awareness and development becomes paramount. By fostering self-awareness and continuously working on personal growth, one can navigate ego-driven dynamics effectively and ensure that progress remains unhindered. Ultimately, it is the pursuit of self-improvement and understanding that paves the way for personal and professional advancement.

The ego system is triggered not only by fear but also by achievement and winning. It is crucial to avoid allowing arrogance to convince you that you are superior, the best, and that no one is better than you. When someone is consistently arrogant and looks down on others, they are unable to recognize the opportunities and successes that can elevate them. If our ego convinces us we are always right and better than we truly are, we become disconnected from the world around us, creating a divide between reality and everything else. Our abilities and skills can serve as either destructive weapons for our ego or constructive tools to achieve our objectives.

People with large egos start to live in their own fantasy worlds. They believe they are making great strides when, in fact, they are doing nothing. Even when someone completes a small or simple task, their ego tells them that they are exceptional, wonderful, or fantastic. The ego is speaking here. I always say, "Never confuse motion with momentum." You are not doing anything until you are making progress or moving the needle. If your ego falsely convinces you that you are making progress when you are not, you need to learn how to control it. Success can be exhilarating, but sustaining it requires clear thinking. If we believe we already know everything, we cannot learn anything.

I want to share an experience with you of how the destructive side of my own ego almost cost me a huge opportunity. In 2017, I released my first book, *Golf: The Untapped Market, Why the Pros Are Failing to Grow the Game.* The book's goal was to educate all golf professionals, affiliated and nonaffiliated, about the four segments of golfers: core, avid, casual, and non-golfer. I had added the category of "non-golfer" to the other three categories, that is, core, avid, and casual, almost twenty years prior to the book's release, when I was still in the health-club business targeting the deconditioned market, that is, nonusers. A non-golfer, as used in this context, is a consumer who has purchased golf-related items such as golf gear, golf paraphernalia, subscriptions to golf magazines, and so on but has yet to make a genuine commitment to the game.

I outlined in detail why the game was withering and not growing as everyone in the industry had hoped. I also gave a long-term plan to turn the industry around by simply targeting untapped segments of the market. Tiger Woods was able to grow the game similarly, but our method takes a different approach. Our strategy involves meticulous data collection, comprehensive consumer profiling, and market-tested introductory offers, all without relying on factors such as popularity, charisma, good looks, or undeniable talent for the game, which Tiger possessed. Our method is firmly rooted in the analysis of both quantitative and qualitative data.

Quantitative data helps comprehend the numbers in each market, including but not limited to market size, what customers (other than golfers) were willing to spend each round, and the realistic number of casual and non-golfers who could be harvested from the researched market. To prequalify your prospects, qualitative data is required. Every company, regardless of industry, has an avatar, if you will, of their ideal prospect. No one wants to squander marketing dollars on customers who will not benefit their company. A campaign cannot be regarded as successful if it disrupts the business's culture. This is why understanding what data is required and how to analyze it is essential for establishing a successful campaign.

Most importantly, I was extremely cautious to demonstrate my respect for the hardworking professionals and my empathy toward their position. I made it clear that I had unwavering confidence that golf professionals were doing their absolute best with the tools and resources at their disposal. I emphasized that no one is more qualified to operate a golf facility than a golf professional. Golf professionals study management methods, course maintenance, public relations, and a variety of other topics related to golf course operations. These are skill sets that I do not possess, nor do I have any interest in acquiring, neither in the past nor in the present. This remains a factual statement.

The point I made in the book was that no one was teaching or giving them the tools and resources they needed to garner customers from these elusive segments of the market. Worse, there was no conversation on targeting these segments until MMC® entered the room. In the leadership's defense, it would have been hard for them to help those employed in the golf industry acquire casual and non-golfers because they were just beginning to understand these segments. The book was meant to teach readers "how to grow your business, career, and the game," rather than a "who's to blame." Most people received the message, but some were so upset by the subtitle that they threw the book away and criticized the model without even turning a single page.

This dismayed group based their entire opinion on the subtitle of the book and used what they had heard through the grapevine about the price point we use as a "hook," to grab the attention of our partnering facilities' market, as the reason for their contempt for the book. Had they just suspended their ego for a minute and read the book, they would have realized the book was written as a tool to assist them in advancing their career as well as the game.

The majority of the reviews were extremely positive, and I got a lot of wonderful feedback. However, there were a small number of people, mostly consisting of golf professionals, who chastised the book, particularly the subtitle of the book. Apparently, they had major issues with the part that read, "Why the Pros Are Failing to Grow the Game." These critics assumed that I was referring to golf professionals, which I was not. I was referring to professionals in the industry from all disciplines, whether they were marketing professionals, sales professionals, consultants, managers, leaders, and so on—in short, those who were considered professionals in the industry. As hard as it may be to fathom, it is not a given to outsiders that golf professionals assume sole responsibility for growing the game.

To demonstrate my ignorance, I should note that, at the time I wrote the book *Golf: The Untapped Market*, I had been working in the golf business for more than ten years, had collaborated with hundreds of owners and operators, and had never once been told who, whom, or what organization was in charge of growing the game. I heard the phrase, "Grow the Game" tossed around a lot, like a hot potato, but I never imagined one association assumed the growth of the entire industry fell under their responsibility, nor was I aware that their members assumed personal responsibility for the mammoth task. My naiveté had me believing it was everyone's responsibility—professionals from all facets of the industry including manufacturers as well as retailers, associations, the Professional Golfers' Association (PGA) Tour, LIV Golf, marketers, salespeople, and, yes, golf professionals. I am not an insider, I do not follow the game, nor do I follow the politics. I am just a casual golfer who happens to have more than thirty years of expertise and experience in growing over one thousand member-based businesses by penetrating untapped markets. The subtitle was meant to encompass "all" professionals in the industry. In short, I just thought it sounded great and was a catchy subtitle for the book.

Similar to how saving and growing the game is not solely a golf professional's responsibility, neither is saving or growing a business solely the golf professional's responsibility. Everyone needs to make a contribution of some kind. Any business that hopes to grow exponentially needs everyone on its payroll to put in their fair share of effort. Leadership begins with the owners taking the initiative and leading by example, contributing in every way they can, including making wise decisions based on accurate data and facts. All employees such as the superintendent, general manager, golf professional(s), bookkeeper, bartender, wait staff, counter staff, cooks, beverage cart drivers, and so on play a significant role on the business's success or failure. "A chain is only as strong as its weakest link," as the saying goes. Teamwork is necessary to save and grow the game, and saving and growing the game starts with growing and saving every business in the industry.

Although some may think that MMC®'s approach is not ideal, the foundation is strong, the principles are solid, and our growth initiative has been proven time and time again to work. By no means am I suggesting that this approach is the only option. I don't claim to have all the answers, I do welcome any constructive input for enhancing any or all facets of the growth initiative—as long as they go beyond mere words and are carried out in a way that advances the game and the industry as a whole. To me, "Saving and Growing the Game" needs to be a team endeavor where the emphasis is on outcomes rather than egos.

After the book had been out for some time, I received a call from an owner who had previously held an important position with one of the industry's major organizations. Unbeknownst to me, my ego was triggered, and I unconsciously classified him as a "hater." This is a common self-preservation maneuver that our egos employ to shield ourselves from experiencing emotional discomfort. At that time, I had just run a series of advertisements on a national radio station. To my surprise, I received a call from my representative who informed me that the station had received a request from this organization expressing their preference for our ads not to be aired in close proximity to each other. Coincidentally, I had also become aware of a few golf professionals expressing discontent with the subtitle of my book shortly before receiving this call.

Without my awareness, my ego had become inflated, leading it to cloud my judgment during the unfolding situation. However, upon careful reflection, I recognized the validity and fairness of their request. Yet, at that particular moment, my thinking was clouded, and I failed to approach the situation with an open mind. It is only with hindsight and a clearer perspective that I could recognize the rationality of their concerns.

When my ego entered the picture, I became defensive and began preparing for an argument. I was adamant about proving myself and my beliefs correct. I was filled with self-doubt and worry about not being able to find the right words to make my points. In my mind, I had already classified him as a hater, and I assumed his call was to criticize me and the program I had been constructing for over twenty-five years. I instantly began looking for strategies to preserve control, direction, and outcome of the talk. Upon my return call, I was fully prepared and motivated to take decisive action.

After the usual greetings and introductions, he began the conversation by expressing how much he appreciated my book. As you can imagine, this compliment caught me off guard because it was unexpected and had not been factored into my ego strategy for dealing with this nonbeliever. I listened closely as he went on, ready for him to launch his attack. He told me about his facility and the issues he and his staff had been facing and how he saw a lot of merit in what I had stated in the book, even though he was not entirely convinced about the program and wanted to discuss some options and adjust certain things to his specific circumstance. *Ah ha!* My ego exclaimed and then added, *Just as I thought, he believes your program is insufficient to complete the task. He believes that because of his background and history in the industry, he understands more about "your" business than you do.*

I had already tuned him out and was mentally going over my rebuttals and plan of attack as he proceeded. He told me about some improvements and ideas he had that he thought could help the campaign's success. Despite being engaged with my defense, I heard his proposals and immediately shut them down because I had tried them before and they had diminished the campaign's outcomes in the past. However, I must admit that during that conversation, I conveyed a sense of pride and defensiveness, immediately criticizing and finding fault in everything he proposed. It is essential to emphasize that he remained composed, professional, kind, and remarkably patient throughout the entire dialogue. Unfortunately, my own ego-driven agenda consumed me, and I cannot say the same about my own behavior. In a moment of arrogance, I conceitedly declared, "If you think you know so much about it, you should just run the campaign on your own."

Deep down, I was well aware that neither he nor anyone else could successfully execute the campaign independently without causing severe damage to their business and future earnings. In my mind, I believed that he was the ideal candidate to demonstrate to the industry the catastrophic consequences of attempting to run the campaign without the intellectual property, experience, and guidance of MMC®.

Yet again, he surprised me with his gracious response to my egotistical remark, stating, "That is not my intention, and I would not have reached out to you if I were not genuinely interested in the campaign."

As we hung up, my ego gave me an *Atta boy! You showed him who the expert was. Are you kidding me? You have spent your entire life developing this program, you have had more than one thousand or so enormously successful campaigns under your belt, you have helped millions of people get healthy and take up the game of golf, and he is going to tell you how to execute your golfer acquisition campaign? He thinks that because you are not a golf professional and he has decades on you in the golf industry, you have no idea what you are doing?* My ego continued, *Well, you are the expert, the greatest; no one has your track record, and no one has ever successfully grown as many golf courses as you have.*

Keep in mind that none of this gibberish was ever spoken or said by either party in the conversation. This delusion was just in my head. The guy was completely focused on the task at hand. He was a consummate professional by all accounts. Looking back, I am confident he was an expert at dealing with overinflated egos since he never, not once, lost track of the conversation's purpose. During the call, he made no mention of his previous triumphs, nor did he appear pompous or conceited. His concerns were valid, but my ego decided to view them as challenges to my level of competence. He was doing what any wise businessman would do: thinking creatively and brainstorming ideas.

I, on the other hand, did not make the most of the chat since my head was too far up my own backside. Hubris and preconceived notions nearly jeopardized everything. Luckily for everyone concerned, he saw past my ego and focused on the value the program provided, and he contacted me a few days later with the decision to proceed.

Fortunately for both me and MMC®, our performance exceeded all expectations, which managed to overshadow my initial poor impression. The campaign not only generated over a million dollars in immediate revenue but also attracted approximately 5,000 new players. Subsequently, we successfully launched two additional campaigns, each achieving significant success in their own right.

It is worth noting that had both of us allowed our egos to interfere, thousands of individuals would have missed out on the joy of a firsthand experience with the game, the community would have missed out on the opportunity, the game would have suffered a loss, vendors would have missed out on new opportunities, and on and on. Moreover, my team and I would have missed out on the rewards we received for orchestrating one of MMC®'s top ten campaigns in our history. Additionally, I would have missed the honor of knowing someone who shares an equal, if not greater, passion for the game and the industry. This individual is truly remarkable and possesses an extensive knowledge of public relations that surpasses my own capabilities. I have gleaned invaluable insights from our interactions and remain genuinely grateful for our friendship.

This episode really took me by surprise. I had not experienced these thoughts and feelings in decades. Of course, we all harbor self-conscious worries and insecurities, but some individuals can manage these thoughts and not let them affect their lives and decision-making; others let their egos guide them. Ego is best described as a persistent preoccupation and concern with one's own self-worth, importance, status, value, and so on. The ego tends to exaggerate your contribution, your value, your importance, etc. Self-importance is humankind's greatest enemy. We, professionals who work in the golf industry should quit if we prioritize our own sense of importance, self-worth, and/or self-image over the advancement of the game. It is incumbent upon us as stewards of the game to ensure that it does grow, as it is required to do. This is what I was doing when I fielded this information call. My ego had me turn a simple call that was initiated by a prospect into an imaginary argument about the validity of MMC®'s golfer acquisition campaign and my contribution to the golf industry.

Let me ask you a question: have you ever caught yourself being more concerned with being right than with what was best for you, for your facility, or for the game? We have this idealized conception of who we ought to be, and we exert every effort to convey that picture. It makes us defensive when someone questions that perception. Then our ego starts to rule our thoughts and decisions.

I will put this into perspective by illustrating just the financial aspects of this partnership that I was perfectly ready and willing to walk away from before even listening to the first word. MMC® covers all of the up-front cost of the setup and launch of our golfer acquisition campaigns, which in most cases runs in the tens of thousands of US dollars. We put up this money so the course owner does not have to. It is called "risk reversal." MMC® accepts 100 percent of the risk. These are hard costs that we factor into every project, and as the campaign builds momentum and success, we have variable expenses such as benchmark goals for the project manager and their team.

Our model incentivizes everyone on performance to encourage total commitment to the project's success. There are no inflated salaries or guarantees here at MMC®. If the campaigns hit their benchmarks, the team is rewarded accordingly. This incentive ensures everyone who is working on a project has skin in the game, and they work as a team focused on a common goal.

On average, our campaigns yield approximately $250,000 in immediate cash within a span of ninety days. Additionally, they generate a substantial range of $200,000 to $500,000 in annual backend revenue over two or three years. This successful outcome not only enables us to recover our initial investment but also allows for the realization of a modest profit. This project closed out just over $1,000,000 in cash collected and at least $2,000,000 in future revenue. In retrospect, I realize that my ego, with all its folly, almost led me to dismiss a lucrative multimillion-dollar opportunity without any valid grounds or factual basis.

Remarkably, this single campaign generated equivalent revenue to what would typically require four campaigns, while our expenses were halved compared to launching four separate campaigns. This, my friend, is how incredibly destructive an overinflated ego can be and how it can ruin a career, a business, and even an entire industry.

The potential disaster that we managed to avoid was my sarcastic remark being taken seriously and the campaign being launched solely based on the price point. This would have had the complete opposite effect of what my ego had falsely presented. Such a campaign would have tarnished the reputation of MMC® because the industry associates certain price points with the marketing hooks we use in our golfer acquisition campaigns.

Whenever a facility attempts a similar approach independently and subsequently fails, with the facility being either sold at a later date or, even worse, going bankrupt, some people tend to attribute it to the campaign in contrast to the human error that would undoubtedly have been the cause of failure. Therefore, had he launched it and it turned into a disaster, we would have unjustly received the blame, leading to a significant blow to our image. Once again, I am immensely thankful for the clear thinking that prevailed in this situation.

His contributions extended far beyond expectations. Not only did he film educational videos for us to share with our clients, but he also wrote compelling articles about the program, emphasizing the significant positive impact it had on his own business and the enhanced experience it provided to all players involved. His dedication to advocate for the program extended to sharing it with numerous facilities that subsequently partnered with MMC®. In the few short years that I have known him, I cannot overstate the profound impact he has had on the game and the industry as a whole.

In fact, as I was writing this book, I could not help but consider him as a potential coauthor. His wealth of untapped knowledge and expertise could undoubtedly benefit the industry in countless ways. While MMC® excels at acquiring golfers, fostering long-term relationships, and cultivating them into passionate advocates for the game and their home facility, we recognize that the industry requires the active involvement of owners, general managers, golf professionals, superintendents, and various other professional services that extend beyond our core capabilities.

In essence, the industry requires more individuals like him, individuals unafraid to challenge the status quo, individuals willing to explore unconventional approaches, and above all, individuals capable of setting their egos aside in pursuit of what is truly best for the business and the game. Together, with leaders like him and a collective mindset focused on growth and innovation, we can shape the future of the golf industry and propel it to new heights.

As I previously stated, I had not had these thoughts or sentiments in decades, and after my mind cleared, I thoroughly investigated why and how this might have occurred. It was not about the money, because I have managed campaigns that generated nearly $2,000,000. Furthermore, even with all the data, research, and experience in the world, you never know when a campaign is going to explode like that. I knew, without a shadow of a doubt, that the campaign was going to do well, but that is par for the course. "What was it?" I kept asking myself. The only explanation I could think of was that it could have been his previous position in the industry.

I found myself competing with an imaginary opponent, even though he never mentioned the organization or his previous role. Due to the recent pushback I had received on the book, I automatically associated the two in my mind. I imagined that he, representing a large institution, was coming to attack me, and I prepared myself for battle. What a paradox! In my mind, I was ready to defend my program against 130 years of entrenched traditional thinking on growing the game. However, it was an organization I deeply respected and desperately wanted to collaborate with to provide MMC®'s growth initiative with distribution channels it needed to achieve my goal of fostering career and business growth in the game on a large scale. Instead of remaining humble and gracious, my ego took control, leading me to become defensive, insecure, and combative. I am grateful that this scenario unfolded solely in my imagination.

Upon realizing my own foolishness, I instinctively resorted to my usual response whenever I make a mistake or encounter deviations from my plans. I posed a crucial question to myself: "What positive aspects can be gleaned from this situation? And what valuable lessons can I extract?" Additionally, I reinforced the importance of remaining vigilant to the warning signs exhibited by my ego, relying on the arsenal of tools and strategies I have acquired throughout my journey to effectively restrain it. The tool that I most often use is to always focus on the big picture rather than the little picture. I am the little picture, and the aim of any project always takes precedence. I

## EGO: EDGING GOLF OUT

never have to question my motives when I am focused on something far larger than myself. The second excellent thing about my temporary brush with lunacy is that whenever the opportunity to collaborate with an organization to launch this growth initiative nationwide arises, I am prepared. I have already fought the giant and made all of the mistakes and corrected them in my head; all that is left to do is the paperwork.

Whether you are conscious of it or not, every day presents you with opportunities to make an impact, whether positive or negative, on million-dollar projects as well. Golf courses, in particular, are substantial investments with high operating costs. Every customer you turn off or turn away represents a portion of that significant financial sum. However, the consequences do not stop there. Your leadership influences the motivation and attitude of those around you, whether you manage a small team of two, five, or ten employees. The financial impact of lost customers multiplies rapidly. Now, consider the scenario of managing multiple facilities, where employee numbers can reach the hundreds. In such cases, the financial losses can easily amount to hundreds of thousands, even millions, of dollars. Expanding further to major corporations with thousands of representatives, the potential lost revenue reaches into the billions. It is crucial to recognize the weight of your actions and decisions and understand the substantial impact they can have on the overall success and financial stability of the projects and organizations you are involved in.

As I have said, the response and reviews for my book have been overwhelmingly positive, particularly from golf professionals. However, there was an occasional mixed review, and one, in particular, stands out as quite amusing. One day, I received a call from a gentleman who wanted to express his love for the book and how it provided a wealth of information. He shared a humorous anecdote with me. He mentioned being the assistant golf professional at a facility where the head pro jokingly handed him a copy of the book, saying, "Here, read this and tell me why you are failing to grow the game." Taking it as a challenge, the assistant pro read the book cover to cover and became incredibly excited about what he had learned. He urged the head pro to read it as well and suggested launching our golfer acquisition campaign, targeting casual and non-golfers. Surprisingly, the head pro had not read the book before handing it to his subordinate, and when he realized that his sarcastic remark had been taken seriously and the book had indeed been read, he abruptly dismissed the idea without even inquiring about its content or the program.

While I found the head pro's response contrary to what one would expect from a leadership role or someone responsible for business growth, I could not help but find the story amusing. I imagined the image of someone arrogantly tossing a book to their subordinate, expecting them to read why they were failing to grow the game, while never bothering to open it themselves. As I hung up the phone, I could not help but wonder why the assistant was not the head pro, but the answer became clear. Despite his current position, if he maintained his positive attitude and would not be negatively influenced by his mentor, he would likely become the head pro in the near future, making him a valuable asset for any facility. I chuckled to myself and thought, *Well, at least one out of two had the right approach.*

Our egos enjoy the rush of adrenaline that comes with having strength, success, knowledge, and control. We experience pride and even superiority when we perform well. Being viewed as weak, soft, inept, or a failure just serves to stoke the fire of the egomaniac inside the head of the person with the inflated ego. A person can get defensive and argumentative when they feel the need to be right and have a strong fear of failing. Accusing, avoiding conflict, exerting control, assuming malice, etc. are the hazards to the ego. Of course, the biggest hazard to the ego is that people would not like or accept you in their network of friends or colleagues.

When someone says they do not care what other people think, they are just being defensive. I once read somewhere that from the time we are born until around the age of thirty, all that matters to us is what other people think of us. From the age of thirty until about sixty we stop caring what other people think of us, and somewhere around the age of sixty, we start to realize no one was ever thinking about us at all. Some people will use sarcasm, but it is still anger-driven; because they want to be liked so badly yet are so insecure, they use "I do not care what people think" as a defense to protect their ego. Naturally, they do. We are social creatures, and our brains are hardwired to be such.

Most of the time, you do not feel confident enough to reveal your weaknesses. It is simply a worry about what other people may think. We constantly work to protect our sense of worth. You may frequently feel as though your life is being dictated by events outside of your control. Your feelings of helplessness, resentment, agitation, fear, stress, anger, and entrapment increase as a result of these emotions. You have a sense of helplessness in the face of these unfavorable conditions and/or duties. Many of us experience this emotion naturally. As a result, we are not even aware it is happening.

Upon entering the golf industry, I experienced similar emotions. Initially, I only considered partnering with facilities that I was absolutely certain would generate substantial returns. However, my decision was driven more by ego than financial logic. Despite investing significant sums into campaign launches, my primary concern was the reputation of MMC®. Instead of being solely concerned with protecting my investment or focusing on assisting businesses, careers, and the growth of the game, I became preoccupied with external perceptions of our campaigns. This distracted me from staying true to our mission, vision, and purpose, which had initially drawn us to the golf industry.

After a few years, my team and I made a deliberate choice to invest in riskier properties with lower earning potential, yet ones that aligned more closely with our core values. Although this decision had a significant impact on our bottom line, as we were no longer making substantial profits from each project and even incurred losses on some, it was more in line with the intended design of our program.

I want to emphasize that it was "We/MMC®" who experienced financial losses, not our partners. Our programs are designed to ensure there is absolutely no way our clients can lose money. We willingly undertook projects that we knew would not cover our expenses, but we had unwavering confidence that the program would revive the businesses and safeguard jobs. We did not enter the industry to play it safe but rather to drive the growth of businesses, foster career advancements, and elevate the game.

There have also been instances when we quickly realized that what seemed like a promising investment was turning sour, yet we chose to remain committed to the project to assist the facility and benefit the community, jobs, and the game. One such example was when we collaborated with a country club that had previously been a private club. After going bankrupt and changing ownership multiple times, the new owner reached out to us out of frustration.

Initially, we saw immense potential in this course—a seemingly easy turnaround that would generate at least $500,000 in immediate cash and over $1,500,000 in the next three years. We launched the campaign, but the results were disheartening. I reached out to the owner and the operator to assess the situation, expecting them to acknowledge the failure. However, to my surprise, neither of them viewed it as a failure. They were ecstatic about having sold approximately fifty memberships within the first week. Yet, my team and I knew that they should have achieved closer to 500 sales. As the one who had invested all the up-front funds for the campaign, I was far from satisfied with the outcome.

I was utterly perplexed as to how these two individuals could be so happy with such dismal results. Determined to uncover the truth, I instructed my team to call the course and inquire about the offer to gain insight into how this was happening and what was being said by the staff. To our astonishment, we discovered that the club had imposed numerous restrictions, limitations, and fees that were never discussed during the campaign's design phase. Essentially, they had completely altered the campaign without consulting us.

At that point, I had invested approximately $20,000 in the campaign. If I had chosen to walk away from the project, I would not only lose my investment (which was inevitable regardless), but it would also impact the golfers who had joined. Additionally, the community would witness the business facing bankruptcy once again, and the industry would suffer another blow with another course closure.

My ego attempted to manipulate me, bombarding me with thoughts like, *How dare they change the campaign without consulting you first? Don't they realize the financial loss they will incur? Don't they understand the opportunity that could have benefited at least two thousand golfers? Don't they care about their community? Do they comprehend the financial implications of altering the campaign?* However, I consciously suppressed those self-serving thoughts and, instead, asked myself, *What good can come out of this?*

The silver lining became evident—the course was saved, providing an opportunity for at least 200 people to experience the game, and the industry was spared from another setback. The owner and operator were very pleased with the outcome, and in their minds, it was very beneficial to the business. Even so, decisions of this nature are challenging because our egos dislike accepting losses. However, it is crucial to consider the greater good beyond ourselves.

In this particular situation, it was crucial for me to set aside my ego and allow theirs to take precedence. Despite their limited resources, they insisted on maintaining the private club status, even though it was becoming increasingly unsustainable. This led them to adopt a semiprivate model, but their egos struggled to accept this new approach. As a result, they unintentionally undermined the entire campaign.

By imposing numerous restrictions and additional fees on the offering, they turned away thousands of golfers, forfeited millions in revenue, and further tarnished a brand that had already endured numerous setbacks. If they had stuck with their initial decision to transition the club to a semiprivate status, they could have generated the necessary revenue to sustain the business. The staff could have utilized the following years to foster relationships with the new players, nurturing them into loyal members. Then, when it was time for their membership renewal, they could have guided them up the membership pyramid.

With two to three thousand introductory members, the management could have simply communicated, "The previous campaign provided an introductory opportunity for you to experience the club firsthand. Now, we invite you to renew your membership at platinum, gold, or silver rates as we return to our private club status." Even if only 20 percent of the players would have renewed, the club would have gained 400–600 new members and established invaluable goodwill within the community.

This approach would have enabled them to swiftly regain the highly coveted prestige of being a private club exclusively for members, requiring minimal sacrifices. The only temporary sacrifice they would have had to make was a small portion of their ego. Within just a couple of years, they could have reclaimed their esteemed status and enjoyed the benefits of being a private club once again. Moreover, this time around, the model would have been truly sustainable, ensuring long-term success and prosperity.

While the owner and operator claimed to be satisfied with the outcomes, it was evident that they were merely applying a temporary fix to a problem that could have been resolved more effectively by embracing the semiprivate model with the right mindset. If I had allowed my ego to guide my actions, the situation would have worsened. Thus, it was in my best interest to accept the financial loss and genuinely wish them the best moving forward.

The difficulty is that most people react to circumstances automatically. When faced with such responses, everything else is put on hold. The ego's knee-jerk response for self-preservation makes it simple for us to dismiss or distrust the source when presented with a better concept or solution or to nitpick the idea to the point where it simply cannot possibly work even though it is unequivocally true and has been amply demonstrated. Any threat assessment can easily be distorted by our ego, which in turn can make us defensive and determined to hold on to our views no matter how unrealistic they may be.

For instance, you may be the operator of a facility that requires an efficient bookkeeper. However, due to financial constraints, you are unable to hire a dedicated employee who would report to you on a daily basis, granting you full control over their every move. Your only alternative is to hire outside aid, which will considerably add to the overall success of the business. Instead of making that decision right away because it is for the betterment of the company, you pause because your thoughts now turn to how this move will affect you, your position of authority, your ability to control how the numbers are perceived and presented, your perceived competence, and whether this decision will jeopardize your position in any way. Your ego is telling you one thing, but the reality is completely different. Of course, you should make the move because you should always do what is best for the whole rather than what appears to be good for you.

Our egos cause us to perceive the threat or danger to be greater than it actually is. Our egos make us believe things to be much bigger or larger than they truly are. This distorted perception often stems from our ego-driven anxieties, particularly the fear of being seen as insignificant or lacking worth.

In the role of a manager, personal superiority should not be the objective. Instead, the focus should be on effectively operating the facility and acquiring the necessary resources for optimal performance. Exceptional managers understand the importance of hiring talented individuals within the budget constraints to achieve success. They do not seek to exert control or manipulate team members. Rather, they aim to build a team of competent individuals who can contribute to their own growth and the overall success of the organization.

When a manager hires someone for a particular role, it is with the expectation that the individual will excel in their responsibilities and reflect positively on the manager's decision-making. This understanding creates a mutual benefit, as employees recognize that their manager's endorsement can lead to future opportunities within the organization. Only an unwise individual would jeopardize this chance for advancement by undermining or mistreating their team members.

In essence, great managers prioritize the operational excellence of the facility they oversee and assemble a talented team that enhances their own effectiveness. They recognize that their success is intertwined with the success of their team, fostering an environment of collaboration and mutual support. At times, we feel uncomfortable when we believe that we are at the mercy of others. When we are driven by our ego, we regularly ask ourselves whether we are competent, bright, attractive, and liked, and the replies for these have become habits. It appears as though they are endangering our comfort and value. We believe that everything will improve if those individuals or those circumstances merely change. So, whether it is people, places, things, circumstances, or anything else, we try to start mending or eliminating what we feel is causing our stress, which is mostly just counterproductive. This immediate reaction is a sign of our ego's negative influence.

You can manage and influence your responses by becoming aware of your current situation and noticing that you are reacting rather than responding to your ego. I can assure you that anytime somebody said something negative about *Golf: The Untapped Market*, my knee-jerk thoughts were to respond with something like "What dummies! Are they not smart enough to know they can learn something from anyone including a janitor if they were just open to listen? Do these egomaniacs not realize that I had just given them the keys to success and they threw them in the trash?"

What I should have really been saying was: their comments and actions hurt. It was unpleasant to hear some of the negative comments because the book's goal was to help golf professionals in advancing their careers by growing the business they represented. So, I got plenty of practice dealing with a lot of ego issues at the time, although the process was a lot easier for me when it came to the book because I was my normal self and immediately applied my ego-check techniques.

One day, the same friend that I mentioned in the first story suggested that I may want to extend an olive branch and change the title of the book to not offend anyone, since my goal was to help people and have them use the book as a tool and/or resource. I thought long and hard about his suggestion. I knew he was much more sensitive to the audience's feelings than I could ever be, but at the same time, I really liked the title, and it conveyed precisely what I wanted it to say. Moreover, the subtitle itself was attention grabbing, and upon reading the book, one would quickly realize the depth of respect and admiration I hold for golf professionals. Nonetheless, I was getting some pushback, and if changing the subtitle could make some people feel better, it was worth considering.

Changing the subtitle of a book affects not only the title but also all of the reviews, clicks, followers, and a slew of other factors that effectively kill the book's sales and momentum. This was not my ego speaking; this was my left brain telling me that this may not be such a good idea. So once again, I defaulted back to my go-to technique and asked myself, "What was/is the goal of the book?" The answer was immediate: provide golf professionals, owners, and operators with new tools, techniques, and resources to grow their careers and business. The book had not been written to sell for profit, clicks, reviews, rankings, recognition, or any other purpose. So, if it lost revenue but helped the industry, then I could consider it a massive success. Once the decision was made, I immediately assigned my staff to make the revisions, and the book was republished under the new title, *Golf: The Untapped Market, Penetrating the Casual and Non-golfer Segments*.

Your ego screams for you to indulge it, and it wants to control everything. Fortunately, because I knew what was going on, I was able to shrug it off quickly and get back to work, focus, keep my head down, and keep pushing forward to fulfill the purpose. That is the saving grace of being able to control your ego! Otherwise, it will drive you mad. It is so much easier to point fingers or be negative, which is something that is quite frightening to me: living life in a negative manner. The prospect of being that kind of person disgusts me.

Whenever I notice my ego emerging, I make a conscious effort to suppress it promptly. However, I acknowledge that I am not immune to its influence, and occasional lapses can occur.

I am aware that this is a topic that is extremely awkward to discuss, and I anticipate facing a great deal of opposition because of this book. Whatever the case is, it must be said to address the problems and advance the golf industry. The likelihood that the golf industry will lose more players and have more golf course closures is guaranteed if the issue is not addressed. The fear of opening up about it is so crippling that it never gets acknowledged, despite the fact that everyone in the golf industry is aware of the existence of a significant problem. Nobody wants to discuss it openly. Because of the ego that is intrinsically linked to the job, everyone in the golf industry is so terrified to deviate from the standard. It is because there is such a deep fear of scorn and embarrassment.

The subject of overinflated egos often comes up in discussions with owners. There have been numerous times I have had an owner tell me the reason they do not have a head golf professional is that they need to attend more classes on empathy and fewer classes on arrogance. If this statement stung a little and caused your defenses to go on high alert, then you are reading the right book. If this statement did not bother you, congratulations; you are very comfortable in your own skin. Nonetheless, keep reading because you will learn how to help your coworkers, employees, colleagues, and most of all—your golfers.

Egos are mostly destructive, but a healthy ego can also be an asset as well. Egos can also be incredibly funny to watch, especially when an ego enters into a friendly round of golf between the teacher and the student. Two good ways to manage your ego are to never take yourself too seriously and be aware that you can always learn something from everyone, regardless of their status.

This lesson reminds me of a story about the guy who taught me how to play golf. I believe it was around 1989. I wrote about him in my first book and referred to him as the "Tom Cruise look-alike." He had a passion for golf and a penchant for gambling. When we first started playing, he always wanted to place bets on the game. Fortunately, he never took advantage of my novice skills and always considered my abilities. He was a great guy, and his love for golf, along with his competitive nature, occasionally fueled his ego.

Every time we played, he would persistently encourage me to bet on something, anything, just to make the round more interesting. It was fortunate that I had learned to manage my own ego because, in essence, he was implying, "You are so bad that I need external stimulation to enjoy this round." Of course, he said it in good humor, and he truly is a wonderful person.

I, on the other hand, have never been inclined toward gambling. As a person who values data and numbers, I base my decisions on what the data tells me. If the numbers do not work, I do not proceed. This gentleman, who was probably a 10-handicap, and I, a novice player with unrefined skills, had vastly different levels of expertise. The data was clear—it was not a favorable wager for me. However, considering his role in introducing me to golf and teaching me the game, I thought it would be a nice gesture to give something back.

One day, I finally relented and said, "All right, let us make a wager. What is the bet?"

He responded, "You know, we do not have to play for much."

At the time, I was earning a lot more money than him, as he was in his final year of college, while I had already begun developing the concepts and programs that would later become MMC® in 1991.

He continued, "Let us play the first hole for a sleeve of Maxfli."

Maxfli were the balls I used, and he often teased me because I kept them impeccably clean and bright white. My intention was primarily to locate them easily since it seemed my shots had a mind of their own once they left the clubface.

Agreeing to his proposal, I replied, "All right, we will play for a sleeve of balls."

Although I was not an experienced golfer, my background as an athlete made me familiar with the concept of skill discrepancies between competitors. In situations where one player significantly outclassed the other (in my case, with no skill to speak of), it was customary for the more skilled player to provide some allowance.

Recognizing this, I asked, "How many strokes will you give me?" It was evident that as a novice, I required some advantage.

He responded with a wide smile, "I will give you four strokes."

To ensure clarity, I inquired, "That is four strokes per hole, correct?"

He chuckled and confirmed, a grin stretching across his face. He appeared ecstatic, as if he were about to enjoy the most entertaining victory of his life, all in good fun, of course.

My companion showcased his remarkable skill immediately, hitting his drive with incredible precision, and the ball sailed 275 yards straight down the fairway. It was a breathtaking shot, one of sheer beauty. Inspired by his prowess, I stepped up to the tee and, as if channeling John Daly himself, unleashed a powerful swing that sent my ball sailing straight and true, rolling just beyond his own. It was a moment of pure exhilaration, one that nearly left me speechless. I had never hit a golf ball so perfectly before. The look of astonishment in his eyes was priceless, and we both erupted in laughter, unable to believe what had just transpired.

Regaining our composure, we hopped into the golf cart, ready to take our next shots. While he continued to play exceptionally well, I found myself hitting the ball better than ever since I had taken up the game just a month or so earlier. Admittedly, I had made a couple of bad shots and ended up 3-putting the hole, but miraculously, I won the hole by a single stroke. It was an absurd, fluke victory that left us in stitches, still marveling at the sheer absurdity of the situation. Naturally, I could not resist teasing him a little, reveling in the unexpected turn of events. He described it as nothing short of insane.

"Okay, let us double the bet," he proposed, his smile widening with mischievous delight. "Double or nothing," he insisted, that infectious grin revealing his eagerness. However, I declined, realizing that it might not be a wise decision.

"This could end up costing you a significant amount of money," I warned him.

I assured him not to worry about the minor loss he had suffered on the first hole since I was covering the expenses for the round and would treat us to lunch and beers afterward. I could afford it at the time, while he was still starting his career. Nevertheless, he persisted, urging me to double the bet on the next hole to at least breakeven.

I relented to his request once more, but little did he know that it marked the beginning of his own personal nightmare on the course.

After winning the first hole by a single stroke, the tide of the game continued to turn in my favor. It almost seemed as though I had been holding back, as my performance improved with each hole, while his game steadily declined. Around the sixth hole, I noticed that his once radiant Tom Cruise smile began to fade a bit. Though he remained enthusiastic and believed he could still turn things around, the signs of stress and anxiety became evident.

Now, we had accumulated several boxes of Maxflis through our bets, and against his better judgment, he decided to double the stakes once again. "This is a terrible idea," I cautioned. "You are losing control, and you cannot afford to be throwing away money on a foolish bet."

Despite my reluctance, he insisted, and half-heartedly, I agreed. To me, the money was insignificant, akin to beer and hot dog money. But for him, it was encroaching on essential expenses such as rent.

Yet again, he lost the hole, but this time, his composure shattered. He threw his golf club in frustration and began berating himself relentlessly. On the other hand, I found myself laughing uncontrollably, not out of malice or spite, but because I had never witnessed him lose his cool in such a manner. His outburst stemmed from disappointment with his game and perhaps the thought of being defeated by someone he had encouraged to try golf and personally taught.

Despite everything that had transpired, he remained persistent and insistent on continuing the round, determined to win back his money. Reluctantly, I agreed once again, and his ongoing nightmare persisted. Through a stroke of luck or perhaps the benevolence of the golf gods, he managed to win a hole or two after the turn. However, by the time we had completed the round, his debt to me had accumulated to nearly $400. Throughout the game, I could not resist teasing him, reminding him that it was his ego that had gotten him into this nightmare in the first place. He had lost every penny he had in his pocket, and the surreal nature of this nightmare playing out in real life left him utterly astounded.

We headed to our usual restaurant, where we enjoyed a delicious meal and shared some beers, all the while laughing and having a great time. He remained a true gentleman throughout the ordeal, accepting his defeat with grace and good sportsmanship. He did not try to avoid paying his debt, but it was evident that it weighed heavily on him. The entire situation arose from his ego getting the best of him. Throughout the game, it was clear that sheer vanity prevented him from accepting the reality of a beginner like me besting him in a round of golf.

In the end, despite the monetary loss, we both shared a memorable experience filled with laughter and camaraderie. It served as a valuable lesson about the perils of unchecked egos and the unpredictable nature of friendly competitions.

From a logical standpoint, I should not have stood a chance of winning that game. The odds were heavily stacked in my favor due to the generous number of strokes he had given me. Essentially, he had diminished my value as a competitor in his mind and, therefore, knew without a shadow of a doubt it would be like taking candy from a baby. He had underestimated my abilities to the point where he believed he could defeat me effortlessly, even without swinging his club. In contrast, he greatly overestimated his own skills. It all boiled down to ego. While he may have learned a valuable lesson from that experience, I frequently observe similar situations in the business world, where inflated egos lead individuals to stubbornly pursue ill-advised decisions rather than admitting mistakes and correcting their course of action.

However, let me tell you, that experience was priceless. If anything, I should have paid him for the sheer entertainment it provided. Every time I recollect that event, laughter overtakes me, leaving my belly aching. It was an incredible spectacle. Those moments on the golf course, alongside many others with him, are cherished memories. Among all the memories I have of him, this particular one stands out as one of my favorites. I am immensely grateful to him for introducing me to the game of golf and providing me with such unforgettable experiences. This anecdote illustrates how the ego's disruptive behavior can cause us to lose everything we own just because we are too proud to acknowledge we made a mistake and how it promotes negative behavior and causes us to lose control, which is the polar opposite of what we want and want to avoid at all costs. It has the opposite effect than what is intended.

On the positive side, a healthy ego can drive individuals to strive for excellence and deliver exceptional customer experiences. Golf course professionals with a strong sense of confidence and pride in their work are likely to be dedicated to providing high-quality services and maintaining course conditions at their best. This commitment to excellence can enhance the overall reputation and appeal of a golf course, attracting more players and generating revenue.

Additionally, a well-managed ego can foster innovation and creativity within the industry. Golf course owners and operators who are confident in their abilities may be more willing to take calculated risks, introducing new amenities, technologies, or sustainability initiatives to enhance the golfing experience. This forward-thinking approach can contribute to the growth and evolution of the industry, attracting a wider audience and ensuring its long-term success.

However, on the negative side, an inflated ego can lead to arrogance, stubbornness, and a resistance to change. Golf professionals, owners, or operators who are excessively focused on their own achievements or status may overlook valuable input from others or dismiss alternative ideas. This unwillingness to adapt or listen can hinder progress and limit the industry's ability to meet the evolving needs and preferences of golfers.

Moreover, an unchecked ego can create a competitive and exclusive environment. Golf courses that prioritize exclusivity and elitism may discourage potential players who feel intimidated or unwelcome. This narrow focus on a select few can restrict the growth and accessibility of the sport, limiting its reach to a broader demographic. During a conversation I had some time ago, one owner described his facility in a way that left a lasting impression on me.

He said, "Chuck, we have the most welcoming and friendly golf course in our market, with just the right touch of snobbishness to make our members feel truly special." I was captivated by this statement because it resonated with our inherent desire to feel valued, important, and accomplished. Embracing these sentiments is entirely natural and human. What's even better is when we extend this sense of importance to every individual we encounter, regardless of whether they are a member, pass holder, green fee player, or simply someone inquiring about our product.

While a healthy ego can drive excellence and innovation within the golf industry, an inflated ego can lead to arrogance, resistance to change, and exclusivity. Striking a balance between confidence and humility is essential for golf professionals, owners, and operators to foster growth, inclusivity, and a thriving industry that caters to the needs of diverse players. Only through a unified effort can the industry regain its former glory and secure its future.

In the upcoming chapter, I will provide you with invaluable tools and techniques that will not only empower your healthy ego but also guide you toward achieving remarkable milestones. These strategies will help you land the job of your dreams, negotiate a highly rewarding compensation package, establish lifelong job security, and attain the financial freedom you desire.

# 2

## CAREER DEVELOPMENT

MMC® ventured into the golf industry with a clear objective: to provide assistance and enhancements to the beloved game that captured my heart during a memorable morning on a South Carolina golf course. As the 1990s unfolded, my passion for golf grew, and I eagerly anticipated each new round, relishing the game and cherishing the overall experience. However, it was disheartening to observe from an external perspective the numerous obstacles and hardships that plagued the industry, hindering its progress as the new millennium drew near.

Golf had been a part of my life since I was nineteen years old, and although I did not play the game until I was twenty-six, I had witnessed both the negative and positive sides of the sport. On one hand, there were many instances when owners and general managers of the health clubs I worked in would prioritize the game over the business, sometimes to the detriment of their own establishments. It seemed as though even when they were physically present in the club, their minds were still on the game. This blatant disregard for the business and its growth appalled me, and I despised the game for it. On the other hand, after experiencing my first round of golf, I could empathize with those who made poor decisions despite the consequences. There is an undeniable allure to the game that can cloud judgment and lead individuals to prioritize their passion for golf over practical considerations. The love and enjoyment derived from playing golf can be so powerful that it becomes challenging to resist, even in the face of potential drawbacks.

Never in my wildest dreams had I planned on being in the golf business. It was never a conscious desire or aspiration. However, from the very name I stumbled upon for my company to its slogan, it felt like fate had guided me toward this path. As I watched the industry implode with a new century rolling in, I felt a strong calling. It was not that I wanted to diversify MMC® and move into other industries; it was quite the opposite. My team and I were very happy and growing every year. Logically, the move made no financial sense because we were already established and the health-club industry had three to four times the potential clients. I just could not shake the feeling that the industry was pulling at me, and I just knew that my team and I could make a difference—that we and our unique approach to growing a business could be of service.

One of the business principles I learned early in my career was strange yet profound. I was told never to go into a business I loved because, once you see the inner workings of an industry, you may lose the love you once had. My hobby is playing guitar, and for years, I reminded myself of that lesson every time I thought about buying or opening a music store. I had also been told to get into a business that I love and one that I would do for free if I had to. It is a fascinating paradox. My love and passion are personal development and the by-products that are garnered from this work. When you grow personally, everything and everyone who enters your life benefits; families are stronger, businesses thrive, communities flourish, and so on.

It is like the health-club industry. The health-club industry was not initially my chosen path, even though I enjoyed working out and living a healthy lifestyle. It felt more like destiny when I walked into a health club one day to apply for a job and immediately felt a deep sense of belonging. It became clear to me that I was meant to be a part of this industry.

As the years went by, I uncovered the true source of my passion. It was not just the act of exercising or maintaining a healthy lifestyle; it was the profound impact that health clubs had on their members. Witnessing the positive benefits and transformations experienced by club members became a driving force behind my love for that industry. Additionally, I found great joy in witnessing the growth, prosperity, and fulfillment of the employees, management, and owners who shared the same deep passion for the health-club industry.

The same applies to the game of golf. I never had a profound love for the game, nor did I ever envision myself being part of the industry. I loved the experience, I loved the connections I made with my friends every time we played a round, and I loved the serenity of being outdoors surrounded by silence and beauty. In short, I loved how I felt before, during, and after a round of golf. Later, when I entered the golf industry as a profession, once again I felt as though I was meant to be there. I take great joy in realizing that my team and I have been, and continue to be, instrumental in imparting those same feelings to a growing number of individuals. What began with a mere 1,200 players has now expanded to millions of new golf enthusiasts. I also love witnessing the success of the golf professional, the operator, the owner, and the community as well. It is funny because I cannot remember playing more than half a dozen rounds of golf since we entered the space, but I have gotten just as much enjoyment out of the game as I would have been playing 100 rounds per year.

Our team is driven by a shared goal: to spread the experience and emotions we have encountered with as many individuals as possible. Within each person, there exists a set of six core emotional needs, which I briefly discussed in my first book and will delve into more comprehensively later in this book. It is a perpetual quest for individuals to fulfill these needs. Remarkably, both golf and health and fitness have the power to satisfy all six of these needs. I firmly believe that these two elements are fundamental to the growth of humanity. By combining the physical health benefits derived from exercise and proper nutrition with the psychological and emotional rewards that golf offers, we can positively transform the lives of every individual.

Deep within every individual resides a longing to achieve greatness, ascend the social hierarchy, mingle with influential figures, and become a part of the esteemed inner circle. This desire stems from the innate need for acceptance, love, significance, importance, value, connection, and a sense of belonging. Remarkably, being a member of a golf club has the power to fulfill all of these emotional needs. Whether it is an exclusive, high-end private club, a public golf course, a municipal course, or even an executive 9-hole facility, in their minds, individuals perceive themselves as bona fide members of a distinguished country club. This newfound sense of belonging elevates their self-esteem, injects a spring in their step, and radiates a broader smile across their face. As participants in the golf industry, we have the incredible opportunity to make these individuals feel a thousand times better about themselves by simply showing them how they too can afford a golf membership. It does not involve lowering the price or giving golf away; rather, it is about presenting golf in a way that even non-golfers can comprehend: an accessible and affordable avenue to enhance their lives.

Throughout the 1990s, I traveled extensively across the United States, crisscrossing the country, visiting health clubs, and occasionally playing golf with the owners. It was during these journeys that I noticed a common missing element in almost every property I visited—a lack of a professional sales system. In fact, if I had not taken the initiative to start conversations, both my companions and I would have gone unnoticed.

This realization struck a chord within me. It became apparent that there was a pressing need for improved sales strategies and systems within the golf industry. With passion and determination, I embarked on a mission to fill this gap and provide the expertise and services necessary to help golf businesses thrive in a highly competitive landscape. A few years later, MMC®'s golf division was born out of this desire—to make a positive impact on the industry that had given me so much joy and fulfillment. We closed our health-club division, and our entire team focused 100 percent of our effort on serving the golf industry.

As the industry started its descent, I became increasingly attentive to the strategies employed by businesses to attract golfers back to the courses. During my travels to various cities and towns, I diligently scoured through all forms of media, seeking out golf course advertisements. Disappointingly, I observed a recurring pattern—the ads were strikingly similar to those I had encountered in previous locations. It became evident to me that there was a weak link in the chain, and it became unquestionably clear that we should step into this space and contribute to the industry's revival. The first crucial step I took was to establish a goal—a purpose, a vision, and a statement we aimed to embody.

My experience with golf professionals had always been great. Throughout the years, my busy travel schedule allowed me to take lessons from several golf professionals. During these valuable moments, I not only honed my skills but also gained insights into the needs and desires of these professionals in their field. One of the most significant needs expressed by these golf professionals was job security and fair compensation. They shared their constant worry about losing their job and having to uproot their families to seek employment elsewhere. This concern mirrored the anxieties faced by individuals in the health-club industry. While relocation can exacerbate the situation, the lack of job security remained a common thread. It became evident to me that addressing this concern could be achieved by mastering the art of growing the business at one's current place of employment. After all, no owner would willingly let go of someone who consistently generates revenue, unless there were serious attitude issues at play. It is crucial to remember that while skill is sought after during the hiring process, it is one's attitude that often determines if they are retained or let go.

Taking into account this valuable insight and recognizing the importance of establishing a strong foundation for any project, the concept for MMC®'s mission, vision, and purpose (MVP) practically developed itself. As the saying goes, "The taller the building, the deeper its foundation must be laid." Golf professionals are the foundation of the golf industry.

MMC®'s mission: *To grow the game, industry careers, and golf facilities by acquiring players from all four segments of golfers, that is, core, avid, casual, and non-golfer.*

MMC®'s vision: *Make golf accessible for everyone and, therefore, all-inclusive.*

MMC®'s purpose: *Save and grow golf facilities, secure gainful employment, fair compensation, and lifelong job and financial security for operators and golf professionals.*

Following solid business principles, I am committed to assisting you in advancing your career. Just as a skyscraper necessitates a sturdy foundation to achieve great heights, the prosperity of the golf industry hinges upon the commitment and knowledge of all individuals involved, including yourself. Recognizing that job security and equitable compensation are predominant concerns for many I believe it is imperative to address these areas as a starting point. The rest of this chapter will be devoted to teaching you how to secure your dream job, negotiate a favorable compensation package, ensure job security, and attain lifelong financial freedom within the golf industry. As a bonus, I will also guide you later in this book on how to acquire your very own golf course with minimal or no upfront capital. I understand that this may initially seem impossible to you, but I can assure you that such opportunities arise frequently, although they often go unnoticed. I have encountered numerous creative purchase agreements and untapped opportunities that remain hidden because people are unaware of where to look and, more significantly, fear rejection too much to give it a try.

For those of you who are reading this book, you may or may not have completed a certification program to acquire the necessary skills to operate a golf facility. If you have not pursued such training yet and you genuinely aspire to build a career in the industry, I highly recommend enrolling in a reputable institution of higher learning. The more knowledge you acquire about the business, the better equipped you will be. While it is not an absolute requirement, if you have the resources and time available, I encourage you to consider enrolling today.

Certification programs provide you with essential skills for managing day-to-day operations, handling public relations, budgeting, and much more. This knowledge will prove invaluable since you have consciously chosen to pursue a career in this industry. It is important to remind yourself that being a part of this industry was a deliberate decision you made, and only you have the power to ensure that it becomes a remarkable and fulfilling journey.

There are six steps you must take to land the job of your dreams.

1. The first step is to determine where it is you and your family want to start building the life of your dreams.
2. The second step is to do your homework (due diligence).
3. The third step is to customize your résumé to sell yourself (your brand) to the owner.
4. The fourth step is to prepare for the first interview; in this interview, you are the one interviewing the owner and staff.
5. The fifth step is to prepare for the second interview; in this interview, you are selling yourself according to the needs of the owner based on the information you gathered while doing your due diligence and the additional intel you gathered in the first interview.
6. The sixth step is to negotiate the deal you deserve—negotiate the compensation package as well as future opportunities based on results.

*The first step* in finding the job of your dreams is to decide where you want to create a life for yourself and your family. It is essential to start with the ultimate outcome of your goal and then work backward, considering the specific details. Begin by asking yourself the question, "Where do my family and I genuinely desire to reside?" Since you are constructing the life of your dreams, aim high. Many individuals fail to realize that when they strive for the moon, even if they fall short, they will still reach the stars. Therefore, contemplate where you would choose to raise your family if you had the opportunity to live anywhere. As a golf professional or someone in the golf industry, you have the advantage of selecting the climate, location, economic area, school district for your children's education, and various other criteria as starting points. There are numerous options available to you, so pinpoint the exact place where you wish to reside, raise your family, or even retire. Additionally, consider your second, third, fourth, fifth, and sixth choices to ensure you have multiple options and ample opportunities, avoiding a scenario where your choices become limited.

The game of golf holds a global appeal, offering countless avenues to establish a prosperous career in the industry. Even if the desired salary may not be immediately attainable, one can offset compensation through various perks and lifestyle choices, such as access to quality education, secure communities, and a wholesome environment. Occasionally, the benefits and advantages associated with a position can outweigh the monetary aspect. It is crucial to maintain a broad perspective and explore creative approaches to achieve what truly matters to you, rather than becoming fixated solely on the salary or a limited set of preferred work locations.

With over 15,000 golf courses in the United States alone, there is an abundance of opportunities to explore. By selecting six to ten cities or towns where you and your family would like to reside, you can potentially uncover more than one hundred properties offering various employment possibilities. By following these steps, you can increase your chances of securing the job of your dreams at one of these properties. It is essential to begin with the desired end result—what holds the most value for you—and then meticulously work through the details.

If ensuring a top-quality public school system for your school-age children is a priority for your family, you can start by researching the top ten public school systems in the United States or even globally. Opting for a strong public school system can result in substantial savings, as it eliminates the need for private school tuition fees. As the saying goes, "A penny saved is a penny earned." To put it in concrete terms, let us consider the financial aspect. If you save $3,000 per year per child by enrolling them in a great public school instead of a private one, and you have two children attending school, your annual savings would amount to $6,000.

Let us consider a scenario where you find a job in your desired area, but the salary falls $10,000 below your expectations. However, since you have already saved $6,000 by enrolling your children in a great public school system, you can take that into account. Additionally, you can explore the possibility of negotiating a compensation package that includes a leased car for the year, valued at an additional $500 per month.

By factoring in the $6,000 savings on school tuition and the $6,000 value of the leased car, you have effectively added $12,000 worth of perks to your overall package. This surpasses the initial $10,000 you were seeking, resulting in an even better compensation package than originally anticipated.

Bartering is an invaluable tool for service-based businesses, and it finds significant usage within the golf industry. It allows for the exchange of goods or services, such as trading rounds of golf for radio spots or newspaper advertisements. However, its application extends far beyond those examples, encompassing housing, clothing, food, cars, and virtually anything else that comes to mind. Golf holds a universal appeal, and while some may not openly admit their fondness for the sport, it is likely because they have not experienced it firsthand. Once someone steps foot on a golf course, they often develop an appreciation for the game, just as we do.

Perks can truly be a game changer, shaping the way we approach our desired lifestyle and career choices. It is crucial to keep an open and creative mindset when deciding on the area where you aspire to build the life of your dreams. By exploring the possibilities of bartering and considering the myriad benefits that can come with it, you can unlock exciting opportunities and create a more fulfilling and rewarding journey within the golf industry.

It is highly advantageous to conduct a job search while you are currently employed. Being employed offers several benefits and helps alleviate considerable pressure, particularly for individuals who are married or have financial responsibilities. It provides a sense of financial stability and affords you the flexibility to explore a wide range of job opportunities that may not be feasible if you were unemployed.

Being employed gives you the freedom to take trips and personally assess potential job prospects. This hands-on approach allows for valuable insights and enables you to make more informed decisions regarding your career path. On the contrary, waiting until you are unemployed may restrict your financial resources and limit your ability to proactively explore job opportunities.

In addition, engaging in a job search while maintaining the current employment helps one avoid the perception of desperation, which can lead to impulsive and uninformed decision-making. Desperation often impairs judgment and may result in accepting suboptimal positions or unfavorable compensation packages. By conducting a job search while already employed, individuals can approach the process with confidence and discernment, ensuring their decisions align with their long-term career goals rather than being driven solely by immediate circumstances.

*The second step* is to do your homework (due diligence). Create a comprehensive list of golf courses based on your geographical preferences, assigning them letter designations such as A, B, C, D, and so on, according to your specific criteria. Begin the list with the golf course where you truly aspire to work, even if there are no current job openings matching your desired position. By thoroughly studying and familiarizing yourself with this material, you will develop an impressive understanding of the business, which can ultimately lead to opportunities even when there are no immediate vacancies. While some headhunters may advise starting with more readily available positions and working your way up, I respectfully disagree. Instead, aim high and prioritize the top choices, shooting for the moon. Your dedication and knowledge will make a lasting impression on golf course owners, potentially leading to the creation of a position tailored to your skills and aspirations.

Subsequently, compile a comprehensive inventory of all golf properties and golf-related businesses within the surrounding areas, including those that may initially seem incongruent with your preferences. Incorporate your newly established criteria into the evaluation process, systematically narrowing down the list while concurrently identifying their respective competitors. To initiate the process, consider approximately twenty cities or towns, enabling you to progressively refine your options based on the established criteria and ultimately yield a selection of fifty to one hundred properties. Aim to identify at least ten to twelve properties where you possess a genuine desire to work.

Additionally, it is essential to include other golf-related businesses in the identified areas. By encompassing a comprehensive understanding of the available options, you can effectively plan for potential career transitions that may necessitate relocating your family across state or national boundaries. Ensuring awareness of all alternatives is vital, as it allows for contingencies in case the original plan encounters unforeseen circumstances. Furthermore, exploring the full spectrum of opportunities becomes particularly advantageous if you contemplate branching out independently within the golf industry. Thoroughly considering all possibilities can help you make informed decisions and ascertain a wide array of opportunities from which to select.

One of the significant challenges in the golf industry, which you should strive to avoid, is the need to frequently uproot your family and relocate across the country in search of new job opportunities. This constant upheaval can be particularly challenging for children and their parents alike. Therefore, it is crucial to conduct thorough research and ensure that you are selecting a destination where you can envision a long-term commitment and where multiple options are available to you. Carefully assessing and selecting a location with a range of viable opportunities can help you confidently establish roots and provide both yourself (in terms of your career) and your family with the opportunity to flourish.

Before investing any resources in travel arrangements, it is crucial to diligently conduct thorough research and maintain meticulous notes. Once you have identified a prospective golf property in a specific area, it is advisable to compile a comprehensive competitive overview of every course within a thirty-mile radius surrounding your selected property. This entails delving into the activities and offerings of each competitor, acquiring knowledge about their membership rates across various tiers, greens fees, cart fees, available amenities, staffing levels, the estimated annual rounds played, the number of rounds played on weekdays versus weekends, the presence of leagues, the frequency of outings, the availability of a driving range and practice putting facilities, specifics regarding the type of greens, and comprehensive ownership details, among other relevant factors. By undertaking this comprehensive analysis, you will arm yourself with essential insights that will aid in making informed decisions and enhance your prospects of securing the desired job opportunity.

Exercise strategic thinking and avoid settling for just any job. Instead, strive to find a golf property that resonates with your passion and aligns with your values. Seek a workplace where you can genuinely connect with your colleagues, relish in the joy of nurturing the business, and contribute to the betterment of the community. While the internet can serve as a valuable resource, exercise caution in relying solely on its information. Recognize that online platforms may present a one-sided perspective and often contain misinformation. To gather accurate data, utilize multiple sources and maintain an open mind. Additionally, do not hesitate to make personal phone calls. You would be surprised by the willingness of employees to share valuable insights, particularly during quieter periods.

When doing your homework, here are a few things to consider:

- Growth potential
- Demographics
- Politics
- Real estate

**Growth potential:** Direct your attention toward economically thriving areas that exhibit consistent business growth. It is essential to prioritize regions where the business community experiences noticeable expansion on an annual basis. Keep in mind that you will play a pivotal role in fostering the future growth of the property; thus, it is crucial to select a location situated within a growing area.

**Demographics**: Consider your target demographic, which will be the driving force in most marketing decisions you make. It is crucial to recognize that profitability relies on attracting consumers with disposable income. However, it is not always necessary to solely target individuals at the pinnacle of the socioeconomic ladder for every golf course. This holds true for the majority of golf properties, as each has its own unique target market. Ensure a thorough understanding of the property and its specific target demographic, guaranteeing there is a sufficient number of individuals within that demographic profile to support the growth of the business.

**Politics:** The political landscape possesses the potential to exert diverse effects on businesses. Its impact can range from heightened risk factors to substantial revenue losses in cases where the political environment is unfavorable for business operations. It is crucial to acknowledge that political factors can instigate changes and shape government policies, encompassing a spectrum that spans from local to federal levels.

The political landscape encompasses various components, such as tax policies, which can have significant implications for businesses. Governments have the authority to adjust tax rates, both increasing and decreasing them, thus affecting different sectors and companies in distinct ways. These decisions directly impact businesses, including the one you aim to work with or establish. It is imperative to remain informed about the political environment you are entering and stay up to date with any changes, as they can have a direct influence on your business operations and career prospects.

**Real estate**: When it comes to purchasing a home or business, the significance of location cannot be emphasized enough. While conventional advice may steer you toward buying in a good and safe neighborhood, it is essential to understand that neighborhoods transform, much like any other aspect of life.

Rather than limiting your focus to simply good or bad neighborhoods, it is more prudent to identify areas with potential for future growth. Opting for a neighborhood that exhibits promising signs of development and progress can be a strategic decision. It is important to note that such neighborhoods may also require less of an initial investment compared to well-established, highly desirable areas. However, by identifying a neighborhood on the precipice of becoming the "next best," you position yourself for a potentially advantageous investment.

Do your homework. There is a saying in construction, "Measure twice and cut once." The more information on the area, the golf courses, and their potential, the better chance you have of maximizing your potential and building the life of your dreams.

*The third step* is putting together an iron-clad sales presentation, which starts with your résumé. Your résumé plays a critical role in making a strong first impression on your potential employer. Consider it as a powerful marketing tool, designed to captivate and engage the hiring personnel. To achieve this, your résumé should be crafted like an advertisement, strategically incorporating hooks that grab attention and leave a lasting impact.

Recognize the importance of tailoring your résumé to the specific industry and organization you are targeting. A generic, one-size-fits-all approach is insufficient. Instead, invest time and effort in customizing your résumé for each business and position you apply for, leveraging the valuable information you have gathered. By doing so, you demonstrate a genuine interest in the company and showcase how your skills and experiences align with their specific needs.

Avoid the temptation to use a blanket résumé and indiscriminately distribute it across various platforms. Instead, adopt a sniper approach, focusing on one target at a time.

One of the most important things to consider when drafting your résumé is the way you convey your primary objectives and prove that you have the ability to grow the business. Incorporate a business plan approach to your résumé and include testimonials from your previous employers. Make a list of your achievements; add a cover letter explaining your vision based on your research and why you want this specific position with this property, why you feel you are qualified for the position, and why you feel you can be an enormous asset to the business.

While topics such as growing the game, public relations, and player development generate enthusiasm, it is important to acknowledge that owners and board members, being business-oriented individuals, prioritize the bottom line. Though they may not explicitly express it, their primary concern lies in identifying candidates who can drive financial success. Your résumé must highlight the pivotal factor that indicates, "I have a proven track record of increasing revenue, rounds, and/or membership at previous courses, and I can replicate and surpass this success at your property. Moreover, my experience and enhanced skill set enable me to achieve these outcomes even more efficiently." This forms the core of your résumé, and as you progress, you can add subtle nuances that align with your chosen property or business.

When it comes to advertising any product, service, or brand, the hook is paramount and must provide a compelling answer to the question, "What's in it for the listener/reader?" People inherently seek to understand the personal benefit or value proposition. Your résumé should address this immediately, with the cover letter often carrying significant weight. It is crucial to recognize that your résumé serves as a sales tool, enabling you to showcase your qualities as a reliable, dependable, honest, hardworking, task-oriented, and team-oriented individual, among other positive attributes. However, these qualities are mere words on paper. To stand out among other applicants, your résumé must demonstrate why you are extraordinary compared to the rest. Your body of work and accomplishments play a crucial role in achieving this. Keeping a diary of your achievements, both significant and small, can be highly beneficial. By documenting your contributions to business growth, you gain a comprehensive understanding of your expertise. Create your own operations manual by capturing these valuable insights. Build a résumé that not only impresses potential employers but also aligns with your own expectations. Reflect on what you seek in an employee, what captures your attention when reviewing résumés, and what improvements you would make if it were your résumé.

Your résumé is an ever-evolving document, and I highly recommend updating it quarterly, even if you are content in your current employment. The future is uncertain, and circumstances can change unexpectedly. Certain tasks or accomplishments that you may overlook or consider routine hold value in the eyes of potential employers. By staying proactive and updating your résumé regularly, you ensure that it accurately reflects your skills and experiences. Additionally, mere words on paper may not be sufficient to convince interviewers. It is crucial to back up your claims with tangible evidence that validates your capabilities. Always be on the lookout for and save supporting documentation, such as testimonials, awards, sales reports, or any other material that substantiates your achievements. These supporting materials add credibility and provide a more substantial foundation for your résumé during the interview process.

Your résumé serves as a representation of your personal brand, which ultimately reflects who you are as a professional. It is crucial to ensure that your résumé tells a comprehensive and relevant story—one that resonates with your future employer's interests. By crafting a compelling narrative that captivates the interviewer's attention right from the moment they pick up your application, you greatly enhance your chances of standing out and securing the job of your dreams. Make your résumé irresistible, compelling the employer to delve further and discover the valuable qualities and experiences you bring to the table. Remember, your résumé is more than just a document; it is an opportunity to showcase your unique story and leave a lasting impression on your potential employer.

*The fourth step* is the interview (gathering information). The absolute best way to start this process is to set up an appointment to tour the property and play a round. This way, you see everything from the consumer's eyes and not from the eyes that are looking through rose-colored glasses. You will also witness firsthand the business's unfiltered sales presentation and customer relations. Granted, this could get costly and time-consuming, but if you have the time, it will prove itself to be well worth it.

If you can't visit the property in person, or if you have already visited the property, the next appropriate step is to contact the owner or operator of the establishment. It would be beneficial to request a meeting, and if feasible, offer to take them out to lunch as a gesture of goodwill. If a lunch meeting is not possible, kindly ask for at least fifteen minutes of their time. When making this request, keep two important factors in mind.

First, understand that most businesspeople have a limited amount of discretionary time, and it may be challenging for them to allocate a full hour or even half an hour for a meeting. However, emphasize that a brief fifteen-minute interaction, even over a quick cup of coffee, can be accommodated in their schedule if the purpose is compelling enough.

Second, it is crucial to address the question of "What's in it for me?" from the perspective of the other person. Immediately convey the reasons behind your request for the meeting and assure them that you possess valuable insights or offerings that they will gain by engaging in the discussion. Approach this request with professional persistence and creativity until they agree to the meeting.

During the allotted time, utilize the opportunity to ask relevant and well-prepared questions, treating the interaction as an interview with the owner or operator, as if you were considering purchasing the business. Seek to unearth as much information about the business as possible, which would enable you to evaluate your skills and capabilities concerning the requirements of the business.

Delve deeper into the conversation with the owner or operator to uncover their underlying challenges and concerns. This will enable you to effectively demonstrate how your abilities can address those pain points during your subsequent interviews. Your objective is to identify what keeps the interviewer awake at night and convincingly present yourself as the comprehensive solution to all their problems. Encourage the owner to discuss various aspects, such as the course itself, their property, aspirations, staff, and personal goals. Prompt them to verbalize their vision of an ideal general manager or golf professional. By asking a series of pertinent questions, you will gather valuable insights that will provide you with the necessary leverage to secure the job.

Furthermore, this initial interview offers the opportunity to assess the compatibility and alignment of visions between you and the owner. Ideally, you seek to work with an individual who possesses a positive attitude, ambition, supportiveness, and a desire to witness both your personal growth and the business's prosperity. It is preferable to collaborate with someone who rewards success not only with recognition but also through tangible incentives. Utilizing this interview to gather extensive information enhances your chances of securing the desired position.

It is critical to avoid accepting a job where the prospect of going to work every day fills you with dread due to an incompatible boss or colleagues. Therefore, it is highly recommended to seize the opportunity to interact with as many staff members as possible during your visit to the property. This does not entail asking the owner or your prospective boss sensitive questions about the staff; rather, it involves being observant. Take the time to look around, introduce yourself to everyone you can, ask relevant questions, and engage in conversations with your potential coworkers. This approach will enable you to make an informed decision that could significantly impact your life.

While you cannot choose your family or parents, you have the power to select your boss, mentor, and coworkers. Assess whether you anticipate having harmonious working relationships and an easy rapport with the team and your supervisor. Regardless of the financial compensation, experiencing happiness when going to work each day holds tremendous importance. Ideally, it is advisable to schedule at least four appointments to make the most of your time and resources. Your objective should be to visit as many properties as possible within your allocated time and budget, prioritizing them based on your ranking system. Employ the same process you followed during your initial interview for each subsequent interview. The information you gather from in-person visits will be invaluable when it is time to make a final decision. It is even possible that your top pick may be reconsidered based on new insights, and you may discover that another property is better suited to your needs.

Moreover, while you are in the area, it is essential to maximize your time and investment by exploring the local area. Visit local businesses, drive through different neighborhoods, and familiarize yourself with the surroundings. Gain an understanding of the local economy. Opt to dine at bustling restaurants, and engage in conversations with the locals while sitting at the bar. Ask for their opinions on the golf courses in the area without disclosing your job-seeking status, as you would not want to influence their answers. Approach inquiries with genuine curiosity, probe deeper, and allow people to express their genuine opinions. The information you gather will help you tailor your presentation, leaving a powerful impression on the owner by showcasing your interest not only in the business but also in the community as a whole.

Now, it is time to return home and tailor your résumé(s) to specifically address the needs and concerns of the owner(s). This customization will demonstrate your ability to meet their requirements and make you better prepared for your second interview. With this step, you are now just two steps away from securing the job of your dreams.

*The fifth step* is the second interview, where you have the opportunity to showcase your abilities and effectively market yourself based on the gathered data aligned with the owner's needs. Before attending this interview, thoroughly review all of your notes and ensure that you are familiar with the material as well as you know the back of your hand. This is not a time to cram for an exam; the information should be deeply ingrained in your mind. It is recommended to review the material the night before and refresh your memory first thing in the morning to ensure it remains fresh in your mind.

In *Golf: The Untapped Market*, you learn how to prepare yourself every day and get into the zone before fielding calls and seeing prospects. Revisit and thoroughly review your notes before entering the interview to ensure you are at the peak of your performance.

Here are the highlights:

- Ask yourself positive affirming questions.
- Be aware of your posture.
- Go through your visualization routine.
- Repeat your affirmations loud, proud, and with intensity.
- Complete some breathing exercises.
- Get focused on the interview.
- Smile and laugh often throughout the morning.
- If you feel nervous, hum your favorite song.

- Prior to the interview, take a few moments to calm yourself through meditation or by engaging in a grounding activity such as rubbing a coin between your fingers.
- Attire (dress sharp and appropriate)—dress for success.

During your initial interview, it is important to assess the dominant social style exhibited by the interviewer and tailor your presentation accordingly. This involves identifying whether the owner demonstrates the personality traits of a director, socializer, relator, or analyzer. Additionally, another valuable insight to extract from the first interview is the owner's preferred communication style. Observe whether they lean toward verbal, nonverbal, written, visual, or auditory communication. Armed with this valuable information, structure your presentation to align with their style and incorporate it into your face-to-face interview.

It is significant to remain adaptable and prepared for unexpected circumstances. While you may anticipate meeting the same person you interviewed with initially, there is a possibility of encountering a change in personnel at the last moment. Therefore, it is essential to be flexible and ready for any scenario that may arise.

Make sure you are able to articulate your plans to grow the business. Validate your statements with supporting documents and research. Demonstrate to the owner how you are going to make it happen and show the difference between what they are doing now and what you can do to improve upon what they are already doing. Do not oversell yourself, but sell the facts. Remember, no one wants to hear what they are doing is wrong, especially from a new person. Tread lightly so you will not step on anyone's ego, and focus on what you can bring to the table.

It is extremely important that you focus mostly on what's in it for the owner, or the business. Yes, your compensation package including perks and benefits is important, but always put the owner's needs, wants, and desires first because the bottom line is that the only way to capture and hold someone's attention is to immediately let them know what's in it for them, and in this presentation, all that matters in the beginning is what the owner is going to gain by hiring you. Every organization can hire as many people as they want as long as those people can pay for themselves by increasing revenue for the business. If you bring more value to the business than it cost them to hire you, you are in! It is that simple. Even if they are not looking to hire someone, you still have an excellent chance of landing the job because you have made the decision a no-brainer for the owner.

At this point, you have sold the owner on hiring you; now it is time to go to the next and final step and negotiate the compensation package you deserve.

*The sixth and final step* is negotiating your compensation package. This is where the rubber meets the road. You must be crystal clear in what it is you want and have many options of how to get what you want. This package should also include a section devoted to future opportunities and earnings based on results. When I used to travel to properties for sales calls, I always went to my meetings with a contract already prepared on a Word document so I could easily edit the agreement as needed right there on the spot. Agreements can also be very intimidating, so make sure it is just an outline of the issues discussed and you only present it when it is time to lock up the relationship. Take really good notes and grade the owner's comments based on not only their verbalized thoughts on specific issues but also on their nonverbal thoughts by paying attention to what their body language is saying.

You must learn the skill of negotiating the right contract. First of all, know exactly what you want and think of creative ways to get it. Be flexible and resourceful. Do not just focus on the money side of things. Focus on the end result, not the path that you will take to get there. Most likely, there are numerous paths available that will get you to the same place. For example, bonuses, percentage of gross revenue, percentage of net revenue, percentage of growth revenue, benefits, etc. all contribute to the bottom line. If you come in and your number is X for a salary, but in the owner's mind, X is way out of his/her budget, you may blow the whole deal when it could have been completely avoided by a simple restructuring of the package. This is a sales presentation, and just as in other sales presentations, it must be guided by feel. As you navigate through the presentation, you should constantly feel the owner out and adjust accordingly.

This is why it is important to have the first interview. In that interview, you uncovered the owner's perceived value of someone in the position for which you are applying. If that number is below what you want, you start with the owner's number and work your way up to your number through bonuses, benefits, perks, etc., and throw in some performance incentives to sweeten the pie. The opposite is also true; most owners will not consider you if you come in way too low. In this scenario, all you are doing is devaluing yourself. If you absolutely know you can grow the business more than anyone else, there is nothing wrong with being creative and suggesting the owner hires you on a thirty-day trial period at a lower salary and if you surpass the benchmarks you both agree to, then the owner signs a long-term contract with you in which you are paid your asking amount. This is called "risk reversal." The owner assumes no risk by hiring you, and now the burden of proof is on you. This offer is not as risky as it sounds because most properties are underperforming primarily due to a lack of three things: innovation, perspiration, and proper education.

Remember, a company cannot pay you more than they can afford to pay you. You must be able to demonstrate that you can bring more value to the business and are willing to defer that additional compensation until you bring that value to the business. No intelligent businessperson is going to turn that offer down.

A lot of golf professionals are either unemployed or underemployed in the industry. When somebody is underemployed, it simply means they are overqualified for the job they are performing and getting paid far less than what they are worth. The reason for this is they do not possess the most important skills, skills that are necessary to grow the business at the rate to satisfy and/or at a very minimum give an owner hope. The only way to overcome this hurdle is by bringing more value to the table. The best way to get the job of your dreams is by possessing marketable skills—skills of great value to the owner.

I often hear people complain about their job or their salary, and I always tell them the same thing, "You are getting paid exactly what you are worth to the owner." Complaining is never going to help them improve their lot in life, nor will "hoping" ever help them achieve their goals. The only thing that is going to help is hard work, learning more about your craft, and being willing to adapt to change.

Many individuals are aware of what they should do but often fail to take action. The first step is to acquire knowledge and understanding and then apply that knowledge effectively. It is important to recognize that the individual who contributes to business growth and generates revenue holds immense value within the organization. Your compensation will be directly correlated to the value you bring to the business. The level of compensation is determined by the tasks you perform, the quality of your work, the complexity of your responsibilities, and the rarity of your skill set. In essence, increasing your income becomes relatively straightforward by driving revenue for the business, a skill that is possessed by only a few. This proficiency sets you apart and positions you in a league of your own. When you possess the skill to grow any business anywhere in the world, you become highly sought after, valuable, and irreplaceable.

Continued education is paramount to success. Before you can develop a business, an industry, or even a player, you must first prioritize your own personal development. In the upcoming chapter, I will delve into several key areas of personal development that have had a profound impact on both my career and personal life. While I do not claim expertise in these subjects, I want to emphasize the importance of seeking out specialists who can offer in-depth knowledge tailored to your specific interests. However, as a dedicated lifelong learner, I have personally benefited from exploring these areas and will do my best to share my insights.

It is crucial to recognize that our learning journey is a never-ending process. We must resist the temptation to rest on our laurels and believe we have reached the zenith of knowledge. The quote "When you are green, you are growing, but when you are ripe, you start to rot" serves as a powerful reminder of the dangers of complacency. By embracing a mindset of perpetual curiosity and continuous growth, we open ourselves up to endless possibilities.

Let us commit to being perpetual students, always hungry for new knowledge and insights. By maintaining a humble curiosity, we can ensure that our personal and professional development knows no limits. Through this dedication to lifelong learning, we can thrive, adapt, and evolve in an ever-changing world.

# 3

## PERSONAL DEVELOPMENT

In the golf industry, we often hear about *player development*, but rarely, if ever, do we hear about *personal development*. Most operators running a golf course focus on growing the business or the game but somehow overlook the importance or do not even realize the necessity of their own personal growth. We all should be doing everything we can to grow in our personal and professional lives to be healthier, happier, and more productive. Most people think of growth in monetary terms, but if you wish to maximize your earning potential, you must invest in your personal growth. As business leaders, we study and work hard to acquire skill sets that will help us in our professional lives. So, why do we not study and work just as hard when it comes to acquiring skill sets that will maximize our personal development? The answer is simple; we have never been taught the facts about personal development.

Throughout our upbringing, parents often emphasize the importance of completing high school or college, but the conversation rarely extends beyond that point. Only a minority of parents who truly understand the value of education may encourage their children to pursue advanced degrees such as an MBA or PhD. As a result, many individuals grow up with the perception that their education is complete once they obtain their degree as if it were a shield against ever having to study again.

However, it is essential to recognize that education is not a finite process that ends with a diploma. One of the biggest travesties in life is that most people cease growing intellectually once they graduate from high school or even college. This is a major intellectual misfortune. Something that was believed or perceived to be true a decade ago might not be true at all. This is consistently demonstrated in the fields of medicine, science, and research, and this also holds true to businesses and other industries.

If you are like everyone else in the industry, what do you really have to offer? What unique contribution do you bring to the table? If everyone is operating in the same exact manner, how can the industry expand? Learning is a lifelong journey that extends far beyond a formal education. Here are a few points to consider:

**Continuous Growth:** Continuous education and personal development offer numerous benefits. They provide opportunities for professional advancement, as certain careers may require advanced degrees or specialized certifications. Ongoing learning helps individuals stay current with industry trends, technologies, and best practices, enhancing their job performance and value to employers.

**Personal Enrichment:** Education extends beyond external expectations and serves as a means of personal fulfillment. Many people find joy and satisfaction in learning new things, expanding their horizons, and challenging themselves intellectually.

**Networking and Collaboration:** Further education often provides opportunities to connect with like-minded individuals, industry experts, and mentors. Building a strong network can offer valuable support, guidance, and potential collaborations.

**Intellectual Curiosity:** Some individuals possess a natural curiosity and a thirst for knowledge. For them, education becomes an ongoing pursuit of understanding, and they find fulfillment in continuously exploring various subjects.

It is crucial to understand that education takes many forms, not limited to traditional schooling. Reading books, attending workshops or seminars, and engaging in self-study are all valid ways to continue learning and growing. Embracing education as a lifelong endeavor can lead to personal and professional growth and a deeper appreciation for the transformative power of knowledge.

For most of us, learning after graduation primarily occurs through magazines, trade journals, newsfeeds, the internet, and even through enjoyable reading such as novels. All of these sources offer valuable information. Nevertheless, it is important to recognize that they all have their own agendas and aim to influence your thoughts, whereas personal development subject matter teaches you how to control your thoughts.

Continuous education, as the term suggests, refers to an ongoing process of learning. Just as our bodies require exercise, our brains also need regular stimulation. Moreover, when considering candidates for leadership positions within your own company, whom would you prefer to promote? Would it be someone actively acquiring leadership skills or someone attempting to navigate the role without formal training? Education spurs innovation while opening doors to opportunities, and the pursuit of ongoing education creates countless possibilities.

To illustrate my points on the importance of continuous education, personal development, and why it matters less how much formal education you have received as long as you are constantly expanding your knowledge to advance yourself and your organization, I will share a sad but true story with you. While reviewing the final edits of this book in early February 2024, I was inundated with calls and emails from friends, employees, clients, and the like regarding an email they had received from a reputable organization—who has been known to "borrow" MMC®'s intellectual property and pass it off as their own—advertising a new service they are launching. Although I don't typically read industry propaganda, over the years, friends and clients have occasionally sent me emails or articles that they believe to be a blatant spin-off of our ideas, content, intellectual property, and so on, that may be constituted as property of MMC®. I felt the same disdain when I opened every single message—it was like a big flashing neon sign. This advertisement screamed, "I brazenly plagiarized MMC®'s new service/marketing campaign with absolutely no remorse at all." Staying true to the spirit of the game, they teed off with some creative twists—tweaking the phrases like a golfer adjusting their stance, aiming to outsmart the rules officials.

In order to raise awareness of the potential that almost every golf course has within their local market, MMC®'s team launched a new service via a marketing campaign. We chose direct mail to be the driving force to announce this new service, mailing to over fifteen thousand (15,000) golf facilities throughout the US multiple times. Additionally, we promoted it on our website and incorporated some email marketing as well to ensure that all owners and operators have access to this free service. We addressed the enormous untapped potential owners and operators have if they just know the real numbers of their market. We offered to conduct an in-depth market analysis within a twenty-five (25) mile radius of the facility, identifying and quantifying the core, avid, casual and non-golfers within the market, we would provide a projected number of rounds that could be garnered from this data, a competitive overview as well as a demographic survey to identify their market, i.e. household, age, gender, income, homeownership, etc. and we would include a projection of their facility's potential based on the data. We announced that we will carry out a thorough study absolutely free and without any obligation whatsoever.

Eight months following the MMC®'s new service launch, the organization unveiled their new campaign that is nearly identical to MMC®'s. They offer detailed market data within a 5, 10, and 25-mile radius. This data includes demographic data such as, golfing household, number of facilities (a.k.a. competitive overview), population by age and gender, number of golfers (current users and interested non-golfers), projected population and rounds potential. It is highly unprofessional and unacceptable for a business to operate in this manner, especially when everyone in the industry knows that MMC® pioneered this program—a fact well-recognized by all who have observed MMC®'s work. How can anyone respect this organization again? How can employees respect their leadership after seeing them act so poorly, tarnishing all regard the industry had for the entire organization? If the leadership is willing to copy a company's programs, what message does that send to their employees, clients, supporters, members, and so on?

The only distinguishing facts between the two campaigns are, MMC®'s campaign only requires the owner and/or operator to call our office to obtain the facility analysis whereas this organization requires them to join their VIP membership for a fee of more than $600. The organization charges a fee, while MMC®, as always, offers this service absolutely free!

It's also important to recognize that MMC® is the company that introduced the concept of targeting the casual and non-golfers. We possess a unique profiling system to pinpoint these individuals with unmatched precision, and to be crystal clear, this system has never been available in the public domain. Hence, it cannot be "borrowed," "copied," "cloned," or "replicated" because we do not share it with anyone. So basically, what you are getting from your VIP membership is the same demographic information that's readily available online at no cost. Furthermore, it should be noted that demographic data plays very little to no impact in identifying any of the four segments of golfers. Demographic data alone is insufficient, unless it is partnered with psychographics, i.e., lifestyle data. Unfortunately, this data comes with a hefty price tag. Thus, businesses or organizations that shy away from investing in innovative programs and ideas will likely hesitate to allocate resources for the crucial data needed to pinpoint potential prospects for golf facilities.

This reminds me of a similar situation that occurred when I first started in the golf industry. We placed an introductory sales system on MMC®'s website as a free service for anyone looking to enhance their professional sales skills. Within a few months, my team informed me that a competitor had cloned the entire system from our website, advertised it as a new program for their company, and charged around $1,000 (if I remember correctly) for it on their member site. While I anticipated potentially unethical conduct from certain competitors, the revelation of such actions emanating from a well-respected organization was beyond my expectations. At least in the past they have been able to cloak their deception, but this time their plagiarism is both overt and appalling.

Regretfully, this is par for the course because people's egos get in the way, and they feel failure so great that they are constantly trolling companies like MMC® for innovative ideas. These organizations' leadership know they are well funded, highly compensated, and are extremely influential with their platforms and are terrified of being discovered that, yes, they too, are just human and don't have all of the answers. Like everybody else, I was initially incensed at the audacity, but as I calmed myself, I felt shame for the organization and sadness that things were so bad they had to result to tactics like this. This same organization has "borrowed" from MMC® numerous times over the last fifteen years or more. Whenever the problems were brought to my attention, I would brush them off as my way of contributing to the industry. I knew this organization was well-established and that, at the very least, our programs were being disseminated throughout the industry, even though the organization was taking credit for, and making money off of our content. Since I wasn't publishing a new book at the time, these instances went unmentioned. I've occasionally considered writing a book detailing all of the unethical practices, alliances, partnerships, politics and so on that are choking the life out of the game but that would not serve the greater good—advancing the game, the industry, or the careers of golf professionals. Similarly, identifying this organization would not accomplish anything more than stroke my ego since, as the saying goes, "Imitation is the sincerest form of flattery."

This organization (under new leadership of course), or maybe a new organization like it, is essential to the industry since it does, for the most part, provide owners, operators, and golfers with much needed services. The leadership only needs to acknowledge that they don't have all of the answers and that during the previous 20 years, they have not been setting the standard in several areas and have been struggling to even play catch-up. As a result, out of desperation, they aren't even making an effort to cover up their plagiaristic nature. Rather than simply reaching out and welcome collaboration, grow the game with honesty and most of all, grow the game with integrity, they let their egos dragged them down to this level.

Leadership demands stepping to the forefront, not trailing behind. We can't let our egos get in the way of progress and we most definitely can't let our egos ruin the game we all cherish.

Many of these leaders, despite holding advanced degrees in business and advocating for civility, integrity, and moral values, fall short by plagiarizing substantial portions of their published work from others, falsely presenting it as their original intellectual contribution.

This true story serves as a paramount illustration of the value of continued education. Had the leadership of the mentioned organization simply collaborated with MMC®, they would have gained access to an array of groundbreaking strategies to enhance their organization, draw new members and subscribers, boost their members' businesses, propel industry advancement, and—crucially—elevate the game to new heights. It's a fact that no lone organization possesses all the solutions; nevertheless, at MMC®, we take pride in being the trailblazers catalyzing growth within the industry. MMC®'s ideas and initiatives are indispensable, hence, without it, organizations such as the one described will always flounder to stay afloat. Our team at MMC® embodies a culture of perpetual growth and self-improvement, aligning with our core values. MMC®'s foundation is built around innovation and implementation.

It's the large companies like this that sets a bad precedent for the entire industry when they engage in practices such as these.

Plagiarizing and copying other people's intellectual property not only undermine innovation but also threaten the viability of smaller businesses—the very pioneers capable of propelling the industry forward. Instead, the leadership should consider taking the ethical approach of forming strategic partnerships with them and recognizing the value of collaboration by saying, "We admire your innovative thinking and ideas, let's join forces to achieve greatness." Fortunately, since its inception in 2006, MMC® has been a stalwart beacon in the industry and golfer acquisition, proving resilience to overcome challenges such as appropriation of most of our ideas by others. Thankfully, we are always learning so our creative minds are always generating new fresh ideas. We are not hyper-focused on the bottom line like some, instead we are hyper-focused on being of service, saving and growing the game. If industry leaders don't exemplify integrity, how can we expect it from anyone else in the industry?

Throughout this book, I will explore various facets of leadership—dedicating a whole chapter to this pivotal skill. I have, and will continue to share my personal growth experiences with you to highlight the significance of self-improvement as a catalyst for advancing not only your own career or business but also elevating the entire industry and the game itself. Consistently absorbing new knowledge ensures a wellspring of innovative ideas. By keeping your focus on long-term objectives, you will soon discover ideas flowing effortlessly, enabling you to forge unique strategies to expand your business. If this mindset becomes the norm within the industry, discarding the outdated practice of merely emulating others, we will witness a renaissance of creativity that will propel our industry forward. This shift will not only revolutionize the game but will also catalyze the rapid expansion of your business, career, and financial success.

While this chapter may seem brief for discussing the multitude of ways personal growth can occur, it serves as the perfect length to introduce the most significant concepts I have encountered during my journey of continuous personal development. These concepts can be applied to various areas of your life. Over the years, I have delved into ideas such as, "What you think about, you bring about," "If you can conceive it, you can achieve it," and "You are what you think." Although I initially struggled to fully grasp these concepts, my belief in them grew so strong through reading and studying that they became ingrained within me. Through consistent practice of controlling my thoughts, I began to witness the manifestation of things I had focused on intensely in my life. While I may not have fully understood the scientific explanation behind this phenomenon, its effectiveness became evident in all aspects of my life.

Years ago, a pivotal day arrived when I gained insight into how the conscious and subconscious aspects of the mind collaborate to form habits, both positive and negative, merely through consistent contemplation. I discovered that the intensity of my thoughts directly influenced the clarity and strength of the mental images and ideas, solidifying them within my subconscious. Basically, the conscious mind is the creator and the subconscious mind is the implementer. Fully understanding this concept gave me a moment of eureka.

Here is an example to help you understand this concept: Imagine there is a straight wide line on level ground and someone asks you to walk the straight line. For most people, this would be very easy and require little to no thought at all. The subconscious mind would take over, knowing you have done this a million times in the past, and you easily accomplish the task. Now, imagine the line has been elevated slightly above ground level but is still very wide and theoretically should pose no difficulty whatsoever. But this is not the case; your conscious mind takes over because now this task is unfamiliar, and you start to focus on the task intensely and start to question things such as balance. Even though there is ample width for you to easily glide across, because this task has not been ingrained in your subconscious mind through repetition and programming, you must rely on your conscious mind to accomplish the task. Think of your conscious mind as the programmer and your subconscious mind as the software; your conscious mind gives the command, and the subconscious mind puts it into action.

The conscious mind focuses on one task at a time, whereas the subconscious mind can think of multiple things at a time. Your subconscious mind is working like an extremely fast processor in a computer, scanning data at a breakneck pace to deliver answers, solutions, and options immediately. The subconscious mind is responsible for coming up with the necessary tools to accomplish the task, bringing most of the things you need to accomplish your goal out to the forefront and shining a light on them. These things have probably always been there but, in most cases, have gone unnoticed. Your subconscious mind is just making you more aware and conscientious now that it knows what to look for.

This is how we create good and bad habits that lead to our personal and professional development or detriment. We are creating habits, good or bad, every time we focus intently on something and then repeat it over and over in our minds whether it is a thought or action. For example, when a person is facing a challenge (problem), in most cases, the person deals with all challenges the same way. Some who have worked on their personal development might immediately think, "What is good about this? How can I make this into something positive?" and another person may immediately think, "Why me? Why do I not ever get a break? Why do bad things always happen to me?" Your reaction or response to the challenge will either be negative or positive depending on how you have programmed your subconscious mind over the years.

Another application for this tool is in goal-setting. I have been setting goals and studying the subject of goal-setting most of my adult life. Even though I have always seen my goals materialize, I still never really understood exactly how and why it worked so well. I knew I was supposed to set specific goals, design a plan to achieve the goal, take immediate action, and adjust along the way, and sure enough the goal would become realized, but I really never knew how or why. Well, here is how and why; when you imagine something in your conscious mind, your subconscious mind does not know if it is reality or not. All the subconscious mind knows is that the conscious mind is giving it a command and a program, and it is the subconscious mind's responsibility to run the program, process the information, and find the relative material to accomplish the goal. This is why when you want something so badly like a new house, all of a sudden you start noticing new homes and real estate ads—this is your subconscious mind obeying the conscious mind.

If you truly believe that it can happen, you can do it; it is your destiny, and you focus intently on it, your subconscious mind will automatically accept whatever it is and start attracting everything you need to make it a reality. So, the key to maximizing this tool is to start by really believing whatever it is in your conscious mind, vividly visualizing it as if it is real, and attaching intense emotions to it so your subconscious mind can take over and get you headed in the right direction.

If you really want a better job, more money, to live in a better house, have a nicer car, and even own a golf course, learn this skill and you will be amazed at how fast you can and will achieve your dreams.

Never forget: if you can conceive it and believe you can achieve it . . . you become what you think about.

It is said the average person has about 65,000 thoughts per day. The challenge for most people is they have the same thoughts every day. Worse, a large majority of those thoughts are negative. Actually, it is not even their fault because we, humans, are built that way. Our minds have been trained throughout evolution to be aware of danger, threats, and/or anything that could harm us. This was needed in man's beginning because he never knew when a wild beast was lurking around the corner to eat him. As a self-defense mechanism, our brains search out possible dangers and problems. This is why the ratio between negative and positive thoughts is so great on the negative side. Of course, in today's society, this self-defense method is overkill. Nonetheless, it is a reality, and we must remain aware of it and cultivate the ability to swiftly replace negative thoughts and images with positive ones.

In the remaining portion of this chapter, I will briefly touch upon several key subjects related to personal development that I believe can enhance an individual's ability to achieve their desired outcomes in life. Each of these subjects has an extensive body of literature, with numerous books offering in-depth exploration. However, due to the limitations of this chapter, I will provide a condensed introduction to these topics, along with practical guidance to help you implement them immediately. It is important to note that while I have studied these subjects for years, I do not claim to be an expert. Therefore, I highly recommend seeking out books written by authoritative figures in the respective fields that resonate with you to gain a comprehensive understanding. I am simply sharing my basic comprehension of these subjects and how they have personally influenced my life. Fear, being a constant obstacle that affects both personal and professional success, seems like an appropriate subject to commence your personal development journey.

## FEAR

### False Evidence Appearing Real

FEAR, which stands for *False Evidence Appearing Real*, challenges the common misconception that it means to *Forget Everything and Run*. In reality, fear is an emotion, akin to anger, and like all emotions, it can be substituted with another. While fear is often viewed as negative, it plays a crucial role in our self-defense system, serving to safeguard us from potential harm. We are all familiar with the fight-or-flight response to fear, but another response often goes unnoticed or unaddressed in certain situations.

When confronted with fear, our brains instinctively present us with three options: fight, flee, or freeze. In a matter of a millisecond, our minds evaluate the situation, almost like a slow-motion scene in a *Matrix* movie, and determine the most suitable course of action. Sometimes, our minds conclude that freezing is the optimal response. It is important to recognize that all three options—fight, flight, and freeze—are valid choices in specific circumstances. However, employing any of these responses at the wrong time can have detrimental consequences.

If you are out hiking and come across a wild animal and fear kicks in, your brain will immediately analyze the three options. To attempt an attack on the animal would not be wise and may end in disfigurement or even death. To run would almost guarantee disfigurement and/or death. The best choice, in most cases, would be to freeze and collect your thoughts, gather the data, analyze the situation, and then make another more educated decision on your next move, if you decide to move at all. On the other hand, if you are being charged by a stampeding herd of bulls, freezing is almost certain to get you disfigured and most likely killed.

Fear is both good and bad. In chapter 1, I discussed how fear of nonacceptance, loss of respect, and failure can make some people who have yet to learn how to manage their ego disrupt both their personal and professional lives. Particularly in the realm of business, fear can be paralyzing, which can, and does, in most cases, kill the business's growth. The fear of making a wrong decision often prevents individuals from making any decision at all. However, in most cases, the absence of a decision proves to be more detrimental than making a flawed one. It is crucial to understand that fear, like ego, can be effectively managed. Similar to business leaders, the world's best golfers also make mistakes on at least one shot per round, or at the very least, the ball isn't placed precisely where they intended. Growing a business day-in and day-out, making decisions all day long means that occasionally you will make some poor choices, and more often than not, some things won't go exactly as planned, but the worst thing you can do is nothing at all. Imagine a touring professional asking to be given a pass on a hole after hitting a bad shot opposed to finishing the hole to the best of their ability. The thought is too absurd to even fathom, yet professional business people fail to play it where it lays all the time. Instead of attempting another shot, they simply opt to move on to the next hole because they are too paralyzed with fear of failure and making a bad decision.

Learning the techniques to overcome and eliminate fear is an important tool you must have in your toolbox, so fear does not stifle your success. Money, happiness, and health are all attainable if you just eliminate fear and push forward with your dreams and goals.

One of the main reasons why fear paralyzes people from achieving their dreams is because they focus on the things they dread and not the outcome they desire. They worry about all the negative "what-ifs." The key is to have the skill set to identify what is happening and turn your thoughts into "Yes, but what if I accomplish it?" "What if I do succeed?" and "What if I do achieve the goal?" Some people fear the journey more than they seek the reward of achievement. In most cases, it is the things that we have not experienced that we fear the most.

Your fears are the manifestation of your beliefs, so the images you put in your mind are due to your beliefs. You are not responding to reality; you are responding to the image that is in your mind, and you have complete control over that image. So when it comes to fear, make sure that you rework that image of any scenario and choose the best outcome to be the picture that you have in your mind. You need to shape it, turn it, twist it, spin it, and do whatever it takes to make the image or short movie playing in your mind positive and portray the desired outcome. When this mental picture becomes so real to you, you will notice fear slipping away.

Another way to eliminate fear is to address it slowly and take it step by step. I love to ask the question, "How do you eat an elephant?" Answer: "One bite at a time." If the fear is paralyzing, then take baby steps to overcome it. Whatever it is that you are trying to achieve, start toward that goal by taking baby steps. This way, you will see that it is highly unlikely that the horrific thoughts you have imagined will ever materialize. It is just like when somebody first learns to swim, there are two schools of thought. One is to throw them in the water and let them sink or swim, assuming they will learn to swim immediately when faced with the alternative . . . death. The other way is they gradually learn how to swim slowly—they first get in the water with their toes touching the edge, gradually working their way up to their knees and then up to their waist, eventually submerging their head underwater while they can still stand—giving them the feeling of control, and therefore, confidence. Eventually, they learn how to hold on to the side and kick their legs quickly, moving on to using a kickboard to propel themselves in different directions. Finally, they learn to use their arms and legs in tandem. With each new step they take, they build more and more confidence and eliminate more and more fear. After considerable time in the water, they swim just as well as anyone else, and they no longer fear the water or swimming.

Another example of confidence eliminating fear could be two golfers playing the final hole and they are both of equal skill, equal experience, and tied for the win. One of the golfers may lay up at a water hazard instead of going for the green, and the other golfer may go for the green. It is my submission that the one that lays up has previously experienced negative results in this scenario whereas the golfer who goes for the green has experienced positive results. The main differences between the two golfers are fear and confidence. The more confidence the golfer has, the more often he goes for the green (the win) and the less fear he has of failing. Some will say it is not that simple; it is all about course management or other factors that come into play. It has been my experience that these are the same people who have a thousand excuses why they are not winning in life either. Yes, sometimes there are underlying circumstances and sometimes you will hit the ball into the water, but the majority of the time, you just have to go for it and be confident everything will turn out all right.

Some people use the technique of acting past the fear, acting the way you want to be, and acting the way you want to respond. I am not referring to what most people call "fake it until you make it." When I am talking about acting your way through it, I am talking about emulation. Find people that you want to look at as mentors, do what they do in the same situation, and act how they act whenever they go through those fears or are faced with similar challenges. You want to condition a response that will neutralize the fear. These are techniques that can be used today to eliminate your fear of failure, fear of loss, fear of rejection, fear of disappointment, fear of coming up short, fear of loneliness, fear of abandonment, and any other perceived fear—when your mind allows false evidence to appear real.

Think of the cost you will pay if you choose not to do the things you fear. What will it cost you? Are you going to overcome your fear and take advantage of the opportunities that are presented to you? Or are you going to let that fear hold you back? The choice is yours to make, and you must make a decision today to incorporate these strategies into your everyday life now that you possess several techniques to overcome and eliminate fear.

Throughout my career, I have personally witnessed numerous instances when the fear of making difficult decisions has resulted in the loss of everything for at least a hundred owners and operators. Not only did the owners and operators lose their businesses and jobs, but golfers also lost their cherished golfing homes, and communities lost beautiful open green spaces that served as sanctuaries for plants and wildlife. This unfortunate outcome was a result of one person's fear of failure, which ultimately became a self-fulfilling prophecy. The firsthand accounts we received from these owners and operators further validate the impact fear can have on decision-making. Some operators expressed regrets about not being more persuasive in their appeals to the owner, while other operators as well as numerous owners wished they had decided to move forward when initially presented with the opportunity, rather than postponing it. These real-life experiences emphasize the crucial role fear plays in shaping outcomes and reinforce the importance of actively managing and confronting fear to prevent such detrimental consequences.

There are thousands of stories like this relating to all kinds of opportunities that I have seen people pass up because they feared ridicule, failure, embarrassment, rejection, and so on. Just think about how many guys and gals never marry the one they truly love because they were too afraid to approach them or too scared to express their true feelings. Think about how many people are in dead-end jobs and careers because they are afraid they may never find another job. Even more tragic, look at the spouses and partners who stay in abusive relationships because they are afraid that they cannot do any better.

Belief systems play a significant role in shaping our fears and overall mindset. In the subsequent section of this chapter, I will delve into the topic of belief systems, highlighting their potential for both positive and negative impacts. Understanding how to effectively manage and reprogram these beliefs can bring about profound changes in one's life. It is important to recognize that everything you learn about your beliefs and fears must be adapted and applied to both your personal and professional spheres. By mastering these aspects of your psyche, you can unlock the potential for transformative growth and create a positive impact in various areas of your life.

The majority of the things that you fear will never materialize, and those that do will seldom be anywhere near as painful or damaging as you may think. The biggest regrets you will ever have in life are the things you failed to do because you let fear hold you back. Once you eliminate the fear of failure, success is your reward. The next step is to embrace empowering beliefs and challenge limiting ones, which will assist us to overcome our fears and give us the courage to take bold actions and achieve our goals with confidence.

**Belief Systems**

A belief shapes your perception of the truth and affects your life in every aspect and in every way. For better or worse, either way, people have beliefs that shape their entire lives. Sometimes those beliefs are instilled from their childhood; they are formed from experiences, and sometimes those beliefs are completely unfounded.

Some people believe that they are helpless, some believe that they are ignorant, and some believe they do not have the strength or that they do not have enough money. On the other hand, some people believe that they are in complete control, that they are geniuses, that they have the strength to move mountains, or that they have enough money and can earn more anytime they choose. People's automatic responses and thoughts in any given situation are driven by their beliefs, which ultimately shape the outcomes they experience. However, it is important to recognize that these beliefs can be altered just as easily as changing one's thoughts.

The great thing about beliefs (good or bad) is that they have been conditioned, and if you want to change them for the better, all you have to do is redesign them and replace them with a belief that is self-serving or for the betterment of mankind.

The reason why some motivational, inspirational, and educational speakers are successful is because of their ability to get you to believe you can do it, whatever "it" is. If an inspirational speaker can get you to believe it truly can happen, then you will make it happen because it now becomes a part of your core belief system. The only difference between you and them is they believe you can do it, and they are using the tools to get you to believe it as well. The key is to eliminate the middleman and learn these techniques so you can apply them to your own life at will. To be successful, you must be able to connect your beliefs to your goals, and, to do that, you have to change what you believe. You must align your goals with your beliefs and align your beliefs with your goals.

You must recognize your beliefs and know which ones are empowering, which ones are destructive, and which ones are your beliefs and not someone else's who may have conditioned you to believe their beliefs.

Here is a quick exercise. Make a list of some of your strongest beliefs and then ask yourself the following questions about each one of the beliefs:

- Are your beliefs empowering or disempowering?
- Are they hindering your success or are they fueling your success?

- Are your beliefs justified?
- Are your beliefs based on facts?
- Are your beliefs based on experience?
- Are your beliefs your own beliefs or were you conditioned to believe them by others?
- Do your beliefs serve you well?
- Do your beliefs serve a higher purpose, for the betterment of mankind?

Your beliefs serve as motivation and inspiration in your life. All of your decisions are shaped by your beliefs.

One of the greatest examples of how powerful your beliefs are is the placebo effect. As I am writing this chapter, the world has pretty much put COVID-19 in the rearview mirror. In an attempt to combat the virus, drug companies across the world rushed to come up with therapeutics and a vaccine to prevent or, at the very least, minimize the negative effects the virus would have on the world's population. Numerous case studies on new drugs and treatments were launched, and all incorporated some components of a placebo.

In most studies, half of the subjects were treated with new drugs and the other half were treated with placebos. In some cases, those subjects who received the placebo experienced the same or similar results as the ones who were administered the actual vaccine because the patient's belief was so strong that they had been given a miracle drug. Because they believed so strongly, their brains had their bodies' internal pharmacy release the exact drug in the exact dosage that was needed to fight off the virus. Two things to note here: As humans, we are gifted with the world's greatest pharmacy and a computer so advanced it knows the exact drug needed to fight an illness, as well as the exact amount of drug needed. Are there exceptions to this rule? Absolutely! Some of us have compromised immune systems or other health problems that hinder or block this process. Others have psychological underlying conditions (such as negative thinking) that can hinder this process as well. I am not a doctor, nor am I giving medical advice here, I am just pointing out that people have been known to heal themselves just by believing they can.

That is what the placebo effect is: it is a belief in the drug, which may be no more than a sugar pill, and that it is going to cure your ailment. Your subconscious mind starts looking for all of the proper drugs from your body's pharmacy and gets your system to release those drugs. The patient emphatically believes that the magic pill is what cured them, when in fact, it was their own body producing the necessary drug in the right dosage that cured the illness and systems to dissipate. The placebo effect is the most credible data and concrete information proving the connection between your belief system, your conscious mind, as well as the subconscious mind, and the ability for you to achieve anything you truly believe. That is why alternative medicine has such a strong following; whether it is a holistic healer or Holy Roller—if there is a strong enough belief—the possibilities are limitless.

Some beliefs should not be blindly embraced, nor should they be ignored. They should be approached with an open mind, analyzed, and researched, and then a decision should be made based on evidence whether the belief(s) are beneficial or detrimental.

A lot of times, people will go to extreme lengths to avoid going against their core beliefs, but they never analyze to see if those beliefs are correct or if there is a reason to believe them in the first place. You must learn the origin of every belief you have and find out how and why you internalized that specific belief and why you made that belief a reality.

Here are the three categories of core beliefs:

1. **Advertisement Beliefs:** One prevalent advertising belief is that owning a particular product will instantly make you happier and more fulfilled. This belief is often perpetuated through advertisements that emphasize the idea that acquiring a specific item will bring joy, success, or social acceptance. However, this belief can be misleading and fail to address the deeper sources of happiness and fulfillment in

life. True contentment comes from meaningful experiences, personal growth, and nurturing relationships, rather than solely relying on material possessions.

Another advertising belief is that popularity or social status can be achieved by using a particular brand or product. Advertisements often create an association between a desired lifestyle and the use of certain products, leading people to believe that owning these items will enhance their social standing. However, true popularity and acceptance come from genuine connections, shared values, and personal qualities, rather than simply relying on external symbols or brands. Individuals must question these beliefs and examine their foundations. Are they truly aligned with personal values and supported by factual evidence? Or have they been ingrained in our psyche by persuasive advertisers or inherited from previous generations? Evaluating these beliefs through the lens of data, education, and personal experience is essential. By consistently challenging and reassessing our beliefs, we empower ourselves to make informed choices rather than being swayed solely by the promises and images presented in advertisements.

Another example is when it comes to politics: both sides want you to have deep-rooted emotional core beliefs about the other party's character and agendas so that you always vote for their party. Some Democrats want people to believe that all Republicans only care about money and have no heart. Some Republicans want you to believe that all Democrats want big government and handouts. Neither one of these stereotypes is universally true when it comes to either party's base, but some politicians try to shape your beliefs through their narrative (advertisements). Remember, when they are trying to condition your beliefs to mirror their beliefs, through their hyperbole and propaganda, they are only trying to sell you on voting for them. They are getting you to buy into these beliefs so they can sell you something (just like a good marketer does). They have an agenda—they want your votes—so make sure that your beliefs are your beliefs and that they are based on education, facts, and your own experience.

2. **Hand-Me-Down Beliefs:** Hand-me-down beliefs can be the most toxic of all the beliefs, but they can also be the most valuable beliefs. Negative beliefs: You cannot teach old dogs new tricks, or you cannot make money unless you have money, or you were born poor and you will die poor, or you will never amount to anything without a college education. These are some of the beliefs that are detrimental to your future.

   Your parents did the best they could with the tools they had, but their negative beliefs should have never been passed down; they should not be your beliefs, even though the people around you may have repeated these beliefs throughout your childhood and maybe even into your adult life. You can change those beliefs by changing what goes into your mind from this day forward. It is crystal clear that anyone in the United States can become anything they want no matter what their socio-economic standing is, their race, the level of formal education they have attained, who their parents are, what their sex is, what their religion is, etc. With the right attitude, education, and drive—everything is possible. Define your own beliefs and make sure they are aligned with your goals, your values, and your objectives in life.

3. **Cultural or Superstitious Beliefs:** Examples of cultural beliefs are things such as religious beliefs and beliefs about family. Certain beliefs about medicine can stem from cultural perspectives, including views that some may consider quackery or unproven practices. There are superstitious beliefs such as "step on a crack and break your mother's back," "walk under a ladder and you will have bad luck," and "break a mirror and you will have seven years of bad luck" or unlucky numbers such as thirteen. I will not spend much time on this one; because I am sure you can come up with many examples on your own.

Analyze the beliefs that are impacting your life at this very moment; what are your beliefs about bosses, course owners, salespeople, marketing, managing staff, your golfers, your relationships, your education, your career choice, your past, your present, and your future? You must know your beliefs and whether they are serving your career or hurting your career objectives. Are your beliefs nurturing or toxic in your personal life? All of these beliefs are going to affect the quality of your life. Once you have a firm understanding of your belief system, then you need to compare your beliefs to your life goals, for example, family and finances, and make sure that they are aligned.

People are unsuccessful because there is a mismatch between their belief and their lifestyles. This conflict causes them to make poor decisions as well as bad choices in their life—producing an undesired effect. It is imperative you make sure your beliefs are correct, the ones you believe, not what you inherited from your childhood or what you were told to believe from an advertisement you have been bombarded with since birth.

People say, "Oh, they are set in their ways; they will never change," and that is because they have that belief ingrained in their core, and therefore, they fail to acquire the tools to change. A great example of this can be illustrated by some of the people in the golf industry—they thrived during the good ole' times—but when the perfect storm hit and golf courses started going out of business by the thousands, these same people fell impotent because of their outdated beliefs of how a golf course should be operated were too conditioned into their core to accept the reality of the change in the industry. They were paralyzed by fear when all they needed to do was change their paradigm and advance their education.

The absolute most important belief to have in business is an extremely positive belief in salespeople and their contribution to your career, the business you represent, the community, the industry, and most importantly, the game. If you have a negative belief about salespeople and selling products and/or services, you are destined for failure. The core skills you must possess are the ability to professionally sell your products and services and successfully bring them to the market, so you must create a new belief about sales; the same goes for marketing and advertising. Those negative beliefs can keep you from achieving the quality of life you deserve. Golf is a sales and service business. You cannot focus on service until you learn sales, because if you cannot acquire new golfers (no matter how well you service customers), your existing golfers will eventually leave, whether they move, lose interest, or perish. Either way, you will need to replace them, and now is the time to learn that skill—not when all of your golfers are already gone.

On a personal note, what are your beliefs about your own game, your performance on the course, your short game, your long game, and your course-management skills? Get to the bottom of your beliefs about your game, and you might just rise to the top.

A belief you must get to your core is that everyone can be successful with the right education and determination—all that matters is you and your desire to change the beliefs that are holding you back from achieving anything and everything you want. You do not have to go back to college or attend an institution of higher learning; you can be self-educated in the field that you are most interested in. It is the smartest way to advance your education because you eliminate all the things that are irrelevant to your goals and you only focus on the things that are pertinent to your goals—it is called accelerated learning. Change your beliefs, and you can change your life!

Ego driven people are those who have one of the three following beliefs:

1. I am what I have, e.g., my possessions, accomplishments, how much I earn;
2. I am what I do, e.g., my profession, career choice, job title;
3. I am my reputation, e.g., what people think of me.

Believing one of these statements means you identify yourself based solely on your ego. Your life is controlled by your ego, not by your true self.

Remember that the majority of your beliefs are not your own; rather, they are given to you by others based on their interpretations and/or experiences (not yours). These beliefs were most likely imparted to them as well, they just never questioned them—rather they accepted them as true and shared them with others. A person needs to recognize their convictions and live their life in accordance with them.

The problem with believing you are your job, your reputation, and/or your achievements is that contrary to your ego which is trying to influence your thoughts, these beliefs in your identity are for the most part, out of your control. If your self-worth is dependent on your profession, ability, title, position, or anything else, there will come a point in your life when you will undoubtedly lose that "status/position." This may happen only when you retire, but, inevitably, you will eventually lose that identity, or at the very least, it will be significantly diminished, and you will then need to find new ways to identify yourself. Attaching your self-worth to your reputation is the worst possible scenario of the three because everyone you meet, know, or even know of you will have a different impression of you and therefore, you will have numerous reputations that you have absolutely no control over.

Believing your identity is attached to either of the three that is position, possessions, and/or reputation will almost always result in edging golf out ego because then it's all about you and not the game or the betterment of it. Being a person of service and always making decisions based on what's best for everyone concerned is the best identity anyone can have. For example, one day you may lose all of your material possessions and subsequently, you will no longer have an identity. This is one of the reasons why so many individuals hurl themselves out skyscraper windows when the stock market crashes.

The next important concept delves into the topic of harnessing the power of your mind for success. By consciously directing your thoughts, beliefs, and mindset toward your desired outcomes, you can unlock your full potential and create a life of extraordinary achievements.

**Program Your Mind for Success**

There are two kinds of laws everyone must know and adhere to: the laws of nature and the laws of society. The laws of society are taught to you from a very young age. These societal laws can vary and evolve over time, across different locations, and among individuals. While it is possible to break societal laws, doing so is highly unwise, and there may or may not be consequences, especially if one goes undetected or unpunished for the violation. On the other hand, we have the laws of nature. Similar to societal laws, the laws of nature exist to assist us and can serve as valuable tools throughout our lives. However, unlike societal laws, the laws of nature are unbreakable, unaffected by geographical differences, and impartial in their application. Unfortunately, nature's laws are not always taught to us as children, and even sadder to say, most adults do not learn these laws until it is too late. The good news is they are built inside of us; they come with every human being just like a program in the operating system of your home computer. In fact, the brain is often referred to as nature's computer. Laws of nature happen naturally and organically, and all we have to do is learn how to use these laws (tools) to our benefit and avoid using them to our detriment.

One such law is the law of attraction. Positive thoughts bring about positive experiences, and negative thoughts bring about negative experiences. In short, you become what you think about the most.

Everything you are and will be is because of the way you think. If you want to change the quality of your life, you have to change the quality of your decisions, and that starts with the quality of thought. Most people like to block out things that they feel are going to be difficult or uncomfortable. A powerful mind accepts things that have possibilities no matter what the difficulty is and then processes the thought in a way that makes you believe that it really can be achieved.

The only things you have 100 percent control of are your thoughts and your mind. Practicing self-discipline and learning to master your mind is the first step to success. A directed mind is the key to accomplishing any goal. You must be able to focus the majority of your concentration on your goals. This is an enormously powerful tool, and that power is sitting on top of your neck every day, and you have complete control of it.

Imagine how happy you would be if you just expected that everything was going to work out well, everything is going to work out in your favor—that the whole world was working in harmony with your goals, your thoughts, and your expectations. It is your responsibility to ensure that your expectations are consistent with your goals and with the things that you want to accomplish. Remember, the power of positive expectation is probably one of the greatest powers in the laws of nature.

Positive expectations must be married to hard work. If you want to be valued more in an organization, you must bring more value to the organization. You must make yourself indispensable; you must be of such great value that it is impossible or even inconceivable for an owner to look elsewhere other than to you to grow his/her business.

Everyone has 168 hours in a week; if you take out the 8 hours for sleep, that is 56 hours per week, and then deduct the 8 hours most people devote to their work, which equates to 40 hours per week; that leaves you with 72 discretionary hours to do and think what you want.

By increasing your knowledge a little each day, you are going to get a little better each day, and that education is going to compound. Think about the guys or gals in the industry who are making $500,000 a year and then compare them to the people making $50,000 per year; ask yourself: Do you really think they are ten times smarter, ten times more educated, ten times better, and are working ten times harder as the lesser paid employees? No, of course not. They give a little more of their time, they work a little smarter, they study a little bit more, they work a little harder—that is what makes the difference—it is the extra . . . effort. The only difference between ordinary and extraordinary is the word "extra."

You are always going to be compensated in direct proportion to the value you bring to the business. You are being paid exactly what you are worth. If you want to earn more, you have to learn more—you have to give more value. You are earning exactly what you should be earning based on the value that you are giving.

Through your mind, you can change anything you want in life. You can change your attitude, you can change your health, you can change your wealth, you can change your status, and you can change your future. If you are sad one day, just simply think of the happy things in your life. One of the things I love to do first thing every morning is to think about all of the things that I am grateful for because someone who is grateful can never be sad for long.

By simply learning how to control your mind, all else can be controlled; all of your moods can be controlled by your thoughts. If you want to be happy, focus on the positive, focus on the happy things, think happy thoughts, focus on a happy future, and think of your happy family. If you think, believe, and put enough emotional intensity into it, it will become a reality.

Free yourself from the constraints of self-limiting ideas. Embrace a mindset of success, popularity, and achievement. Cultivate unwavering expectations that propel you toward your goals. Unlock the power of utilizing the abundant tools and resources provided by nature, and harness the laws of the universe to work in your favor. With these foundational principles in place, let us now venture into the next topic: the art of goal-setting. Discover the artistry of crafting clear, compelling goals that ignite your passion and drive. Learn proven techniques to set meaningful objectives, create actionable plans, and navigate the path toward your desired outcomes. Goal-setting is a powerful tool that propels you toward success, and we will explore it to equip you with the knowledge and strategies to make your aspirations a reality.

**Goal-Setting**

It is impossible to get somewhere if you do not know where you are going. Most people spend more time planning their vacations than they do their futures. Setting goals is fundamental to success, and if you are serious about your success, you must write your goals down. It is one thing to imagine what you want, but putting your goals down on paper in black and white takes your goals to a new level. Regrettably, the only time most people write down their goals is at the beginning of the year, during New Year's. Goals are something you need to have in front of you all the time. The more you write a goal down, the more you are going to ingrain it into your subconscious mind and the faster it is going to be realized.

You must condition your subconscious mind to focus on the goal constantly. When a goal is ingrained in your subconscious mind, your brain will start to get hypersensitive to anything associated with that goal and will signal your conscious mind to be alert. Resources such as people, places, and things that could assist you in achieving a goal will now start to appear everywhere.

Case in point, in the early days of MMC®, I could not afford a marketing budget for direct mail, magazine ads, radio ads, and so on like I can today. Back then, I was on the road almost every day of the year driving across the United States, knocking on doors. One day, I was passing through Santa Fe, New Mexico; a beautiful little quaint city, and I decided to stop and eat lunch before going to my meeting later that day. Just a few steps away from the restaurant stood an adorable boutique store that caught my attention. Among its collection of trinkets and treasures, my gaze fixated on a stunning globe that immediately captivated me. Without a doubt, it was the most exquisite globe I had ever laid eyes upon.

I went inside to inquire about the globe and was told by the salesperson that it was a limited edition; it was made from precious stones, and each country was made of a different precious stone.

The salesperson continued by saying it was their only one. Of course, I knew I was getting the big sales pitch, but I did not care because it truly was the most beautiful globe I had ever seen. Then the price was revealed, and it almost floored me. At this point in my career, I was living on a shoestring budget, sleeping in cheap motels and eating fast food. Besides, the globe was delicate, which could pose shipping issues and would definitely require special care when packaging, incurring even more cost, so I decided the purchase was just too illogical, and I passed on it.

Throughout the rest of the day, I could not stop thinking about that globe. This obsession continued as I drove further out west and tried to remember if I had ever seen a globe like that in all of my travels, and the answer was no. I had crisscrossed the United States numerous times from New York to LA and from Chicago to New Orleans but could not remember ever seeing such a beautiful globe. Finally, I could not take it any longer, so I called the store, gave them a credit card, and told them to ship the globe to my office in Jacksonville.

Even though I had purchased the globe, I still thought of it often while on this business trip and was looking forward to getting back to my office to position the globe perfectly on my office cabinet.

Several days later when I was in Los Angeles, and, of course, the globe was still on my mind, I met with an owner, and lo and behold, there it was—my globe (although in a different finish) was sitting in the owner's office. I was taken aback for a second, but I did not say anything to the owner. Once back in my car, I shrugged it off as being a coincidence, but it did not end there. As I traveled back across the States, I saw the same globe at least two more times. Again, I did not care because the globe was so incredibly beautiful, and up to the time I had bought it, I had never seen one.

I finally arrived back in Jacksonville and went straight to my office as usual, but this time, I was there to decorate it with my prized possession, "the globe." It matched the decor beautifully, and I was ecstatic. I marveled over the globe for a while and then decided to go to a quaint area, San Marco in Jacksonville, for lunch with my secretary. By this time, my secretary was sick of hearing about this globe; she was just glad it was finally over. As we strolled down the street toward the restaurant, something caught my eye in a store window. Son of a gun, it was my globe, not one similar to it but one that was exactly like it. I could not believe my eyes. I bolted through the front door of the store, and I was greeted by a minimum of fifty of this "limited" number, precious stone globes! My secretary could not contain her laughter and burst into a hysterical laughing fit. I was not amused, to say the least. My precious limited edition, impossible-to-find globe was just one of the millions of mass-produced globes that could have been purchased just minutes from my office.

The crux of this story is that if you ingrain any goal into your subconscious mind, even though the resources were probably there all along, your subconscious mind will start to make you more aware of them. Although the globe was not a goal per se, once I had a clear picture in my head of the globe and thought of it in detail often, my subconscious mind started heightening my awareness similar to setting a goal, bringing it out in plain sight. Goal-setting makes you commit the goal to your subconscious mind, and then your subconscious mind will make you hypersensitive to the available resources necessary to achieve that goal.

I have always said there are four phases to successful goal-setting:

1. Set specific goals. Do not just say, "I want to be rich." Being rich is a subjective term. Some people feel as though they are rich if they are surrounded by family, some people think they will be rich if they make a million dollars, and some think they will be rich when their money works for them and they no longer have to work for money. Be specific and identify your goals in detail.
2. Develop a strategy. How, what, when and why are the four questions you must answer in detail. Within what time frame do you want the goal to be accomplished? And why do you want to accomplish the goal? The "why" being the most important. Your desire to reach the objective will be stronger the more motivation you have to do so.

3. Go for it! Execute your plan.
4. Once you implement your strategy, check on your progress daily to make sure you are making inroads. If you are not getting the desired result, be prepared to make adjustments and try new things. Be flexible in the approach but not with the goal.

Start setting goals for every facet of your life and look at them daily or at a very minimum weekly. Turn your goals into a vivid motion picture in your mind with as much detail as possible. Add sound, colors, and textures if possible. Always make your goals in the present tense. Remember, if you can conceive it, and you believe it, you can achieve it!

Similar to how your goals need to have a time frame, it is equally important to establish time frames for everything else in your life if you want to maximize your personal or business endeavors. Time management is an essential skill that propels you toward success, and we will delve deeper into its principles to equip you with the tools and mindset required to make each moment count.

**Time Management**

Time is an invaluable asset for any businessperson. However, it is often in limited supply, which is why effective time management is crucial. Just like the saying goes, "Rome wasn't built in a day," you must approach your day as a whole and then break it down into manageable chunks. By tackling tasks one step at a time, and allocating sufficient time for each item on your to-do list, you can make progress toward your goals without feeling overwhelmed. Remember, great accomplishments are the result of consistent effort over time.

There is never enough time to do everything, but there is always enough time to do the most important things. It is a matter of prioritizing. What is most important to you? Is growing your business, growing the game, and growing your golf career the most important thing you can do with your time to support yourself, your family, and your owner? If yes, then a large portion of your day should be devoted to activities that will align with your goals.

Time management is a key element to success. You have to consider the long-term consequences as well as the short-term consequences of your decisions on how to use your time or how to allocate your time. Everyone knows time is money—a great example of this can be illustrated by looking at how professionals, such as attorneys, bill their clients for their time. Most attorneys bill their time in blocks of ten minutes. If you only need three minutes, you are still billed for ten minutes. If you need eleven minutes, you are billed for twenty minutes because you have now entered a new block of time. You must develop a sense of urgency when it comes to time because if you do not, you lose that time forever.

Start by scheduling the tasks, appointments, calls, and so on that you are avoiding or are not excited about but know they are crucial to your success. People think, "Oh, I can do it tomorrow," but "There is no tomorrow!" as Sylvester Stallone says in one of his *Rocky* movies, and "Tomorrow never comes" as Garth Brooks sings in one of his hit songs. People want to put things off until tomorrow because they think they may never have to do it, and that is absurd. The faster you do it, the quicker you get it off your desk and the more successful you are going to be.

Everyone must look at the secondary consequences of their actions of how they spend their time. If a golf professional chooses to throw his feet up on the desk and surf the internet for two, three, or four hours a day as opposed to taking time to make some calls, send some emails, put out some flyers, call some businesses, or even just study an educational program, he/she, in essence, is choosing failure over success.

The same goes for a golf professional who chooses to spend all of their time chatting with golfers who are already loyal committed members of the club instead of going out and chatting with guests and new members. Yes, it is important to socialize with all the members, but the new members or guests need just a little more attention for them to feel welcomed, appreciated, and valued. A great example of this is a golfer who has a great long game but is weak around the greens. He/she spends their practice time at the range in hopes of impressing their friends with their powerful long drives instead of practicing their short game, which is where they really need to improve.

When you are socializing, especially at work, remember that time has to come from somewhere, which could have been spent on anything. When you are taking that time from more productive work, such as engaging prospective members—you are never going to get that time back. There are only 24 hours in a day. We all have 168 hours a week. It is a matter of how you allocate that time that is going to determine your success or lack thereof.

Often, I hear owners, managers, and staff complaining about the excessive hours they are forced to work at the course. One of the things I always try to bring to their attention is that it is not the quantity of time you spend at work; it is the quality of the time you spend at work. One of my favorite sayings is, "Do not confuse motion for momentum." Just because you are busy at work, that time does not qualify as quality time spent on doing important work or work that is going to contribute to the bottom line. Learning time-management skills will allow you the time to grow the business, which in the end is really all that matters because when you grow the business, you are not only supporting the course, all of the members, all of the golfers, your salary, all of your employees' salaries, the owners' profit, the owners' families' lifestyle, but everybody who is in the industry can be affected either positively or negatively by your work ethic.

Look at growing the business through my eyes for a moment. Every time we acquire a new golfer for a facility, that revenue pays salaries for people such as the ground crew, the superintendent, the counter staff, the bookkeeper, the golf professional, the management, the wait staff, the cooks, and the janitors, and these new golfers may buy new clubs, balls, apparel, tees, books, and lessons, which of course contributes to those companies' employees' salaries. These new players will rent carts, and possibly book banquets and weddings, and now these businesses would have additional revenue to pay their employees. This is why I believe if you have any extra time in your day, devote it to acquiring new golfers, and each time you do, you will be contributing to the growth of the entire industry.

You must learn to allocate your time wisely. You need to prioritize what is most important to you. In this section of the chapter, I focused on time management at work, but it is equally important to manage your personal time so you will thrive in all areas of your life including the quality of life you will have with your family.

Most people stop growing personally after they finish college. They fail to continue reading and learning outside of trade magazines or things that they love and enjoy for pleasure. You must make learning in all areas of your personal and professional development a priority. Since the golf industry is your chosen field, you need to be sharpening your tools every day. Allocate your time wisely and eliminate distractions in your life that are not producing the results that you desire. Learn to manage your time, and you will create the future that you desire.

You are where you are and who you are because of what has gone into your mind. The same holds true for time. You are where you are because of how you have chosen to use your time. Choose wisely. Choose to stop hoping to get all your rounds in this season, choose to stop hoping for good weather, but instead, choose to educate yourself and learn ways to grow the business and set time aside every day to do exactly that . . . grow the business by managing your time well. As I stated earlier, we all have 168 hours a week; it is up to you how you decide to use them.

Procrastination poses a significant obstacle to effective time management. In the following section, we will examine the root causes of procrastination and explore practical strategies to conquer this prevalent challenge. By addressing procrastination head-on, you can reclaim control over your time and propel yourself toward greater success and fulfillment.

**Procrastination**

Contrary to what most people believe, procrastination is not always a bad thing. You can make procrastinating work for you. In this section, I will show you how to take something that most people view as a negative and turn it into a positive. On the negative side, procrastination can create havoc in your personal and business life. If used as a tool, procrastination can be a great motivator.

Procrastination can also be defined as the "Mañana habit." *Mañana* is a Spanish word for tomorrow. Proactive people live by the creed, "Never put off until tomorrow what you can do today." Those who procrastinate think that if they can put the task, decision, etc. off until tomorrow, they may never have to do it at all. Putting off important tasks and/or decisions can devastate your life. You must take action steps toward eliminating procrastination in your life because it can destroy your career, your relationships, and even your outlook on life if you let it. Procrastination, in most scenarios, is linked to a fear of doing something. The goal is to turn that fear into fuel.

As with any problem, the first step is identifying that you have a problem. Next, you want to start identifying when you are procrastinating and take immediate action. One of the best ways to avoid procrastinating is to always follow the old Nike slogan "Just Do It" and get it out of the way. Every day, I write a to-do list of the things I need to accomplish, and one of the things I do to avoid procrastinating is that I always try to do the things that are least enjoyable first. This way, I get the least enjoyable tasks out of the way, and I do not procrastinate and let them hover over me like a dark cloud and ruin the entire day or week.

It is very easy for people to immediately do the things that are the most fun on their to-do lists and put the things off that they least enjoy, but when you do that, you will always regret it, because the undesirable tasks and/or decisions will start to pile up, and soon you will start to feel overwhelmed. I had come across this scenario numerous times while speaking with operators, especially when it came to marketing and sales. They knew something needed to be done, but they feared making a bad decision and inevitably only made the situation worse. Often, I will have an operator tell me that they had planned on calling MMC® for years but just never made the call. Unfortunately, they needlessly suffered through a few more seasons just because they procrastinated.

A perfect example of procrastination is when you go into a pro shop and you see the staff scrolling through social media, and not making phone calls, sending out emails, or doing something that can be productive to grow the business. It is much easier to divert your attention to something that is comforting as opposed to something a little challenging.

Another thing you can do is try to identify what it is about the task that you are avoiding or that you dislike. Does it make you feel like you are unqualified? Does it feel like it is going to be overwhelming? Do you feel like it is going to take too long, or could it be that you unconsciously feel you are not worthy of success and, therefore, sabotage your efforts by procrastinating? No matter what it is, if it has to be done, you have to get your head into the game and know that this is something you have got to do.

It is just like on the golf course; you may not be great at bunker shots, and you might avoid hitting into a bunker at all costs, but no matter what, there are always going to be times when you are golfing that you are going to end up in the bunker, and if you keep avoiding practicing bunker shots, you are always going to perform poorly, which means you are always going to play subpar golf. Moreover, it is often the very things people fear the most that they inadvertently attract into their lives. This is due to them being hyper-focused on the thing they fear when they should be hyper-focused on the desired result instead. The only way to get rid of this fear, whatever it may be, is by doing it now and if necessary by doing it often.

As I have stated many times in the past, we do things either out of pain or pleasure. Most people procrastinate because there is something painful that they associate the task or decision with. But just like with anything else, you have got to look at the long game. By doing the task, whatever it may be, and getting it off your to-do list, you can then move straight to something a lot more pleasurable. This is what I mean when I say you can use procrastination as a motivational tool. Reward yourself every time you do something you would normally put off with something you love doing.

A great example of this is, let us say, you need to sell at least one golf membership every day. You also know you need to make ten calls to get two appointments. Since you close 50 percent of your presentations, you can feel pretty confident that ten calls will produce one membership sale. Unfortunately, you have been procrastinating when it comes to making your daily calls; therefore, you fail to sell your quota of one golf membership per day. From now on, reward yourself with ten minutes of social media for every successful call you make. This way, you can browse social media guilt-free and you have turned a negative (procrastination) into a positive.

Always try to do the things that are least pleasurable in the beginning and find something or anything that can be associated with that task or decision that is pleasurable so that it will not be so painful for you to do.

Frequently, after starting something you have been putting off, you will find that you exaggerated how unpleasant it was and that the task is actually fun to do. When asked, people say, "That was not nearly as hard as I thought it was going to be."

Every time that you conquer a task that you originally started to procrastinate about, it becomes a habit, and the more you overcome procrastination, the more you will reinforce that habit.

Overcoming this challenge can propel you closer to achieving your goal of financial freedom. Embrace the opportunity to transform procrastination into a driving force and seize your full potential, and you'll start producing the numbers that one day may make you a self-made millionaire.

**Think Like a Self-Made Millionaire**

I remember reading a book years ago called *The Millionaire Next Door*, and one of the things that stood out to me from that book was that anyone can become a millionaire and that most millionaires are people you would never suspect of being a millionaire—they are the people who own things such as dry cleaners, laundromats, mom-and-pop stores, and salespeople.

Everyone thinks that celebrities, musicians, professional athletes, real estate developers, or executives of Fortune 500 companies are millionaires, and yes, some of them are, but the majority of millionaires are hardworking people who have learned how to invest well, save, and continued their education within their industry and have the ability to keep their primary focus on forward thinking. Not every self-made millionaire went to college. In fact, most of them did not. What matters when it comes to education is: are you educated? This does not mean you have to attend an institution of higher learning; it means you have to have an appetite for knowledge that can never be satisfied, especially in the area of growing your business.

The intelligence of most self-made millionaires is generally average. Rather than relying solely on their intellect, they understand the importance of acquiring relevant education in their respective fields. They work diligently, employ smart strategies, and go the extra mile to achieve success. The differentiating factor between ordinary individuals and extraordinary ones lies in the additional effort they invest. Self-made millionaires recognize the need to dedicate extra time and effort, particularly in acquiring knowledge and skills related to attracting new customers and growing their businesses.

You can absolutely start from nothing and become a self-made millionaire within a few years in any field. As long as you learn the skills of sales and marketing, you will be able to promote and bring your ideas, products, and services to the masses.

If you want to earn more, give more value. If you want to earn a lot more, give a lot more value to a lot more people.

Here I have listed eighteen attributes that you must have to become a self-made millionaire:

> *The first* must-have attribute is common sense. If you do not have common sense, you automatically have a weak foundation.
>
> *The second* must-have attribute is courage—to go for what you want, to take risks, and to make difficult decisions. You need courage to ignore the naysayers and to make mistakes because you are definitely going to make them, so just be prepared to fix them along the way and move on.
>
> *The third* must-have attribute is education—you need to continually educate yourself in your field of industry and your position. If you manage a golf course, it does not mean that you only study facility-management systems; you should study every position you are responsible for as well as those positions above and below you. The most important subject matter you must study is acquiring new business and becoming proficient at it because the bottom line is—the bottom line, and the only way to change it is by growing the business and being responsible for the actions of those who are under your management.
>
> *The fourth* must-have attribute is you must be responsible—you must take responsibility for the results of your decisions (good and bad). If the business is performing poorly, it is your responsibility to make it

perform well. If the business is performing well, it is your responsibility to make it perform even better.

*The fifth* must-have attribute is belief—you have to believe in yourself, you have to believe in your dreams and ideas, and you have to believe they can and will materialize. Whatever you can conceive in your mind, you can achieve. Your subconscious mind does not know the difference between what is happening in reality and what you are imagining. Create the world you want, create the future you want, and create the life that you want. Just know that if you believe it really can happen, that you can make it happen, it will happen.

*The sixth* must-have attribute is the ability to trust your gut feelings—for example, are you in a field that you absolutely love? You would think this is a no-brainer for those who are in the golf industry. They love the game of golf, and when you love something, you are going to excel at it. But this is not always the case. Some in the industry may have lost the passion because of mundane day-to-day operations or the pressures of running a business, or they just prefer playing the game over the business side of the game. Either way, you need to follow your gut feeling. If you love golf as well as the business of golf, you will excel in this field, but if you do not have a passion for the business, you need to rethink your career choice and trust your gut. Adapt to your surroundings, and adapt to your situation. The golf industry is changing; there are no ifs and buts about it. It is happening, and it is happening before your very eyes. The traditional field of dreams is gone. If you build it, people will come to check out the bells and whistles because it is new, but they will not stay unless you give them a reason to. So, stop relying on the field of dreams.

*The seventh* must-have attribute is the ability to adapt—stop depending on some of the systems of the past. Learn that you are now in an industry that is more competitive than at any other time. Think outside the box and adapt to the changes in demographics, buying habits, cultural changes, and life in general. Winners do not complain; they adapt.

*The eighth* must-have attribute is curiosity—ask questions and ask more questions. For example, the key to succeeding in the golf industry is being able to lock up long-term relationships with golfers. Asking great questions will help you unearth golfers' needs and wants. This way, you can demonstrate how your products and services are far superior to any other offered in the same category. All questions are not created equal, so learn how to ask well-structured questions to get the exact answers needed.

*The ninth* must-have attribute is communication skills—written, oral, nonverbal, etc. are all tools that need sharpening. Customer relations, public relations, as well as personal relations, all depend on good communication skills. Communication skills go far beyond conversations. Communication skills include listening, asking questions, reading body language as well as knowing how to communicate with your own body language.

*The tenth* must-have attribute is the ability to think creatively. If you are doing the same thing as your competitor, you are not being creative. Most people live paycheck to paycheck, season to season, or month to month. Follow them, and you will end up living hand to mouth also. Be creative, and keep coming up with new ideas, especially those that can grow your business.

*The eleventh* must-have attribute is the willingness to make sacrifices. You can always spot the winners and losers in an organization by their willingness to work late and on weekends, holidays, vacations and miss ballgames, social functions, and so on. Self-made millionaires put their goals at the forefront and graft in everything around them. This does not mean missing every one of your children's school events or family get-togethers. It does mean prioritizing everything in your life and making necessary sacrifices when they arise. There are numerous sacrifices you must be willing to make, especially when first starting on your journey, which could include not buying the nice car you want at the time and settling for a less expensive car, not buying the new home you want but maybe buying a much smaller one with a much smaller more manageable mortgage. There are thousands, if not millions, of examples you will face, but the main question will always be: are you willing to make that sacrifice to achieve your dream?

*The twelfth* must-have attribute is loyalty—loyalty is the key. You will never see a successful businessperson who is not loyal stay at the top. You must be loyal to your customers and loyal to your employees, and especially your boss. There are a lot of self-made millionaires who work for other people, and they are very loyal to their bosses and their companies. It is probably one of the most important attributes a person can have to help them become successful because when you are loyal, people will trust you, and when people trust you, they are going to bestow opportunities upon you because they know you are going to be loyal to them, and in the end, this one attribute will bring you a wealth of opportunities. One of the worst things you will ever hear is somebody who is in a leadership position bad-mouthing the company, the owner, or the employees; this will get you nowhere fast. You may be able to hold on to that position temporarily, and, believe me, it is only because the owner does not have any other options better than you at the moment. But once the owner is presented with a better option, you will be out. So, make sure that you are always loyal to your staff, the owner, and the company. And make sure that loyalty is based on hierarchy; you are always loyal to the owner first. The owner is the most important person; then comes your senior management and then your subordinates.

*The thirteenth* must-have attribute is having a positive attitude and positive outlook on life. You should look at things positively. Keep positive images in your mind. Always think of positive results. Think positive, and you will see an immediate change in your life. If you improve your thinking, you will also improve the quality of your life. There is always something positive in everything in life. It is up to you to look for it and bring it to the forefront.

*The fourteenth* must-have attribute is confidence. Self-made millionaires have an abundance of self-confidence. It may not show in all aspects of their lives, but they definitely demonstrate confidence in their chosen profession. They get their confidence from experience, from studying, and from knowledge of their product and industry. They are confident because they know what they are doing and not just guessing. They are not feeling their way through life; they are in control of their destiny, and they are confident they will succeed.

*The fifteenth* essential attribute is possessing an exceptional vocabulary. It is crucial not only to use words that carry strong meanings but also to employ positive language. Opt for positive words over negative ones. Proficiency in the English language, both written and spoken, holds immense value.

*The sixteenth* must-have attribute is you must know how to delegate and assign things to people who are experts in their field. Do not try to be an expert in every field. Yes, you should know a little bit about everything, but do not try to be in authority on all things. Know what your real strengths are, focus on them, and delegate the rest to people who can do those things far better than yourself.

*The seventeenth* must-have attribute is dedication. Self-made millionaires do not watch the clock—they will work on their goals from the time their feet hit the floor until the time their heads lie on the pillow. They know that in the first forty hours, they will work just to earn a living and in the second forty hours, they will work to create a life. The beautiful thing about success is that when doing something you love, it never seems like work because you are always doing something you enjoy.

*The eighteenth* must-have attribute is the ability to choose your friends wisely. Socialize with people who are striving and doing everything possible to become successful. Make sure that you are socializing with the people who you want to be like. Negative attitudes, negative people, and negative thoughts are the source of almost everything that goes wrong in life. Do not socialize with people that radiate negative energy, get away from them like they have an infectious disease, and run as far and as fast as you can. The people whom you choose to associate with are going to affect your success whether it is for the good or bad, so choose your friends wisely.

All of these attributes can be acquired. You do not have to be born with these attributes; they can all be learned. Like talent, some of us are born with some of these attributes and characteristics, and like skill, some of these must be acquired. Nonetheless, they must be incorporated into your core being. Of course, there are a million more things a person can work on to improve their chances of becoming a self-made millionaire, and most of them are little things that compound into gigantic things. Often you will hear, "Do not sweat the small stuff," but I disagree. The Tao (pronounced Dow) is in the details—the Tao is enlightenment. Pay attention to the little things as well as the big things and you will achieve financial enlightenment. Acquire the eighteen must-have attributes and you too will become a self-made millionaire.

It is through continuous personal development that we unlock our true potential and pave the way for a fulfilling and successful life. By addressing our fears, managing our beliefs, and cultivating empowering mindsets, we can overcome obstacles, seize opportunities, and create positive change. Remember, change begins within us. As we strive to grow and evolve, we not only enhance our own lives but also inspire and uplift those around us. Embrace personal development as a lifelong journey, and let it guide you toward a future filled with limitless possibilities.

Now, let us explore the strategies to cultivate and expand your business, unlocking financial rewards beyond your wildest imagination.

# 4

## DEVELOPING NEW SKILL SETS

In *Golf: The Untapped Market*, I have established a solid groundwork for professional sales and marketing, unlocking untapped opportunities. As you embark on this chapter, allow me to guide you through the intricate framework of advanced selling and marketing techniques. Just as I divided chapter 3 into insightful topics on personal development, I will employ the same systematic approach to illuminate the next phase of professional sales and marketing in this chapter. For those who have not yet obtained a copy of my book, *Golf: The Untapped Market*, you can visit www.golfmarketingMMC®.com and secure your copy today.

One of the most captivating facets of the golf industry, both historically and presently, is its inherent association with robust moral and ethical standards. From the initial moment I set foot on a golf course, I discerned a profound affinity between the game and my personal values. This intrinsic connection has served as a compelling factor, driving my interest and fascination with the sport. When I established MMC® in 1991, my unwavering commitment was to infuse membership sales with dignity and integrity. Golf, being a sport that demands unwavering adherence to ethical principles, fits my business philosophy like a glove. I believe that ethical selling and marketing are the only pathways to acquiring and professionally selling a golf product and/or golf service. By upholding the highest standards of honesty, fairness, and transparency, we can forge meaningful connections with customers, foster trust, and cultivate a sustainable business built on principles that remain steadfast over time.

In today's business landscape, where golfers have numerous options to choose from, it is crucial for companies to strictly adhere to a strong code of ethics. Customers can explore various alternatives until they are assured that they are pledging their loyalty to a business operated by honest and fair people. One of the topics I have spoken about in the past is finding your niche market or specialty within the golf industry that allows you to stand out from your competitors. Operating your business with a strong emphasis on good moral conduct is a great place to start.

It is important to emphasize that your staff, as well as anyone representing your golf course, adopts an ethical approach when performing their tasks, regardless of their role in food and beverage, range management, or maintenance. Telling the truth and treating people with fairness and dignity should be universal principles practiced by all individuals, regardless of their involvement in business, personal life, or any other aspect of daily living. Building a life or operating a business on a solid foundation of morals and principles ensures its enduring strength.

Regrettably, some individuals resort to bending the truth to achieve their goals in life. This tendency also extends to marketing golf courses and establishing relationships with golfers. Regardless of the condition of a golf course, there are always positive aspects that can be highlighted to excite golfers and capture their attention, ultimately leading them to visit the property. It is important to maintain honesty and integrity throughout this process, without misleading anyone. Not every relationship is a perfect fit, so do not try to force a square peg into a round hole. By telling the truth, understanding how your product can meet the customer's needs, and ethically locking up that relationship, you can secure a valuable connection.

Let us take a scenario as an example. During a sales call, you have successfully built rapport with the prospect. However, when they ask for more information about your product or services, you may feel tempted to provide exactly what they want to hear, even if it involves stretching the truth. At that moment, you may question the potential harm and think that nothing could go wrong. But the reality is that a lot can go wrong, and it will have severe repercussions on the brand reputation of the business as well as your personal integrity.

When the customer eventually uses your golf product or service, they will not only realize the dishonesty but also lose trust in the entire business. Instead of gaining a satisfied and happy customer, you will end up with an irate customer who is likely to share their negative experience with ten friends, and those friends will further spread the word.

It is important to understand that dishonesty not only damages the relationship with the customer but also tarnishes the reputation of the business. It is always better to prioritize honesty and maintain trust, even if it means losing a potential sale. Building a strong and trustworthy brand is a long-term endeavor that relies on ethical practices and genuine customer satisfaction.

"Why should I choose your course over your competitor?" is a question you will hear more often than you want. When that happens, you have two options:

1. **Slander and criticize your competitor:** This approach involves speaking negatively about your competitor, highlighting their weaknesses or shortcomings. However, this strategy can come across as unprofessional and may reflect poorly on your integrity. It is generally advisable to avoid engaging in negative tactics that tarnish the reputation of others.
2. **Showcase your unique value proposition:** Instead of focusing on criticizing competitors, it is more effective to utilize this opportunity to demonstrate why your golf course is the best choice for the prospect. Emphasize the qualities that set you apart, such as your honesty, dedication, and commitment to serving golfers. Highlight the unique aspects of your golf

course that align with the prospect's specific needs and preferences. By taking this positive and customer-centric approach, you can showcase your strengths without resorting to negative tactics.

Ultimately, by focusing on the positive attributes of your own golf course and how it caters to the prospect's requirements, you can build trust and establish a genuine connection that resonates with the customer.

Belittling your competitors will not improve your standing in the eyes of your prospects. Instead, it will portray you as dishonest and unethical. Golfers seek interactions with proactive staff and operators who possess a deep understanding of their needs. They desire someone who listens attentively and comprehends their desires, goals, and requirements. The objective is to engage in an honest and open dialogue that is founded on trust and respect. As an operator, your aim should be to cultivate long-lasting relationships with golfers. Demonstrating trustworthiness is essential, and this trust should be established from the very first encounter.

Developing a code of ethics for your business helps build a culture of ethical selling. Your code of ethics may simply be a statement of principles defining the way you operate, make decisions, and treat your staff and customers. The code of ethics that guides your actions may encompass the following principles:

- Prioritize the significance of your actions over mere words.
- Provide golfers with truthful and precise information.
- Ensure that the purchasing decisions of your golfers are driven by their preferences, free from any undue pressure from your side.
- Cultivate enduring and loyal relationships with your players.
- Compete in the market based on the strengths of your business and reputation, without resorting to damaging the reputation of your competitors.

It is easy to sell and market your golf course ethically without bending or exaggerating the truth; all you need to do is look for the little things that separate you from your competitors and make sure you highlight the FABs—features, advantages, and benefits of golfing at your course. The truth is that everyone should golf at your property because it is managed with an emphasis on ethics.

When a product advisor possesses the necessary skill sets to market and sell a product and/or service, ethical selling will no longer require a conscious thought but instead, will be woven into the marketing and sales process automatically.

**Mastering New Skill Sets**

To achieve mastery in a specific skill set such as golf marketing or professional membership sales, it is essential to possess a high level of competence in the field. Competence can manifest in various forms and proficiency levels. I have read somewhere that we go through four stages in mastering a given skill: unconscious incompetence, conscious incompetence, conscious competence, and unconscious competence. This is the natural progression we all must go through when acquiring a new skill, including professional golf membership sales as well as golf marketing.

**Unconscious Incompetence**

The initial stage is commonly referred to as "unconscious incompetence," wherein individuals lack awareness and skills in a particular task. For example, when appointed as a teaching professional by an owner and entrusted with the responsibility of expanding the business, one may find themselves attempting to navigate unfamiliar territory without proper education, expertise, or knowledge of where to begin. This stage is often encountered by numerous golf course operators today, who are thrust into their roles without adequate training specifically in business growth. While these operators may possess training in other areas such as public relations, budgeting, and the game itself, they are unfairly expected to possess the requisite knowledge to attract new golfers and drive the expansion of the golf course. Faced with the pressure to increase rounds and revenue, coupled with a lack of understanding, operators often experience a sense of incompetence and overwhelming challenges in effectively developing the business. At this pivotal point, operators may choose to either relinquish marketing and sales endeavors altogether or persist, regardless of the associated costs to the business, and progress to the subsequent stage.

**Conscious Incompetence**

The second stage in the mastery of a skill is referred to as "conscious incompetence," wherein individuals become aware of their lack of proficiency in a given task. At this stage, you begin to recognize that you are ill-equipped to successfully undertake the assigned task. It becomes evident that you lack the necessary tools and knowledge to effectively grow the business. Consequently, you embark on a quest for additional information and seek guidance from industry experts to acquire the relevant skills and expertise in attracting golfers and nurturing relationships with them.

This stage marks a significant turning point as you become consciously aware of your limitations. It serves as a crucial realization in your career journey because acknowledging your lack of expertise is the catalyst for growth and development.

**Conscious Competence**

Upon entering the stage of conscious competence, you begin to develop a heightened awareness of your actions, both correct and incorrect. Things start to fall into place, albeit without a complete understanding of the underlying mechanisms. Your marketing campaigns yield better results, leading to increased revenue for the business. At this point, you are likely experiencing success through a process of trial and error. It is crucial to take detailed notes and gather data during this phase.

This stage marks the beginning of mastering your craft. You actively acquire additional tools, skills, and education to build upon the modest success you have achieved. As you delve deeper into golf course marketing, you strive for excellence and enhance your competence in the field. This involves expanding your knowledge beyond marketing and sales, encompassing subjects such as history, sciences, psychology, and more. This broader education enables you to deepen your understanding of the art of growing a business.

During this stage, you realize that golf course marketing is not merely a matter of sending a few emails, posting on social media platforms, or placing ads in the local paper, expecting prospective golfers to flock to your course. The outdated notion of "build it and they shall come" no longer applies to the golf industry. Instead, you recognize that golf course marketing is an intricate art that demands strategic and thoughtful approaches.

**Unconscious Competence**

The final stage in mastering a given skill set is known as "unconscious competence." At this stage, individuals possess a profound awareness of their full capability and are equipped with the necessary tools to accomplish a specific task, such as growing a business. Having accumulated numerous successes, they can now undertake tasks without apprehension about the outcome. The skills acquired in golf marketing become ingrained habits, enabling them to perform with effortless ease and automatic proficiency. This stage is characterized by exceptional performance and unwavering confidence in the realm of golf club marketing.

As you develop your marketing campaigns for your golf course, you will be astounded by how effortlessly they come together. Recognizable patterns will emerge, and systems can be implemented and adapted to market other products and services. You will possess insights into the media and platforms that yield the best results. A plethora of hooks and compelling call-to-action statements will be at your disposal, capturing the golfer's attention and motivating immediate action. The proficiency in creating campaigns will be so innate that questioning their efficacy will no longer be necessary. The self-doubt and second-guessing that plagued you in the past will fade into insignificance.

At this stage, you can focus on considerations such as formulating your future tagline, packaging new products or services, enhancing the effectiveness of your advertisements in capturing prospects' attention, increasing website traffic, and exploring other avenues for growth.

Golf marketing and professional membership sales are dynamic fields that continually evolve, demanding ongoing adaptation and growth. As a professional in these domains, you must embrace the mindset of perpetual learning and innovation to ensure continued success. While staying at the forefront of industry trends and strategies, you will consistently refine your approach. However, when it comes to the fundamental aspects of golf course marketing and locking up relationships with golfers, your expertise will reach a level of unconscious competence. This means that performing competently in these areas will become second nature, as your mastery becomes an effortless and instinctive process.

The first step on the staircase leading to competence is knowing the needs of your audience.

**Identifying the Needs**

The process of need identification can be summarized as the identification of the player's needs. Crucially, this involves uncovering both their emotional and logical requirements, which are fundamental in selling any golf product or service. It is universally recognized that without understanding the genuine needs or problems of the player, it becomes impossible to offer a meaningful solution, thus, hindering the establishment of a solid relationship. Effective questioning and active listening play vital roles in revealing needs and problems.

Every golfer who visits your golf course has certain core emotional and/or logical needs that they seek to fulfill. For instance, some may desire to engage in golf to foster camaraderie with their colleagues or to play a round of golf with their superiors. These needs can be classified as logical and career-oriented motivations that prompt golfers to inquire about joining your golf course. During the need analysis phase, it is crucial to explore the golfer's fears, the positive emotions associated with the game of golf or with being a member of a golf course, as well as their desires, hopes, and aspirations. Delving deeper enables you to understand their concerns about potential losses, what they aspire to gain, and their ultimate objectives. Armed with this understanding, you can tailor your sales presentation to address their needs and effectively demonstrate how your product meets those requirements.

The rational reasons may attract individuals to your doorstep, but it is the emotional needs that ultimately persuade them to become members, purchase season passes, punch cards, or play a round or two. For instance, a customer who sees golf as a means to enhance their career is initially driven by logical motivations. However, it is the emotional reasons associated with this desire that will solidify their commitment. How will playing a round with their boss make them feel? What emotions will arise from golfing alongside their superior? These questions are pivotal in establishing a strong relationship.

Throughout my studies, I have discovered six fundamental emotional needs that our subconscious minds consistently seek to fulfill. These needs act as internal motivators, prompting consumers to seek products and services that can address these desires. The six core emotional needs are security, significance, belonging, variety, contribution, and accomplishment. Identifying these needs is crucial, as everyone seeks to satisfy each of these core emotional drivers. However, the hierarchy and priority of these needs may vary based on an individual's psychological makeup. For one golfer, feeling important might be their primary focus, while another golfer may prioritize feeling loved. As a golf membership advisor, it is your responsibility to uncover which of the six core emotional needs is guiding the customer you are addressing during the presentation.

Golfers choose specific golf courses to play and invest their time and money based on their quest to satisfy these emotional needs.

Frequently, golfers find themselves caught between conflicting emotions. They fear the possibility of loss while they simultaneously desire to gain something valuable. It becomes your responsibility to guide them away from the fear of loss and steer them toward the path of pleasure. The golfer must experience the sheer joy of the game and the unparalleled benefits of being a member of your club. Your task is to condition the golfer to associate your course with exclusively pleasurable emotions. By unearthing the golfer's core need and consistently addressing it throughout the entire presentation, you ensure that their purchase decision is solely driven by immense pleasure, eliminating any potential regrets.

By asking a series of well-crafted questions, you allow the customer to reveal their needs. Open-ended questions that begin with words such as "who, what, when, where, how, and why" encourage thoughtful and detailed responses. When customers are presented with these relevant questions about their needs, they provide a wealth of valuable information.

As a product advisor, it is crucial to determine the benefits that golfers are willing to invest their hard-earned money in and what they seek in return. The decision to purchase a product is not solely based on its features or functionalities but rather on how those products benefit the individuals or elicit an emotional response from them. Emotions play a significant role in the purchasing process, as customers often buy products not out of necessity but to satisfy their emotional desires. For example, while individuals may desire wealth, it is not merely the physical currency they seek but rather the feeling of security that comes with it. The pursuit of this emotional satisfaction drives their purchasing decisions.

Consider the scenario where you possess the perfect product, competitive pricing, and a strong rapport with the customer, and have successfully addressed their needs. If you can create an environment where the golfer perceives minimal risk and feels a sense of certainty, the likelihood of establishing a long-term relationship becomes considerably higher. By satisfying all of the golfer's needs, they will experience a positive sentiment regarding the purchase, leading to a higher probability of locking up the relationship.

Emotions play a significant role in the consumer's evaluation of a product or service. People seek to satisfy their emotional desires and experiences through their purchases. For instance, someone may buy a luxury watch not solely because they need to know the time but because it evokes a sense of prestige, status, and self-worth. The emotional appeal of the product creates a connection with the consumer's desired self-image and gratifies their need for significance.

Emotional factors heavily influence the decision-making process. People make purchases based on how they believe the product or service will make them feel. They seek pleasure, joy, excitement, or a sense of fulfillment. By understanding and addressing these emotional needs, businesses can effectively engage with their customers and establish strong connections.

At the core of human behavior, individuals are driven by a desire to fulfill their psychological needs. These needs encompass various aspects such as security, significance, belonging, variety, contribution, and accomplishment. While logical reasoning plays a role in decision-making, emotions often serve as the primary motivator for purchasing decisions.

However, it is important to note that emotions alone may not be sufficient to drive a purchase. Customers often rationalize their emotional choices by aligning them with logical reasons. They seek to justify their decisions by evaluating the practical benefits and value derived from the product. These logical justifications serve as a means to validate their emotional desires and reduce any potential feelings of regret or uncertainty.

Therefore, successful marketing and sales strategies acknowledge the interplay between emotions and logic. They aim to evoke positive emotions, align with the customers' psychological needs, and provide logical arguments that support emotional desires. By appealing to both the emotional and logical aspects, businesses can create compelling narratives that resonate with consumers and drive their purchasing behavior.

**Emotional Drivers**

The expression "selling ice to an Eskimo" is often used to depict a salesperson's ability to persuade someone to buy something they do not need. However, true professionals in sales would never make such a claim, as their approach is centered on selling products or services they genuinely believe in and that address the customer's genuine needs. Professional salespeople are not manipulative or dishonest; instead, they recognize that individuals have inherent emotional needs that influence their purchasing decisions.

The goal is not to sell unnecessary items but to identify the customer's genuine requirements and present suitable solutions that align with their emotional and practical needs. In the realm of sales, it is essential to uncover the customer's motivations, understand their specific needs, and determine how golf professionals can assist them in fulfilling those needs. This understanding of the customer's core emotional drivers distinguishes professionals from amateurs in the sales field. Professional salespeople focus on creating meaningful connections with customers and offering products or services that genuinely meet their needs.

As individuals, we inherently desire a sense of belonging, acceptance, importance, love, value, connection, achievement, and growth. These fundamental emotional needs apply to all humans. When marketing or selling golf products and services, it is critical to uncover and address these needs. However, it is important to recognize that the significance attributed to each need can greatly differ from one consumer to another. For instance, one golfer may prioritize feeling respected (important) above all else, while another may value belonging (connectedness) the most. Skilled salespeople comprehend this and employ specific questions to discern which core emotions drive the customer they are engaging with.

Instinctively, an experienced golf professional possesses an innate understanding of how to fulfill a golfer's need for significance, importance, and connection with the game and fellow players, as well as facilitating their growth and achievement. This expertise is acquired through comprehensive training and guidance provided by instructors during the accreditation process. As a result, the golf professional is not starting from scratch but is rather building upon a foundation of knowledge. The key now lies in effectively applying these insights during sales presentations. The initial step is to identify the specific emotion that motivates the golfer and then showcase how enrolling today will fulfill those needs. It cannot be emphasized enough that consumers make purchases primarily based on their emotional needs and subsequently rationalize them with logical justifications.

If it is your goal to have job security for the rest of your life and to thrive in the golf industry, knowing how to satisfy the golfers' emotional drivers is paramount. Every golfer that steps on your property is different, and at the same time, every golfer that steps on your property shares or has numerous things in common. There are patterns and systems to everything in life—tangible and intangible. Be absolutely sure that the entire time you spend with your golfers, he/she is experiencing those core emotional needs and can without a shadow of a doubt realize the best place to feel those emotions, again and again, is by being a member of your golf course. The word "membership" alone encompasses and evokes, most of all, the core emotional needs. This is why I always use and repeat the words "member" and "membership" in most of MMC®'s golfer acquisition campaigns, whether the course offers memberships or not.

For example, a client's course may be a public course and only offers punch cards, annual passes, season passes, or preferred player's cards. I will do my very best to get the owner to realize that any of these purchase options have some type of membership component attached, and therefore, it would not be a stretch to graft in a membership category as well. Golf is so much more than a game; it truly is an experience. Golfers yearn to belong and feel connected. Membership satisfies this desire instantly.

Understandably, many golf courses are hesitant to offer traditional "memberships" due to concerns about some golfers exploiting the system or feeling entitled to criticize and complain. However, it is essential to recognize that such golfers represent a small minority, although admittedly, they are the loudest. Many core and avid golfers do join memberships because they anticipate playing a certain number of rounds each year and understand that membership offers the best value. Unfortunately, these segments often contribute less to the profit centers. Nevertheless, despite this data, pursuing membership is still the recommended approach.

Loyalty is a mutual commitment. If you desire golfers to be loyal to your business, you must reciprocate that loyalty. However, it is crucial to understand that the definition of loyalty may vary among golfers. One effective way to discern their perception of loyalty is by identifying and addressing their emotional needs. By focusing on the desires, wants, and needs of golfers, you can foster their connection and engagement with your brand and business. During your presentation, pinpoint the emotions that drive their decision-making process and dedicate a significant portion of your time to ensure they consistently experience those emotions. The easiest way to master this tool is through active listening. Once you truly start to listen to your golfers, you will cultivate stronger relationships and accelerate the growth of your business beyond your expectations.

**Active Listening**

Can you imagine how difficult it would be to run a business without communication? Communication is not only crucial in our daily lives but also plays a critical role in the functioning of society, especially within a business context. It is nearly impossible to envision our lives without constant communication. In the realm of selling golf products and services, the absence of excellent communication skills can significantly hinder the growth of your business. Both speaking effectively and actively listening are vital components of successful communication, with active listening potentially even more important.

Active listening serves as a powerful strategy for establishing trust and fostering customer loyalty. Workplace communication, when deliberate, can be effective without being overly complicated. It involves honing good listening skills, as golfers' thoughts and expressions may not always be logical, articulate, or well organized. As a product advisor, it is your responsibility to create a comfortable environment for your customers, assisting them in articulating their thoughts and identifying their needs. It is common for individuals to have ideas in their minds but struggle to put them into words during communication. Listening, therefore, emerges as one of the most potent tools in your communication arsenal. By actively listening, you can truly understand the message your golfers are attempting to convey.

Listening and hearing are distinct processes. While hearing is the physical act of perceiving sound, understanding requires mental engagement. Listening goes beyond comprehending the words being spoken; it involves grasping the underlying reasons and intentions behind the questions or statements. Moreover, passive listening, where one simply hears without active attention, falls short compared to the depth of active listening. Establishing solid relationships is built upon active listening, where genuine engagement in the conversation is present. The disparity between active and passive listening holds true in all settings, be it professional or personal. Active listening forms the foundation of effective communication—it goes beyond speaking clearly and choosing the right words. It begins with active listening and being fully present in the conversation.

Astute small business owners recognize and prioritize the development of their employees' listening skills. For a small business, losing customers can have significant repercussions, making listening skills vital. Customer interactions are directly impacted by effective listening, and in some cases, they can determine whether customers choose to stay or leave. By attentively listening to players as they express their needs and opinions about your product, a wealth of valuable information can be gleaned at no cost. Listening becomes a powerful tool to understand your players and enhance their experience.

I often emphasize the importance of using our two ears and one mouth proportionately, meaning we should listen actively twice as much as we speak. An effective practice for honing active listening skills is to genuinely take an interest in what your golfer is expressing. By actively listening to your players and demonstrating respect and value for their thoughts, you create an environment where they feel welcome to share their input and observations and contribute to the success of the course. The more authentic your interest is in understanding what the customer is saying, the stronger the connection you will establish with them. Sincerity allows you to genuinely assess and evaluate the information they provide, leading to a fair scrutiny of their input.

Consider incorporating the following active listening tips into your sales presentation to become a better communicator:

1. Keep your eyes peeled. Avoid being distracted by environmental factors by facing your golfer and giving them your complete and undivided attention.
2. Show your golfers that you are listening to them with attentiveness through your body language by sitting up straight, smiling, using other facial expressions, and making sure that your posture is inviting.
3. Respond appropriately to show that you understand by nodding your head in agreement and encouraging your customer to continue with small verbal comments such as "Yes," "Uh-huh," and "I see."
4. Provide feedback. Use open-ended questions such as, "How did you feel when that happened?" to entice your customer to provide more details. The longer you can get your golfers

to talk about themselves, the more you will learn about their emotional and logical needs.
5. Do not interrupt. Allow your golfers to finish their sentences before you ask a question or decide whether or not you agree with them. Interrupting with counterarguments is not a good idea.
6. The more questions you ask, the more interested you will seem. Active listening is not an interrogation, so limit your questions to relevant issues.
7. Probe deeper when possible. Remember, everyone's favorite subject is themselves. Let the golfer talk as long as he/she wants. You are a product advisor, and the only way you can competently give someone advice is if you know what they want. The only way to know what your customer wants is by actively listening to your customer.

Inadequate communication leads to more mistakes being made, relationship breakdowns with your customers, and missed sales opportunities. Active listening skills are required to improve your business's image as well as your relationship with your golfers. Although it is considered a soft skill, it is still a solid foundation for effectively increasing your sales.

**Profiling Your Customers**

Failure to connect with golfers and prospective customers will put a golf course out of business quicker than anything else. We all want to acquire new players, and therefore, we must learn a new skill set. Presentations are either successful or unsuccessful for hundreds of reasons, far more than I can list in this chapter, but the number one reason usually boils down to compatibility, that is, does the salesperson and the prospect like each other? People speak and act differently, but just as in everything else in life, there are patterns people tend to follow and categories people tend to fall into.

In *Golf: The Untapped Market*, I briefly touched on the subject of the four social styles: the director, the socialist, the relator, and the analytical. Each style has a preferred way of communicating as well as a host of other common behavioral characteristics with others who fall into the same social style. Social styles matter; people like people who are like themselves and prefer to do business with people whom they like.

Knowing each style and their preferred communication style will not only assist you in locking up more relationships with golfers but having this skill set will also help you communicate better with your owner, your staff, your coworkers, your spouse, your children as well as anyone else you choose to cultivate a relationship with.

Identifying another individual's social style can provide a golf professional with a wealth of information about certain aspects of that individual's life. For example, people get very comfortable with the way they conduct business. They get into a rhythm and a pattern of their preferred way of doing business, and if you interrupt that pattern, it will be as though you have just run your fingernails down a chalkboard. You want to avoid interrupting your customer's rhythms and patterns at all costs. Your goal is to make sure everything goes as smoothly as possible. If you can, you want to jump onto the back of their surfboard and ride their waves with them. Let the customer lead the conversation and you follow. Listen and ask poignant questions. Let the customer dictate the pace and direction of the conversation in the beginning. This way, you will avoid a lot of resistance. This initial dialogue will give you some insight into their preferred communication style.

People normally have a pattern that they stick with when communicating, and you will be able to see this repetition in the way they speak, the words they choose, their body language, their mannerisms, and so on. If you are astute, you will easily identify this pretty quickly in most conversations, whether it is face-to-face, on the phone, or through emails. Once you identify the pattern, start honing in on the keywords, phrasing, intensity, and so on. Once you recognize the patterns, start mirroring them, and eventually, you will be able to adapt your communication style to align with your customer's style.

Knowing how to identify and then adapt to the four social styles helps you to determine your golfers' interpersonal interactions. If you, as a representative of your golf course, try to force your social style on your prospect, it will only end in a poor representation of your product and will most likely leave both you and the prospect feeling awkward. This use of this behavioral model is suggested to make both parties (you and the golfer) more compatible, therefore making it easy for both parties to get what they want out of the relationship.

The best salesperson is the person who is the most adaptive. It does not matter what your social style is, what matters is if you can recognize different kinds of customers and be able to adapt to their communication style, which is how you are going to become enormously successful. With that said, you must first start by identifying your own social style.

Customers differ in personality, style of communication, thought process, behavior, and method of making decisions. It is imperative that you recognize the characteristic social style of individual customers and approach them accordingly. By adapting your approach to the customer's style, you can enhance your chance of achieving the successful outcome you desire. The more adaptive you are, the better the results will be.

Once you have adapted your style to the customer's communication style, the presentation will flow beautifully. This skill will take time to develop just like any other, but this skill will pay greater dividends than any other because it is, more often than not, the deal-breaker or the deal-clincher.

The golf business is a relationship business, and the best way to cultivate relationships is by knowing your customers and how they prefer to communicate.

## Communication Styles

Successful business leaders are master communicators, whether in oral or written form. Communication should be professional, clear, and concise. When I teach any subject, you can bet it will be focused on business. This segment was written to address business communication. Effective business communication is essential for the success and growth of your business, as well as your golf career. Unlike everyday communications, business communication is always goal-oriented.

Good communication skills are essential for selling, marketing, customer service as well as managerial effectiveness. A large portion of an operator's day is spent communicating his/her ideas, plans, goals, and policies, whether it is via email, telephone, text, person-to-person, and so on. Operators are expected to lead meetings and motivate their employees. Today, electronic mail dominates the business world; therefore, written communication skills are equally essential for operators. Great communication skills have the power to create and maintain meaningful connections—a crucial aspect of growing any business. Effective communication reduces errors.

In previous lessons, I talked about the four social styles: the socialist, the relator, the director, and the analytical. Just as there are four social styles, there are four communication styles: the passive, the aggressive, the passive-aggressive, and the assertive. By understanding your customers' preferred communication style, as well as their needs, you will be able to build rapport easier, which will help you move your prospective clients through the buying process.

The four communication styles are:

1. *The Passive Communication Style*
   This type of communication is also known as the "submissive style" of communication or a people-pleaser type. The aforementioned is a type of communication that is self-effacing, conflict-avoidance, and easygoing.

   A passive communicator is often quiet and is always considered to be a display, blending into the background. Passive communicators tend to step back and let other more assertive or aggressive people lead the way because they find it challenging to adequately express themselves. You can quickly identify a passive communicator based on their behaviors, which usually include their inability to say no, being happy-go-lucky, lacking eye contact, having an apologetic demeanor, and so on.

Examples of phrases that those who use a passive communication style would say or may believe include:
- "It is no big deal."
- "I just want to keep the peace."

2. *The Aggressive Communication Style*

An aggressive communication style can be hostile, combative, and comes from a place of wanting to win despite everything. An aggressive communicator behaves as if their contribution to the conversation is more important than anyone else, and the content of their message is frequently lost because of the tone of their delivery, which results in people feeling disparaged, steamrolled, and threatened. In positions of authority, they may be more of a boss versus a leader. Another way of describing it is the authoritarian style. They also tend to ask questions rudely but then demand respect from others. The signs that someone is an aggressive communicator are: poor listening and interfering frequently, frowning, using aggressive gestures, and making intense eye contact.

It is often apparent when someone communicates aggressively. You will hear it. You will see it. You may even feel it. Examples of phrases that an aggressive communicator would use include:
- "I am right, and you are wrong."
- "I will get my way no matter what."
- "It is all your fault."

3. *The Passive-Aggressive Communication Style*

The passive-aggressive communication style falls amid being passive and aggressive. A passive-aggressive communicator seems passive on the surface but reveals a hidden resentment that comes through in subtle, indirect ways. They are quite manipulative and try to turn the situation into where they would be the ones to benefit.

This type of communication is, ironically, pretty easy to recognize through their behaviors and the way they act, which usually do not align with their actions, their frequent use of sarcasm during the conversation, and when they are struggling in acknowledging their own emotions.

Examples of phrases that passive-aggressive people commonly use are:
- "That is fine with me, but do not be surprised if someone else gets mad."
- "I guess I could do that, but is that not meant to be your job?"
- "Fine, whatever."

4. *The Assertive Communication Style*

The assertive communication style is the most compelling among all the communication styles. Assertive communicators can express their needs, desires, and ideas while being able to consider other people's perspectives. This positive attitude manifests itself through speaking with confidence about their desires and needs. They can say no calmly, use "I" statements rather than placing blame on others, and maintain good eye contact.

Examples of phrases you might hear from an assertive communicator are:
- "Here is what I think . . ."
- "I respect the needs and opinions of others."
- "I realize I have choices in my life, and I consider my options."

Having at least a basic understanding of your own style is very important to building better relationships in your personal and professional life. You may find yourself in situations where someone's communication style clashes with your own. Alternatively, you may have a communication style that other people find difficult to understand, which means that you could struggle to get your message across.

Product advisors must understand all four communication styles and practice adapting their personal styles to the other three instantly to align with their customers and make the buying decision a no-brainer.

**Closing the Sale**

People have three choices when it comes to buying a product. They can buy from you, buy from your competitor, or make a choice not to buy at all. Buyer indecision kills businesses. The main reason a buyer is indecisive is that the product advisor, most commonly referred to as the salesperson, fails to close the sale. Statistics prove that in 50 percent of all sales presentations, the product advisor never tries to close the sale. This is primarily due to fear of rejection, but ignorance plays a major role as well. In short, some product advisors do not know when or how to close a sale.

It is important to mention that contrary to most people's belief, egotistical maniacs are seldom great in marketing or sales. For those who have inflated egos, it is extremely difficult for them to set their wants, desires, opinions, and so forth in the shadows while illuminating the wants, desires, and opinions of their customers. In addition, ego maniacs fear rejection like the plague, and rejection is synonymous with sales. This is just another reason why those who are in charge of growing the business better start taming their ego pronto.

In this section, I am going to outline a very simple process for closing the sale. The first thing you need to know is that the "closing" of any sale starts immediately after being introduced to a prospect and continues throughout the presentation. There is a term in sales called "The ABCs of Selling," which means ALWAYS BE CLOSING.

The simplest way to close a sale is by immediately identifying the golfer's emotional needs. Once you know the core reason for them visiting your property, you can refer to it throughout the presentation. This is called the "hot button close." The hot button close is the path of least resistance. Once you identify what the prospect truly wants and needs, you can then build your presentation around those hot buttons. Even though it may seem like there are several hot buttons at the beginning of the presentation, you will see that number dwindling as you move through the presentation to one or two core hot buttons, at which point you will narrow your focus and 90 percent of the presentation in that direction.

For example, most golf professionals and/or operators prefer to start by highlighting things such as course conditions. Product quality is a logical decision. People buy for emotional reasons. The only time course conditions are really going to come into play in the presentation is when you are comparing apples to apples, that is, your property to your competitor's golf course. It is also important to point out that course conditions are usually only relevant when you are presenting to core and avid golfers. If a golfer's main concern is not course conditions, do not waste his/her time on the subject. Do not think for one minute that everyone you speak with is going to have the same needs. This is not about you; this is about the customer, and the only way you will know what the customer wants is by asking quality, qualifying questions.

For example, if a casual golfer visits your course, his/her interest may be solely in the experience. He/she does not take the game seriously, or at least, nowhere near as seriously as you or your coworkers. He/she may care less about what their score is. The golfer may just want to have fun with their friends for the day and just take in the beauty of it all. A conversation about course conditions would probably ruin their experience.

When you feel you need to bring quality into the conversation, add an emotional component to it and explain the benefits of why course conditions are so important and how the customer will benefit by having a good playing surface. But if you do not first appeal to their emotional needs, everything you say will just be background noise.

Keep in mind that if somebody has made the effort to drive to your property to visit or to play a round, they have a true interest, and whatever that interest is, you need to know it. Once you know it, then you need to repeat that over and over and demonstrate how your property is the place where they will achieve those goals and experience those emotions. Try to think of your current golfers who had similar goals or needs and pull up their testimonials on your computer, or even better yet, see if there is a golfer on the property you can call in your office and get them to share their experience. Let the prospect see that you actually have accomplished everything that this golfer wants to accomplish. You will be amazed when you witness the impact a satisfied customer can have on helping you close a sale.

There is absolutely no steadfast rule that you must adhere to when it comes to the time to close a sale. Listen to your customer; if the customer is giving you buying signals, it is time to close the sale. If a customer comes in and says, "I want to buy a golf membership," that is a buying decision, and the sale is closed. Go straight to the paperwork. You do not have to go through the entire process. This is true no matter what stage of the presentation you are in. If you are halfway through the process and the golfer starts showing he/she has made the buying decision, close the sale. Align with the customer and take their buying cues. Be aware of them. Be sensitive to them. Listen to the cues, stop selling, and start writing up the agreement. Do not oversell the product.

Although the sale is officially closed when the golfer pays for his/her membership and the financial transaction has been completed, I personally define a sale as being closed when the product advisor and/or operator transfers his/her enthusiasm about their product to the prospect.

Sadly, most people in sales are really order takers. A golfer comes into the clubhouse and says he or she wants to join, and the order taker fills out the paperwork. A professional salesperson/product advisor knows they really aren't in a sales presentation until they have heard, and overcome at least five objections.

## Overcoming Objections

Overcoming objections is the process of successfully handling reasons given by prospects/golfers for not buying today. Learning to overcome objections in a sales presentation is absolutely crucial if you want to be successful in business. Prospects raise objections to purchasing for numerous reasons, but mainly the objections are just ways for the prospect to avoid making a possible bad decision. Every decision we make is made in an attempt to make our condition in life better.

When someone presents an objection such as, "I want to think about it," "Let me talk it over with my spouse," "I'm not sure if I have the time," or "I'm not sure if I have the money," it indicates that they have not yet been fully convinced that the proposed decision is the best choice for them at the moment. It suggests that there is a need for further evidence and assurance that making the decision now will not lead to regrets or losses but rather will offer an opportunity for improvement and advancement in their life. Simply put, an objection is just a buyer's indecision.

Buyers are terrified of making mistakes and/or bad purchase decisions, so it is your responsibility to make the purchase decision so positively powerful that it overrides any fear the golfer may have and gets them feeling 100 percent confident that this is the best decision they could ever make. When you get a golfer to that point, the sale is closed, and all that is left to do is the paperwork.

One of the objections that you certainly need to start overcoming at the beginning of the presentation is, "I want to think it over." Salespeople have to be incredibly vain to believe that when a golfer says, "I want to think it over," they actually mean it. Most of the time, that is just a knee-jerk excuse used to avoid making a decision. The reality is that the golfer is never going to give you or your product a second thought. Once they leave your property, if you ever see them again, there is a good chance they will not even remember your name.

Address this objection head-on by asking, "What is it exactly that you need to think about?" Dig deeper and find out specifically what it is that they are thinking about and get them to think about it right then. There is no better place to think about your product than when you are there in person to answer any and all questions. One of the tools I have provided you in *Golf: The Untapped Market* was the Tour Sheet, which is a questionnaire form for you to identify the golfers' needs as well as their possible objections. There are ten questions on the Tour Sheet designed to assist you in creating value while eliminating objections just like the "I need to think about it." "How long have you been considering a golf membership?" is one of the questions on the Tour Sheet. Most golfers will tell you they have been thinking about it for years, if not decades. This initial question gets a bit of the objection out of the way, but then you need to dig deeper with follow-up questions to get them to remind themselves they have been thinking about this purchase decision long enough and it is time to do something about it today!

Just as important as identifying the golfer's needs, you must also identify the fundamental objection. It will be far more difficult to close the sale if you are unable to recognize the golfer's objections before they are vocalized. Ninety percent of why somebody will not buy something will boil down to just one or maybe two things. This means there are only one or maybe two things that are stopping the golfer from feeling 100 percent confident in the purchase. Anyone who loves the game, whether they are trained professional salespeople or not, can overcome one or two objections, especially if they identify them immediately and focus on overcoming them throughout the entire time they spend with the golfer.

It is imperative to understand the statistics when it comes to sales. Eighty percent of all sales are closed or finalized after at least five objections have been raised. This does not mean five separate objections on five different issues. More often than not, it will be the same issue causing the five similar objections. You are going to come across objections, and it is just an inevitable part of being in business.

Unfortunately, the statistics also show that in at least half of the presentations, the product advisor does not even try to close the sale one time. Again, this is out of fear of rejection. Most people fear rejection and will do anything to avoid it. This is why most people hate sales. They are so afraid of being rejected; they do not want to be told no, and when they are, they take it personally. But the reality is, an objection is not a no; it is a "not yet" because I do not "know" the right decision at this moment or I don't "know" enough to make the decision right now. In essence, the golfer is asking you to give him/her more information. The golfer is objecting to buying the product right now, at this moment.

Think of objections as opportunities for engagement and interest. When a golfer raises concerns or asks questions, it signifies his/her active involvement and indicates his/her level of interest. Instead of viewing objections as obstacles, consider them as invitations for further discussion and clarification. Addressing these concerns not only shows your attentiveness to their needs but also demonstrates your commitment to providing satisfactory solutions. Embrace objections as a chance to deepen the conversation and strengthen the golfer's engagement with your golf course.

Being in the golf business, we have the opportunity to interact with numerous golfers and listen to their concerns regularly. By carefully observing them, just as MMC® has done, you can identify the primary objections they commonly raise when it comes to making a purchase. These objections can typically be categorized into four main types: "I do not know if I have the time," "I do not know if I have the money," "Let me speak to my spouse," and "I need to think about it." With proper training, you can proactively address these objections and have a repertoire of at least twelve effective responses for each objection.

After dedicating over four decades to studying professional sales, I continue to embrace the mindset of a perpetual student, consistently learning something new each day. While I do not consider myself an exceptional salesperson, I have come to realize that sales and marketing are merely tools that have allowed me to pursue my true passion: empowering individuals to grow personally and professionally.

It is not necessary to have an overwhelming love for the sales profession to utilize the skills it offers, just as one does not have to adore mowing grass to work at a golf course. Both are vital aspects of any business, and, while the grass may grow without attention, the business will never thrive without a well-developed sales system and effective marketing strategy.

On a personal level, it is crucial to understand that if the business does not experience growth, neither will your career. Selling does not require adopting a different persona; in fact, authenticity is key. Be genuine, humble, and compassionate. Listen attentively to your customers, uncover their desires and needs, and demonstrate how you and your facility can assist them in achieving their golfing goals. By showing them how to attain everything they desire, you will naturally find yourself on the path to immense success.

Remember, your ultimate satisfaction will come from helping others achieve their goals, and in return, you will attain your own aspirations.

# 5

## DEVELOPING YOUR BUSINESS

In the sphere of business growth, there are essentially three primary strategies: customer acquisition, increasing the price per unit, and boosting the frequency of purchases. Regrettably, for golf course owners and operators who adhere to conventional methods of business expansion, acquiring new golfers proves to be a slow and arduous process, barely keeping up with the attrition rate and offering little hope for substantial growth. The second option, raising prices for core and avid golfers, can have detrimental effects as they often choose to play elsewhere when faced with higher rates. Consequently, the third alternative, increasing the frequency of purchases, remains the most viable option. However, it is widely known that core and avid golfers have found ways to circumvent this approach by bringing their own refreshments and making most of their equipment and apparel purchases from big-box discount stores.

To achieve favorable outcomes, a change in strategy is imperative. The objective should be to excel in all three areas: acquiring players, conditioning them to spend liberally and frequently in profit centers from the outset, and gradually increasing their membership fees over time until they match or surpass those of core and avid golfers. Throughout this chapter, the term "memberships" is employed to encompass all prepackaged options, including punch cards, season passes, and preferred player's cards. This terminology is chosen to effectively address golfers' fundamental emotional needs, such as connection, security, status, growth, variety, and contribution. Whether or not a golf facility currently offers a formal membership option is inconsequential. Daily fee operators have the liberty to label their offerings to the community using any terminology they prefer, be it a season pass or preferred player's card. At present, our focus should be less on the specific "label" and more on increasing the rounds played and the revenue generated.

Many owners and operators in the golf industry initially feel apprehensive about golfer acquisition efforts and unconventional expansion strategies. The industry is not accustomed to this approach, which makes it challenging for them to embrace new methods of growing their businesses. However, as you delve further into this book and explore the additional material provided on our websites, as well as *Golf: The Untapped Market*, you will realize the accuracy of my assessment regarding the current state of the golf industry and the vital role played by golf facilities. Through my analysis, I present a proven and sustainable plan for the industry's growth. I am confident that as you progress, you will have an "Aha moment" and gain a deeper understanding of MMC®'s strategy.

By now, most people in the industry already know that MMC® has identified four different types (categories) of golfers, and they are core, avid, casual, and non-golfers (aka new golfers). We use psychographics to identify and categorize the non-golfer group rather than demographics, which is how most marketing companies identify their prospects. Age, income, homeownership, and education are the traditional demographics on which marketers construct their consumer profiles. This is a fairly basic method of identifying customers. They do this because it fits both their budget and their level of expertise. The cost of buying demographic data is low, and it does not call for much ingenuity or thought. Although it is inexpensive to gather, this information is very expensive to the bottom line because it does not provide the necessary data that gives you the full image of your potential customer.

Psychographics are what truly count. It is significantly more important to know a person's lifestyle, spending patterns, buying tendencies, and buying behaviors than to know their age, whether they are homeowners or renters, how much money they make annually, or how much schooling they have received.

It is frequently seen that wealthy individuals spend a great deal of their income, which forces them to live month to month as well. Simply put, at the end of the month, they have more month than they do money. You want a customer with disposable income, not customers who cannot afford to even pay attention. Most essentially, you need to locate, interact with, and establish long-term connections with customers who make purchases from golf-related categories. MMC® uses this method to find new players for the golf facilities it partners with. However, MMC® digs far deeper into the customer profile to find those who buy things related to golf but have not started playing. These consumers are the game's future growth.

The initial considerations for consumers are centered on two key factors: the benefits they will receive and the associated cost. It is crucial to note that approximately 90 percent of your target market will dismiss a product or service if the price exceeds its perceived value. Conversely, if the price is perceived as significantly lower than the anticipated benefits, you will capture their attention. However, it is important to emphasize that the success of a campaign does not solely hinge on the price point, contrary to some beliefs within the industry. The price point plays a minimal role in the overall success of the campaign. The notion that this offer is excessively generous and undervalued is primarily held by industry professionals and core and avid golfers. Casual and non-golfers do not perceive the membership as an overwhelmingly favorable value proposition since they have not engaged extensively in the sport. For individuals who have never played golf or engaged in the activity infrequently, the price point appears reasonable.

It is important to acknowledge that most people who have never played golf would not anticipate playing more than once or twice per month. Playing more than a few rounds a year may even seem inconceivable to them. This is a challenging reality for industry professionals and regular golfers to grasp, as they assume that everyone who plays golf does so as frequently as they do. However, pricing serves as a mere enticement to attract customers. Therefore, I strongly advise against lowering costs unless you are confident in your strategic approach. Lowering prices without considering the other 99 percent of the criteria will only attract core and avid players who will not contribute significantly to the profit centers. Such a move would be financially detrimental to any business.

I acknowledge that there is a small percentage of consumers who prioritize quality and prestige and are willing to pay accordingly. However, this group represents a minor fraction of the overall consumer base. In fact, even within the core group of golfers, it is important to critically examine the figures. Our research indicates that approximately 80 percent of core golfers actually spend significantly less relative to the value they receive compared to casual and non-golfers. When faced with the decision to join or renew a golf membership or season pass, the majority of core golfers assess the benefit-cost ratio. They determine whether they can outsmart the system by playing a substantial number of rounds at a lower membership or pass cost. If they can achieve a significant financial advantage, they opt in; otherwise, they decline. While they may claim to support the club, their motivations often revolve primarily around financial considerations.

Furthermore, our findings reveal that core and avid golfers are the ones most likely to bring their own six-pack of beer and a sandwich instead of spending money on food and beverages at the facility. These players rarely utilize the driving range, make purchases at the pro shop, or engage with other profit centers. Instead, they prefer to buy golf accessories such as tees, clubs, balls, gloves, and other items from discount golf stores. I understand that these facts can be misconstrued, so allow me to clarify. Golf enthusiasts, including core and avid golfers, are undoubtedly vital to the golf industry, as their support sustains its existence. We rely on core and avid golfers for revenue to maintain the operations. However, I am simply highlighting that even with a reduced entry barrier, casual and non-golfers can contribute equal or greater financial value to the facility through their playing habits and consumption patterns.

To illustrate this point, the average number of rounds played by casual and non-golfers is approximately six rounds, allowing for a potential 20:1 ratio of these players compared to core golfers. These players actively purchase beverages and food items such as hotdogs, sodas, burgers, and sandwiches, as well as golfing essentials such as tees, balls, clubs, apparel, caps, and ball markers, and even utilize the driving range facilities. They exhibit a "spend freely" mentality when they play, understanding that it is a limited occurrence throughout the year. Therefore, it is crucial to recognize the potential financial impact that casual and non-golfers can have on the facility, as their consumption patterns can generate substantial revenue.

Achieving profitability in the current business landscape, and beyond, relies on effectively balancing your tee sheet to encompass all four golfer segments: core, avid, casual, and non-golfer. By encompassing a diverse demographic range, you can expand your reach and significantly boost operational revenue. Throughout my experience, I have developed an optimal mix of golfers that can be tailored to suit each facility's specific needs. It is important to note that these numbers are not set in stone and should be adjusted based on individual circumstances. Despite their appearance, they provide a solid starting point for owners and operators.

For most 18-hole facilities, the ideal target lies around 2,350 members and/or season pass holders. During a 30-week season, such a facility can accommodate approximately 53,000 rounds of golf while still ensuring a satisfactory pace of play. These figures serve as a benchmark, allowing room for adjustments based on the unique characteristics and goals of each establishment.

Possible membership classifications:

- **Diamond:** 50 members playing at most 150 rounds per season = 7,500 rounds per season. Diamond members pay a premium for an all-inclusive membership.

- **Platinum:** 150 core golfers playing at most 100 rounds per season = 15,000 rounds per season. Platinum members pay a premium for privilege and perks.
- **Gold:** 200 avid golfers playing at most 50 rounds per season = 10,000 rounds per season. Gold members pay relative fees for their play and member services.
- **Silver:** 1,950 casual and new/non-golfers playing on average six rounds per season = 11,700 rounds per season. Silver members pay relative fees for their play and member services.

Total rounds committed per facility: 44,200. This leaves a surplus of about 9,000 rounds open for green fee play of the 53,000 possible rounds in a 30-week season. Another important note to consider is that our data shows that these casual and non-golfers spend from $30 to $50 per round and play during the facilities' off-peak times.

A typical facility's audience is made up of about 20 percent of the population within a thirty-mile radius of the business consisting of core, avid, casual, and non-golfers. The largest group is casual and non-golfers who represent 80 percent of the market. I strongly suggest, if you fall short in any category, it would be advisable to offer the extra rounds to casual and non-golfers to develop them as customers and as players in hopes of moving them up the membership pyramid.

The revenue potential derived from 44,200 annual rounds can be quite substantial for the operational backend of a golf facility. To illustrate this, let us consider the example of car rentals. If only 80 percent of silver members (1,560 members) rented a car each time they played 9,360 rounds, and the car fee was set at $18, the annual car revenue would increase by $168,480. This demonstrates the untapped revenue from customers who might have been overlooked in the past. It is important to note that this is just one profit center, and maximizing revenue from other areas such as clinics, outings, events, food and beverage, lessons, merchandise, and more can significantly contribute to the overall revenue potential.

When considering the potential revenue, it is crucial to develop these players as loyal customers. Interestingly, although casual and non-golfers may make up 80 percent of your membership, they may only account for about 20 percent of rounds played. However, they can generate a substantial 80 percent of your business's revenue. This model highlights the significance of targeting and engaging with these customer segments.

Identifying and reaching out to casual and non-golfers requires a strategic approach, as not all consumers are interested in golf. Simply relying on untargeted advertising would be a financial mistake and could potentially harm your business. A successful campaign necessitates expertise from various disciplines, including, but not limited to, research, data interpretation, consumer profiling, marketing, sales, web design, search engine optimization (SEO), integrated mail services, printing, ad copywriting, and design layout. While it may not be an easy task, investing in a comprehensive approach is worthwhile for long-term success.

Sometimes, I encounter resistance regarding the cost of our campaigns, even though they are 100 percent self-funding and have low acquisition costs, as low as 7 percent of the generated revenue. However, when questioned about the cost, I always respond by saying that it is better to address the cost up front in our presentation than to ask for forgiveness multiple times due to poor campaign results.

Growing a business is not rocket science. As I have emphasized before, if you learn the fundamentals of business, such as personal development, sales, and marketing, and gain a basic understanding of your market, and if you are willing to put in the necessary work, most golf facilities can achieve a respectable return on investment (ROI). Unfortunately, some businesses choose to try everything except what is truly essential.

For instance, the other day, while finalizing this book, I spoke with an owner who had contacted us before the COVID-19 pandemic. At that time, the business had desperately needed revenue, and the owner had been enthusiastic about our program, so I was confident that he would reach out to us again. However, due to the impact of COVID-19, I never heard from him until recently. This situation was similar to what other owners and operators experienced, as they had contacted us before the pandemic. My team and I did not reach out to them because we assumed they had benefited from the pandemic's social distancing measures, and we were genuinely happy for them. Besides, we were already occupied with assisting less fortunate facilities.

During our conversation, as we moved past the usual pleasantries, the owner began to summarize the past three years of his business and the extensive measures he had taken, along with his several partners, to keep their business afloat. I listened in amazement as he shared his experiences and the challenges they had faced.

He said, "Chuck, we are fully committed to completing this deal. We have invested a significant amount of money and are deeply entrenched in it. We initially started with thirteen partners, but now we have fifteen because we needed additional funds. There have been five capital calls since then, although not all partners have been able to meet them. I do not force everyone to make the capital call. In addition, we secured two PPP loans totaling $266,000. We also obtained an SBA loan amounting to $150,000. Toward the end of last year, we faced accounts payable of $350,000, and I had to arrange another payment of $200,000 to settle them. Despite a subsequent capital call that did not raise enough, I approached the bank and borrowed an additional $200,000. Initially, I had invested $100,000, and now I have $250,000 in it. Two other partners have also invested $250,000 each." He concluded the conversation by saying, "I got them involved in this venture, so I need to find a way to get them out at some point, and I am currently working on that."

As I hung up the phone, I sank back into my chair, replaying the conversation in my mind like a repetitive recording. Throughout our discussion, he mentioned that he had read my book and found it to be excellent, gaining valuable insights from it. Furthermore, he reminded me that we had presented him with a proposal that could have generated over $250,000 in immediate cash from new business, along with an estimated annual operational revenue of over $300,000 for the next three years. Remarkably, this $1.2 million opportunity would have entailed no risk for him or his partners whatsoever.

The total acquisition cost would have been a mere 7 percent, which is significantly lower than the interest rates on business loans. Additionally, the golfers would have spent approximately $48 per round, eliminating the need for fees, applications, or any additional work. There would have been no capital calls, no SBA loans, no requirement for new investors, and no out-of-pocket injection of cash. In essence, he and his partners could have raised the same, if not more, capital in just ninety days through the sale of the product for which they had initially purchased the business—rounds, memberships, food and beverage, and so on.

Curiously, I asked him why he had not reached out to us, and his response was all too familiar and disheartening. He said, "I kept hearing stories about how other facilities were benefiting from COVID, and people started saying that the industry was turning a corner. I believed that our time would come if we could just hold on a little longer." It was like the metaphorical frog in a pot of boiling water, unaware that the temperature was gradually rising, putting its life in danger.

Update: During the final edits of this book, I had a few more conversations with this owner. He actually took it to the next step and had me on a conference call with his employees and one or two of his investors. At this point, he was already up to 17 investors. Since I had spoken to him just a few months ago, he had already sold two more people on investing in this titanic. The entire staff was all for launching the campaign which I think took the owner by surprise. I'm not sure but it seemed as though he just knew his team would shoot the idea down immediately giving himself a clear cut excuse not to move forward. However, they were extremely excited and wanted to do it immediately. The golf pro even knew a golf course that we had worked with that was not too far from this facility. The course was not in their market and was not a private club. It is a muni course that we had literally pulled out of the depths of financial ruin. And now it's an enormously successful business for the owners as well as the city and community. The pro said he knew one of the owners of the leased muni course very well and if he did the campaign, then they too should do the campaign.

After the conference call, the owner and I spoke again and I was confident from the feedback, the owner was ready to give the campaign the greenlight. He said he was very excited but he still needed to think about it. A few days later I made a follow up call and the owner said he spoke to the owner of the muni course and he gave us rave reviews. However, he felt that because his course is private and the other course was a muni; the testimonial didn't carry much water. He proceeded and asked me to provide him with another testimonial that mirrored his facility. I know he must consider moving to a semi-private facility if he has any hopes of surviving much less thriving so I gave him the perfect testimonial from a course that was private and dying by their own sword that went semi-private and is thriving today. Once again I followed up with the owner in a few days and once again he told me how happy the manager/golf pro was with our campaign and how going semi-private was the best thing that could have ever happened.

By this time I was already designing his campaign in my head because I just knew he was sending in the paperwork as soon as we got off the phone. But oh no, the owner said he still needed more time to think about it. I was flabbergasted. I couldn't believe what I was hearing. So of course I did exactly what I am teaching you and I started digging deeper. Finally, the real reason for all of the pushback was revealed. The managing partner, the one who put the deal together, really doesn't like the idea of being semi-private. I would imagine he has the support of a few of his 17 investors but I can assure you it is not the majority.

A few of the investors are sacrificing the financial future of the club, the employees, the existence of the golf course, etc., just because their egos are getting in the way of what is best for the business, community, the game, and the industry. I know it is their egos because the course only plays a few thousand rounds per year. It is like a ghost town most of the time. It can't be the image of the club in the public's eye because everyone knows they are on the verge of bankruptcy. The employees know their jobs are at-risk, the majority of investors know they are almost sure to lose their investments, the government has no more bailouts, the state and the banks won't loan them money anymore, and they may even lose their own families because of the business. Everyone remotely associated with that property sees the iceberg ahead with the exception of the managing partner and a few of his supporters.

Now, there is, of course, a much better solution if they move forward with the campaign. They can be semi-private, which is not really semi-private since the new golfers will be brought in as members on an introductory membership. The owner could launch MMC®'s campaign once or twice over the next few years, get the business financially stable, build a surplus of introductory members, golfers that they could then move up the membership ladder, and the business would begin to thrive. Unfortunately, it is still extremely difficult for the owner to wrap his head around the idea of being semi-private for even just a few years, even if it means saving the business, jobs, investor's money, and so on. But the ego, the thought, the idea, the perception that his course will no longer be a private facility is just more than he can bear at this moment.

Instead of dragging this nightmare out for several years, all he would have done was suspend his ego, partner with MMC®, launch the campaign and start cultivating the relationships with his new members. This entire process would have been accomplished within ninety days or less. The golfer acquisition campaign would give him all the cash that he needs as well as the backend operational revenue he would need to sustain the business for two to three years. During this period, his team would have ample time to cultivate the relationships with their new golfers/saviors. And if the label and status of being a private club is still important, he could always take the course back to a private facility, but this time, with financial stability.

# EGO: EDGING GOLF OUT

A truly wise person once remarked, "It's not the things you don't know that will harm you, but rather the things you are absolutely certain of, that are not so, that can cause real damage." Blinded by the hype surrounding the COVID Bump, this owner placed a high-stakes bet on its potential to save both his business and his investors' money when all he had to do was look in his own backyard for the solution.

I have come across a fable called "Acres of Diamonds," which resonates with me and holds valuable lessons, especially in light of the COVID-19 pandemic. It amazes me how some business owners fail to recognize the hidden potential within their own ventures.

The story revolves around an African farmer who hears tales of other farmers discovering diamond mines and amassing great wealth. Driven by these stories, he sells his farm and embarks on a lifelong quest for those precious stones. Despite his relentless search across the African continent, he never finds any diamonds and tragically meets his demise by hurling himself into a river out of frustration.

Meanwhile, the person who purchased the farmer's land casually stumbles upon a gleaming stone at the bottom of a stream on the property. Initially considering it a decorative item, they place it on their fireplace mantle. A few weeks later, a knowledgeable friend visits and identifies the stone as an exceptional diamond, leaving the property owner in shock. It turns out that the very diamonds the farmer had sought far and wide were abundantly present in the creek bed of the farm he hastily sold without ever once looking in his own backyard.

This fable serves as a powerful reminder that often the most valuable opportunities lie right in front of us, waiting to be recognized. It cautions against overlooking or undervaluing the untapped potential within our own endeavors. Instead of incessantly pursuing external solutions, success can be found by acknowledging and harnessing the hidden treasures within our own businesses.

I share this story with you, as it has provided me with valuable insights over the years, and I hope you can derive wisdom from it as well. The fable is easily accessible online and can be found in numerous books. I encourage you to explore it further.

This situation occurs far too frequently in the golf industry, and it is entirely avoidable. Each owner and operator possesses a valuable asset within their golf course, akin to having their own acre of diamonds. By proactively identifying and leveraging these assets, and effectively marketing them to potential buyers, there is no longer a necessity for operators to seek additional funds from investors, shareholders, partners, or financial institutions.

Many golf courses face the challenge of operating below their maximum capacity, with over 50 percent of the facility's tee times going unsold. This represents a significant loss of potential revenue for the business. The issue often lies in the fact that core and avid golfers have established preferences for specific days and times to play, such as Saturday and Sunday mornings or certain weekdays and afternoons for league play. As a result, the remaining tee times become less desirable and are often overlooked.

To address this situation, many golf courses offer discounted tee times, typically marketed as Early Bird, Twilight, Senior, Junior, or other similar packages. These discounted rates can be found on the golf course's own website or through third-party tee time vendors. Prices can range from $18 to $100 per round, with most local golf facilities falling within the $28 to $60 range. However, core and avid golfers, who make up a significant portion of the customer base, often do not purchase these discounted packages. They may find it challenging to adjust their playing schedules or they play frequently enough that non-prime-time opportunities do not hold much appeal to them. This has been the traditional approach to filling slow times and seasons for many years.

The underlying challenge is clear: we are trying to sell tee times that our core and avid golfers are not interested in to the same core and avid golfers. Naturally, this approach is unlikely to yield results because we are targeting the wrong audience. Regardless of how affordable the packages may be, if they do not align with the preferences and needs of the customers, they will not be inclined to make a purchase.

The underperformance of the golf industry cannot be attributed to the product itself, but rather to the outdated thinking and approaches used in acquiring golfers. Some individuals within the industry are entrenched in traditional practices and struggle to envision the future. However, the future of golf lies in attracting and engaging the casual and non-golfer segment, who have the potential to develop into core and avid golfers.

It is essential for us, as the stewards of the game, to actively invite these new customers into the golfing community. The days of relying solely on individuals following in their parents' footsteps are long gone. To grow the industry, we must embrace a more inclusive mindset and create opportunities for individuals who may not have a history of golfing in their families or social circles.

By recognizing the changing dynamics and preferences of potential golfers, we can develop innovative strategies to attract and retain new players. This may involve reevaluating our marketing tactics, designing beginner-friendly programs, offering affordable and flexible options, and creating a welcoming environment that appeals to a diverse range of individuals.

Embracing the casual and non-golfer segment as the future of the industry is crucial for its growth and sustainability. By breaking away from antiquated thinking and embracing new approaches, we can pave the way for a vibrant and thriving golf community that appeals to a broader audience.

In today's market, the golf industry faces intense competition for the attention and patronage of the current generation. We must recognize that our competitors are not limited to the golf course just a few miles away. In fact, in this interconnected world, our competition can emerge from any corner of the globe. Unlike the past, when our predecessors had to contend with a local steak house taking away from their food and beverage sales, the landscape has changed dramatically. Growing the game and sustaining its success now requires us to adopt a broader perspective.

We must question whether reverting to a limited product offering, reminiscent of earlier times, is truly in the best interest of the game. By doing so, we risk stifling its growth and eventually harming its vitality. Instead, we should embrace innovation and diversity, seeking to expand the appeal and accessibility of golf to a wider audience. By adapting to the evolving market and embracing change, we can ensure the game thrives and continues to capture the imagination of generations to come.

Growing a golf facility is simple. By effectively communicating your facility's availability and showcasing its offerings at a competitive price point, you can engage the community and generate interest. It is important to note that this approach does not necessitate further discounting, as some may suggest. Rather, it entails understanding how to effectively present your product to the target audience that seeks it.

I introduced a fresh perspective on a traditional marketing strategy called "Loss leader" marketing, where businesses sell a product at a loss to generate future profits. However, I propose an alternative approach called "Lost leader" marketing, which focuses on discovering overlooked or forgotten products or services within a business's offerings, eliminating the need for accepting losses. Golf facilities already implement a variation of this strategy by offering discounted rounds during Early Bird and Twilight hours. As mentioned earlier, the individuals attracted to golf through MMC®—casual and non-golfers—spend between $30 and $50 per round. Therefore, there is no requirement for discounts or incurring any losses. These individuals represent a new segment of golfers, not previously engaged, which means the revenue generated from them is an entirely new income for the business.

Let us take a moment to calculate and use rounded numbers for simplicity. Suppose your facility currently plays 25,000 rounds per year. If your location has a season lasting about thirty weeks, your facility could easily play 53,000 rounds each season. Basic calculations indicate that your facility is operating at approximately 50 percent of its capacity.

Now, imagine that you have sold passes or introductory memberships to casual and non-golfers who, as a group, are projected to play around 10,000 rounds. Based on their spending average of $50 per round, your business would generate approximately $500,000 in revenue. As a result, your facility would play 35,000 rounds out of a potential 53,000 rounds. This exemplifies an effective strategy for business growth.

The process of finding underperforming products, repackaging them, and targeting the right audience is indeed a straightforward approach that can yield significant business growth. I speak with absolute confidence in this matter, as my team and I have successfully executed this strategy over a thousand times. Contrary to any concerns you may have, there are no downsides to implementing this strategy.

The rounds played by the new customers are scheduled during off-peak times when the demand is low, ensuring that the pace of play for other golfers remains unaffected. Furthermore, the selection of these new players follows a carefully formulated criteria-based formula, ensuring that there are no disruptions to the existing golfing culture. These new players willingly adhere to a code of conduct, dress code, and consumption guidelines.

Acquiring golfers from the casual and non-golfer segments brings balance to your business. While they may only occupy 20 percent of the tee sheet, they can contribute as much as a staggering 80 percent to your business's revenue. Importantly, these casual and non-golfers do not overshadow or interfere with the core and avid golfers or disrupt the natural flow of your business. Instead, they fill the tee times that would otherwise remain vacant, seamlessly fitting in like drops of water filling divots.

In writing this book, I have been mindful of not overly promoting MMC® and instead focusing on delivering valuable content to readers without making them feel like they are being sold something. However, I must be transparent and acknowledge that my intention is indeed to sell you something through this book, although it is not specifically related to MMC®'s golfer acquisition campaigns. It is inevitable to mention MMC® from time to time because everything I teach is derived from my career experience.

At this moment, what I aim to sell you on is the concept of exploring alternative methods for growing your business beyond what you may have learned in the past or the traditional approaches prevalent in the industry.

To initiate exponential business growth, the first step is to conduct a comprehensive market analysis, including a thorough examination of your target customer base, a demographic survey, and a competitive overview specific to your facility. By gathering relevant data and aligning it with your business objectives, you can gain insights into the market landscape and identify areas where you can differentiate yourself to increase your market share. It is crucial to consider both quantitative and qualitative data in this process.

Quantitative data, when combined with demographic data encompassing factors such as age, income, and homeownership, provides a solid foundation for market analysis. This data offers measurable insights into the characteristics and trends of the target audience. On the other hand, qualitative data plays a crucial role in refining and eliminating certain aspects. By gathering subjective information through methods such as interviews, surveys, and observations, we can gain a deeper understanding of the motivations, preferences, and behaviors of individuals within the target audience.

One significant aspect to focus on during the market analysis is psychographics, specifically the lifestyles of potential consumers. This involves identifying individuals who exhibit the purchasing habits associated with golfers, such as their choices in clothing, subscriptions, games, gadgets, and more, even if they have never played the game itself. Humans naturally seek ways to conserve energy and find shortcuts in their daily lives, which is reflected in the brain's ability to form habits. Golfers, like everyone else, develop routines and patterns of playing and spending in various aspects of their lives, including where they buy gas, shop for groceries, and what morning rituals they follow. These activities typically begin as conscious thoughts, evolve into routines, and eventually solidify into habits that require minimal effort or conscious decision-making.

Habits can be both beneficial and detrimental, depending on their impact. Some habits are desirable and bring joy and fulfillment, while others may hinder personal growth or prevent positive change. For instance, consider Joe, who has been golfing with his three buddies on the same day of the week, at the same time of the day, for an extended period. This established habit has become a source of tremendous joy for Joe and his friends, and it has been reinforced over the years. Disrupting this habit would be unthinkable because it has become deeply ingrained and provides a consistent source of happiness.

Once you have gathered all the necessary data and determined the offer based on your business needs, it is time to involve your staff if you have not done so already. Assign your most capable individual as the project manager, and their team can begin working on the materials for your campaign. This includes developing a dedicated website specifically for your golfer acquisition campaign. The team should delve deeper into the market analysis; conduct a comprehensive competitive overview; draft correspondence emails; create ad copy; design signage for the property's exterior and interior areas; develop Facebook ads, newspaper ads, radio ads, text message ads, phone scripts, answering machine messages, sales presentation scripts, and direct mail ad copy and design; and coordinate with necessary vendors, among countless other essential details to ensure a successful campaign.

The project manager will facilitate meetings with all departments to ensure seamless communication and collaboration, eliminating any potential delays. It is crucial to thoroughly review all materials and gather input from as many team members as possible to avoid double expenses due to mistakes and prevent unnecessary time delays. Any last-minute changes should be promptly communicated to everyone involved to keep everyone informed and up to date. Schedule a training meeting to prepare your staff for the upcoming program. It is vital to have everyone on board and be supportive of your efforts. You and your team should strive to deliver your best performance because, even if you may not realize it yet, every phone call and every person-to-person interaction holds a minimum value of $1,000 for your business.

Similar to popular restaurants or nightclubs, golfers are drawn to courses that are bustling with activity and where everyone is enjoying themselves. An empty tee sheet does not convey exclusivity; instead, it projects a sense of fragility. While core and avid golfers may outwardly appreciate the lack of crowds, deep down, they recognize the potential implications of a deserted course and hope that it can weather the prolonged period of neglect. However, it is crucial not to overlook the remaining 80 percent of golfers, as they contribute significantly to your profits and share these same concerns, even if they have not yet set foot on your beautifully vacant greens.

An empty tee sheet is far from appealing for any golfer. It loudly proclaims a struggling business, akin to a duck on a roller coaster. Just as no one wants to purchase a ticket for the ill-fated Titanic, golfers have no desire to play on a course that lacks popularity. However, when your tee sheet is filled to the brim with enthusiastic golfers, the story takes a different turn. Suddenly, everyone wants to be a part of the vibrant atmosphere and experience the joy of playing on a highly sought-after course.

Golf courses often have the misconception that an empty tee sheet indicates success. However, it is primarily the core and avid golfers who hold this belief, while the general public sees it differently. If you aim to capture the attention of the general public and market to them effectively, you need to convey the message that your course is vibrant and filled with excitement.

While it is important to appease your existing golfers by assuring them that there is still available space on the tee sheet and that it will

# EGO: EDGING GOLF OUT

not slow down play, it is equally important to create an atmosphere that attracts a wider audience. Using tools such as LED ticker displays to communicate accurate pace of play information such as "4 hours and 15 minutes" can prevent misconceptions and rumors about slower play times. Claims that slower play will occur are often made by individuals who want to maintain a sense of exclusivity and have the golf course all to themselves. Their concerns about a few extra minutes of playtime are not representative of the general public's perspective.

As the saying goes, "Everyone wants a piece of the action!" A thriving golf course acts like a magnet, attracting golfers from all walks of life. If your tee sheet resembles a barren desert or, even worse, does not exist, it is time to reconsider your strategy. After all, who wants to play on a golf course where the only companions are tumbleweeds?

In Los Angeles, bars and restaurants often hire movie extras to create the illusion of a packed house, with queues stretching down the street and around the block. Some lawyers have been known to instruct their secretaries to lie when answering calls, claiming they are either in court or with a client, all in an effort to appear busy or important. Have you ever wondered why doctor's offices often have long waiting times? It is because some physicians purposely overbook their schedules to convey the message that their services are highly sought after and worth the wait. Businesses go to great lengths to create the perception of being busy, even when they are not, to avoid the perception that they are hosting a party that no one will attend.

Perception plays a significant role in shaping people's reality. Consider two nightclubs located across the street from each other, similar in size, decor, DJ, and service. However, one nightclub has a line extending down the block, while the other appears empty and deserted. Which one do you find more appealing? Despite their similarities, most people would be drawn to the nightclub with the bustling queue. We all have that desire to be part of something exciting and exclusive. If your golf course lacks energy and a crowd, it will be an uphill battle. For your facility to ascend the social ladder, you need to create buzz and attract a swarm of enthusiastic golfers. Teach golfers to indulge in your offerings, gradually increase membership fees while nurturing their loyalty, and guide them up the tiers of membership.

Avoid the rookie mistake of advertising a blank tee sheet, as it will only drive golfers to your competitors' facilities. Instead, fill any gaps in your schedule with paying golfers who are passionate about the game. These golfers will not only become loyal ambassadors for your club when they are in their office or out about town, but they will also bring their friends to play and spend freely in your profit centers. Let your community know that your establishment is the place to be, where a vibrant and lively golf experience awaits them. Make it clear that your facility is hosting an extraordinary event that everyone wants to be a part of.

The process of growing a business is akin to playing the game of golf itself. Just when you think you have mastered it, the next day on the course reveals that there is still more to learn. It requires ongoing lessons, instructions, practice, and dedicated effort. Similarly, growing the industry demands continuous learning, adaptation, and perseverance.

Just as golfers seek improvement through lessons and practice, your business must also draw lessons from its own journey and apply them to the task of expanding the business. It requires a willingness to learn from both successes and failures, constantly refining strategies, and staying committed to the long-term goal of growth. In chapter 6, I will equip you with a comprehensive tool kit to help you build a marketable brand, streamlining the process of growing your business and career even further.

# 6

## DEVELOPING YOUR GROWTH TOOL KIT

The golf industry places significant importance on branding, image, perception, and status within the community. The way a company presents itself and its brand is crucial for establishing credibility and fostering customer loyalty. Unfortunately, many individuals and businesses fail to fully grasp the process of developing a strong brand and effectively managing it. In this chapter on "Developing Your Growth Tool Kit," I aim to provide valuable insights into building a marketable brand.

Creating a marketable brand is equally vital for individuals as it is for companies. Your personal brand is essentially the perception others have of you, and it is essential to be conscious of how you are being perceived. To build a marketable brand, four key areas deserve your focus: brand language, brand management, brand audit, and brand preference.

When delving into brand marketing, your first step is to carefully consider the language you will employ to create a strong connection between the public and your brand. Brand language serves as a powerful tool in marketing by associating specific words or concepts with particular companies or products. Developing a brand language entails focusing on two fundamental components: word choice and tone.

Word choice encompasses the vocabulary utilized in marketing and advertising materials. Selecting the right words can significantly impact how your brand is perceived and remembered by your target audience. Think about your local golfers and the characteristics that would resonate with them. Imagine yourself in their shoes, envisioning the ideal golf property or future golfing experience. Consider the elements that would attract and captivate you. Identify emotional words that can evoke positive sentiments within your customers, and incorporate them strategically into your golf marketing and advertising endeavors to establish a compelling brand.

Additionally, tone plays a vital role in brand language. It encompasses the overall attitude and demeanor conveyed through your advertisements and marketing materials. Tone can be expressed not only through language but also through visual elements and delivery methods. A consistent and appropriate tone will help shape how your brand is perceived and ensure that your messaging resonates effectively with your audience.

Ensuring that your golfers and community associate your golf property with positive emotions and good feelings is essential, and it falls upon you to shape these perceptions through effective branding. Select keywords that effectively convey the intended message of your golf property to golfers. These keywords should align with the emotional needs of golfers and the experiences they seek. Additionally, consider the keywords you want people to associate with your brand in relation to your golf products and services.

Building a strong relationship with your target market is a crucial aspect of brand positioning and maintaining a favorable reputation in the marketplace. It is important to cultivate a positive and lasting connection with your audience, aligning your brand with their values and aspirations.

The next step is brand management, which can often be a source of confusion for many golf courses. In reality, every individual involved with your golf property has a role to play in brand management. It is a collective responsibility to uphold and enhance the brand's image, ensuring consistency in messaging, service quality, and customer experience across all touch points.

From the groundskeepers to the front desk staff, from the golf instructors to the restaurant servers, each person contributes to the overall brand perception. By fostering a culture that values and supports the brand identity, you can create a cohesive and authentic brand experience for golfers.

To project professionalism and enhance your brand reputation, it is crucial to provide exceptional service to your golfers. This begins with effective communication, whether it is answering phone calls promptly or assisting them when they visit your golf course. By offering attentive and personalized service, you create a positive and welcoming experience that reflects well on your brand. It is important to make your golfers feel valued and important by providing guidance, support, and excellent service throughout their visit.

Brand management encompasses more than just marketing campaigns and pricing structures. It involves understanding and catering to the emotions and needs of golfers when they visit your golf course. This requires being attentive, alert, accessible, and of service at all times. By consistently delivering exceptional experiences, you can cultivate a strong reputation for your brand.

Conducting a brand audit, such as a survey, is an effective way to gauge the preferences of your local market. By sending a short questionnaire to a sample group of your existing customer base, you can gain insights into how golfers perceive your golf course. Pay attention to their feedback, thoughts, and associations with your brand. This information will help you understand the strengths and weaknesses of your brand and identify areas for improvement.

If the results of the brand audit do not favor your property, use the feedback to create another questionnaire that addresses the identified areas for improvement. This proactive approach allows you to take steps to make your brand the preferred choice in the market.

Building brand preference requires dedicated effort and an understanding of your customers' needs. While course conditions are important, it is crucial to recognize that not all golfers prioritize them above everything else. Casual golfers seek an enjoyable experience where they can have a good time and feel welcome. Just like the familiar theme song from the sitcom *Cheers*, where everyone knows your name, creating a welcoming and personal atmosphere can go a long way in building brand preference. Taking the time to learn and use your customers' names is a simple yet effective way to make them feel valued and connected to your brand.

Solidifying brand preference in the market means ensuring that customers choose your golf course over competitors when making a decision. It reflects the strength of your brand in customers' hearts and minds, considering factors such as amenities, pricing, location, dependability, operating hours, and more.

While these tips can help you build a marketable brand, the ultimate branding tool is your golfers themselves. Happy and satisfied golfers who consistently enjoy their experience at your golf course will naturally become advocates for your brand, spreading positive word-of-mouth and attracting new customers.

Once you have a clear understanding of what you want your brand to represent, it is important to disseminate it effectively. A great starting point is establishing an online presence through a well-designed website. The internet offers a wide reach and allows you to showcase your brand, facilities, services, and any unique selling points to potential customers. Utilizing online platforms and digital marketing strategies can significantly enhance your brand visibility and attract new golfers to your course.

**Build Your Own Website**

In this section, I would like to discuss the process of building your own website, addressing the concerns and misconceptions that some operators may have about technology and the role of tech companies. It is important to realize that the complexity of building and hosting a website has been exaggerated by some tech companies to justify their high prices.

Fortunately, in today's digital age, creating a website does not require advanced coding skills. Whether you are building a personal website or one for your business, there are accessible tools available to help you achieve your goals. You do not necessarily need a background in computer coding to create a beautiful and functional website. In fact, even high school students can often put together an impressive website at a fraction of the cost charged by most tech companies. In some cases, you may even be able to negotiate a trade, such as offering a golf membership in exchange for the website development work.

I understand that the idea of building your own website may initially seem daunting, but the truth is that many website platforms provide user-friendly templates that you can easily customize. These platforms also offer guidance and support throughout the website creation process. Additionally, you can find numerous tutorials on platforms such as YouTube, which provide step-by-step instructions on building websites. It is worth noting that you will be working with a hosting company, not a website company. Hosting companies primarily generate revenue by hosting websites over extended periods, and they often include templates, tools, and tutorials to facilitate the creation of your own website as part of their hosting services.

Websites are powerful marketing tools because they work tirelessly to promote your business. They operate 24/7, 365 days a year, regardless of whether you are awake or asleep, at home or away. Treat your website as a sales tool with the goal of being informative, welcoming, user-friendly, and revenue-generating. While selling products and services online will be discussed later, it is crucial to understand the significance of having a well-designed website that is easily discoverable. The more accessible your website is, the more traffic it will attract, and as we know, increased traffic often leads to higher revenue.

Make your website an enjoyable destination for visitors. Continuously add fresh content and do not hesitate to share free information. Consider filming video lessons; writing blogs; publishing newsletters; and showcasing pictures, videos, and testimonials from satisfied customers. Demonstrate to the community that your golfers are having unforgettable experiences. Guide your website visitors through a sales presentation without making it feel like a sales pitch. Above all, prioritize attracting attention to your website.

To create a functional website, you will need four essential components: a domain (the web address), a web hosting account (to store your website's files and make them accessible online), a web publishing platform (such as a content management system), and a payment system (if you plan to sell products and services directly through your website). These components work together to establish and maintain your online presence effectively.

1. **Domain:** Picking the right domain will play an important role in your website. The domain name is your website name and address. That address will be used by visitors when they try to find your site or a golf course in your area, through their web browsers. Basically, it is your online address through which people can find you.

    A domain name is the location of an entity on the internet. This is a subject I am sure most of you in the golf industry are very familiar with and may consider this subject elementary at best, but if you do, you would be making a big mistake. I wanted to devote an entire chapter to understanding the importance of a domain name because even in today's society, there are thousands of golf courses out there that still have not made a presence on the internet. There are even more golf courses out there that have chosen poorly when it comes to domain names for their websites. For those of you who do not have a website, the first decision you need to make is the domain name. This decision will require some thought because the success of your website will depend on your decision.

    Since most tech companies are billing you a flat fee for building your website and then an ongoing charge for hosting your site, they have no incentive to educate you on choosing a

## EGO: EDGING GOLF OUT

URL. Most operators choose the name of their golf course for their URL and this is logical on the surface, but when it comes to maximizing your effectiveness in garnering new business, choosing the name of your course falls short.

One of the things you want to take into consideration is SEO. SEO is maximizing your search engine visibility, as it is extremely important to maintain an online presence. SEO is the system or strategy used to get better rankings with search engines such as Google and Bing. When someone is looking for something online, they go to their search engine, which is probably Google or Bing, and type in words to find whatever it is they are looking for. The most important thing you need to understand about SEO is your goal to get to be a top-ranked golf course within your market. For example, if you are located in Chicago, and someone types in "golf courses in Chicago," your goal is to be ranked number one with the top search engines. This way, when a golfer searches online to get information about golf properties within a certain area (if you have worked on your SEO), your golf course's website will be the first one to come up.

Golfers frequently use keywords and phrases such as "golf," "golf club," and "golf 18" in their search engine queries to find golf courses in their area. To further refine their search, they may also include specific location-based keywords such as the name of the county, city, or town they are interested in. For example, terms such as "Golf Chicago," "Golf Course Chicago," or "Golf 18 Chicago" effectively target golfers seeking courses in the Chicago area. By incorporating these keywords, golfers can more easily find courses located in their desired location, resulting in more accurate search and relevant search results.

Only the golfers who are already familiar with the business are going to search for the name of the business. New players and prospects are most likely going to search for something such as "GolfABCCounty" or "GolfWhatever." Search engines find businesses based on key search words such as golf, the name of a city, a town, a county, and so on. The best way to increase business is by choosing your URL made up of key search words relevant to your property. Even third-party tee time vendors who build sites for their clients could care less what your URL address is. They only promote their own URL, which is, of course, made up of key search words because they know the strength of this important detail.

The most fundamental step an operator can take to optimize his search engine rankings is to incorporate keywords as part of their domain name. For example, MMC®'s domain name for our golf site is "www.golfmarketingMMC®.com," and I chose this domain name because when operators search for "golf marketing," we want our website to pop up in Google's listings as well as on other search engines. The goal is to be on the first page, but when you are a national company, it is much more difficult because you are competing with hundreds of thousands, if not millions, of other people and companies for first page ranking. For example, when people search the phrase "golf marketing," they will see as many as 337,000 results. If someone searches for a golf course, they may see as many as 1,820,000 results. When you are creating a domain name, be specific as to what the keywords of the search are going to be when golfers look for a golf course in your area, and you will have a much better chance of them finding your information. Getting to the top of the search engines' list will be much easier for the operators if they just stick to the keywords because they will only be competing with a few other properties in their area, and if their competitors do not know this little nugget, they may not even make it on the page at all.

There are numerous things you can do when it comes to SEO to get your business positioned in the number one spot, on the first page, of the search results whether it is Google, Yahoo, MSN, or any other search engine. You can set up backlinks, write blogs, emphasize keywords on your site, get involved with social media, etc. These are all essential elements to help you get a better ranking with the major search engines. Make sure you provide education and information on your site. Always add exciting new content. "Content" does not need to be only text. Use illustrations, product photos, how-to videos, etc. This is one of the key reasons why businesses and individuals load up on social media. They want more traffic to their site to get better rankings with the search engines within their niche market.

As I stated earlier, one of the most overlooked and simplest ways to get great rankings is with your URL. Your URL is your website address. Most hosting platforms include a free URL with their hosting packages. I reiterate that you take some time and put yourself in the shoes of a new golfer and think, "What would be the words he/she would type into a search engine if he/she were looking for a new golfing home?"

Maximizing the potential of the internet as a marketing resource is crucial for generating new business. While choosing the name of your golf course as the website's URL may not directly generate new business, it is still important for brand consistency and recognition. However, it is also beneficial to have a second URL that is search engine-friendly and auto-forward to your existing URL. This increases the chances of attracting prospective golfers who are searching the web for a place to play.

Achieving a first-page ranking in search engine results is highly desirable because the majority of users rarely venture beyond the first page. Ideally, you want your website to be among the top three results, if not the first. The percentage of views and clicks varies day-to-day based on your ranking, but generally, being in the number one spot can result in 50 percent or more clicks, while lower positions may receive as little as 3 percent on the first page. Incorporating SEO techniques is essential to establish a strong online presence and improve your website's visibility.

As mentioned previously, improving your search engine ranking requires time, consistency, and a certain level of skill. You have two options: invest time in learning SEO yourself or hire someone with expertise in the field. It is important to be cautious when considering SEO companies, as many make grand promises and charge high fees without delivering satisfactory results.

Fortunately, in the golf industry, you generally have a smaller pool of local competitors, typically around twenty, compared to nationwide companies with hundreds or thousands of competitors. This means that by implementing effective SEO strategies, you can outperform these local competitors. A crucial factor in this process is owning a suitable URL, which can significantly contribute to boosting your website's ranking within a few months. Instead of spending unnecessary funds on SEO companies, it is advisable to take matters into your own hands and implement the following key steps:

- **Secure a great URL:** Invest in a memorable and relevant domain name, which can be purchased for as little as $10 per year.
- **Create and publish compelling blogs:** Regularly write informative and engaging blog posts that incorporate relevant keywords and provide value to your audience.
- **Distribute a monthly newsletter:** Keep your subscribers updated with valuable content, special offers, and news related to your golf course.
- **Produce instructional videos:** Utilize your mobile device to film and share videos that offer golfing tips, techniques, and insights. These videos can be embedded on your website to enhance its appeal and engagement.

Becoming an SEO expert is not necessary to achieve favorable results. By implementing the basic SEO principles outlined in this chapter, you can position your golf course on the first page of major search engines without incurring additional costs. It is important to consider the value of your time, effort, and investment to determine the ROI and assess whether the clicks generated are worthwhile.

At MMC®, we prioritize our marketing efforts based on ROI, and we have found that dedicating extensive time and resources to SEO yields limited returns compared to other strategies. By focusing on the fundamental SEO practices shared with you, you can achieve positive outcomes, especially considering the relatively small number of competing golf properties in your local market.

While having a well-designed website that serves as a sales presentation is advantageous, your website must be easily discoverable on the internet. Without a strong domain name, your website's visibility and impact will be diminished, rendering your efforts less effective. Just as a peanut butter sandwich lacks the complementary element of jelly, a website without a great domain name fails to reach its full potential.

By incorporating the basics of SEO, ensuring a strong online presence, and optimizing your website's discoverability, you can enhance your chances of attracting potential customers and maximizing the benefits of your digital marketing efforts.

2. **Web hosting account:** Web hosting is a service that hosts and stores your website files (content) on a secure server that is always up and running. Without a web host, your site will not be accessible for others to read and browse.

This is the situation in which many tech companies take advantage of operators. Most tech companies use platforms such as WordPress to host and build their clients' websites. Some of these unethical shysters lead operators to believe they are hosting the site and charge a monthly hosting fee between $50 and $100 per month. Just to be clear, the average business site needed by a golf property costs $300 annually if you work with WordPress. This package includes all of the plugins, templates, a URL, and hosting for an entire year.

In short, most tech companies charge thousands of dollars to build a website, whether you pay cash or in tee times, and then thousands of dollars in hosting fees, when, in fact, they probably contribute less than a couple of hours in the setup of your website and have nothing to do with the hosting.

3. **Web publishing platform:** Web publishing or online publishing is the process of publishing content on the internet. It includes creating and uploading websites, updating webpages, and posting blogs online. The published content may include text, images, videos, and other types of media. This service, too, comes free with most hosting packages.
4. **Payment system:** The most popular payment systems include PayPal, Square, Stripe, Amazon Pay, and so on. Yes, you want to offer your customers an option to pay for products and services online. The easier you make it for customers to buy, the more they will buy.

Many golf course websites are built on the WordPress platform, which is widely popular and commonly used for web publishing. With WordPress, you can easily handle domain registration, hosting, and web publishing, and there are numerous compatible plugins available for integrating payment systems. At MMC®, we offer to build our clients a website for their campaign absolutely free as part of our services.

Paying exorbitant amounts of money to have someone else build your website is unnecessary when the process is straightforward and can cost as little as $25 per month. By taking control and building your own website, you can eliminate wasteful spending and have the freedom to make changes and updates quickly and easily. Tech companies often create dependencies and delays, even for simple tasks such as changing a sentence or adding an image. They may take 48–72 hours to respond to such requests, making a two- or three-minute fix turn into a multiday process. Moreover, these companies often assign themselves as the "admin" of your website, granting them complete control. If you decide to part ways with them, you may fear losing everything. However, in reality, most websites are better off being abandoned as they mainly serve to promote the tech company.

Taking control of your website design and management is a crucial skill for every business operator. It is one of the most important marketing tools you can have. Alongside a great website, having a reliable email platform is essential for business growth. Companies such as Mailchimp, BenchmarkEmail, and MailerLite offer affordable email platforms that often come at significantly lower rates compared to what third-party tee time vendors, website developers, and freelancers charge. Depending on the size of your email list, operators can expect to pay as little as $100 per year, and those starting with a small list may even enjoy free services.

In conclusion, numerous hosting companies provide these services at a fraction of the cost charged by some vendors. I always encourage conducting your research and exploring the options available. Take advantage of the free trial templates offered by various companies and experience firsthand how easy it is to use. You might discover a way to save your business thousands of dollars annually, acquire a new skill set, and gain complete control over your business's future.

**E-Commerce**

E-commerce refers to the electronic selling of golf products and services, similar to a pro shop selling merchandise over the internet. Once the online store is set up, it offers numerous advantages such as no employee salaries, personnel conflicts, health insurance requirements, scheduling challenges, real estate taxes, water bills, workman's compensation, or excuses. Additionally, an online store is open 24/7, 365 days a year, providing convenience for customers and creating an additional revenue stream for the operator.

In the current economic climate, it is essential for golf operators to explore every opportunity to sell products and services, and the internet offers a promising avenue. E-commerce serves as an excellent way to generate additional revenue for your golf course. While it may require some initial setup time to connect and operationalize the online store, the effort is worthwhile as this profit center is often overlooked and underdeveloped.

Online stores are suitable for selling a wide range of products and services in the golf industry. These can include logo caps, golf shirts, balls, tees, shoes, towels, divot removers, ball markers, gift cards, punch cards, lessons, clinics, tournaments, outings, social events, and more. It is important to note that online stores should not replace physical pro shops but complement them. Ideally, having both a physical and online store provides the best of both worlds.

Unlike a brick-and-mortar store, starting an online store is super easy. There are only three things required to start an online store. A website, a shopping cart, and a merchant account. Most website hosts offer a shopping cart component to their software. If not, and you do not want to switch hosts, just search "shopping cart" on the internet, and it will give you a list of different companies that offer shopping cart products and services. These companies always provide great tutorials on YouTube and Google. The function of the shopping cart is to take the customer through the buying process.

You can go to your local bank and set up a merchant account and the shopping cart with them, and they can set it all up for you in-house, where you are in complete control. But when you partner with a bank, you will be subjected to a lot more regulations, which could lead to some headaches as well. So, in most cases, it is better just to set up a PayPal, Square, or Stripe account or something similar to it.

When determining which products and services are viable candidates for online purchases, it is important to consider the preferences and needs of your target customers. While some items, such as golf clubs, may require a hands-on experience and are better suited for in-person sales, some other products and services lend themselves well to online transactions.

For products, items such as golf balls, tees, caps, and other accessories are ideal for online sales. These items do not typically require physical interaction or testing, as golfers are already familiar with their features and functionality. Customers can easily browse and make a purchase online, enjoying the convenience of having these products delivered to their doorstep.

When it comes to services such as banquets and lessons, online sales can also be effective. For lessons, providing sample video lessons on your website allows potential students to get a sense of your teaching style and expertise. The online store can serve as an introduction to your lesson packages, with the ultimate goal of bringing the student face-to-face with the instructor for personalized instruction.

It is worth considering that certain products and services such as high-end sets of golf clubs may still benefit from a combination of online and in-person sales approaches. While core golfers may understand the value of playing with quality equipment, the average consumer may require a more hands-on experience to fully appreciate the benefits. In such cases, using the online store to generate interest and educate customers about the product can be a valuable strategy, with the intention of guiding them to visit your physical location for a more personalized consultation or fitting.

One of the common mistakes made by online businesses is focusing solely on one-time sales. While customers may visit your store, make a purchase, and leave, it is important to leverage the opportunity to build long-term relationships and encourage repeat business.

To achieve this, always strive to collect customer information, such as their name and email address. Let them know that you value their support and would like to follow-up with them. Building a relationship with customers is key to fostering loyalty and generating ongoing revenue. By engaging with them through email marketing, you can nurture the relationship, provide relevant updates, and offer exclusive promotions or discounts.

Retaining customers is critical for business growth. For instance, instead of a golfer buying just one sleeve of balls, engaging with them and building a relationship may lead to them purchasing a hundred sleeves of balls over their lifetime. By focusing on customer retention, you can maximize the lifetime value of each customer.

It is important to recognize the difference between a buyer and a prospect. A buyer is one who has already shown interest and trust in your brand and products. These individuals should be treated as valued customers, as they contribute to your revenue. Consider offering special perks or incentives to show appreciation for their support. Provide them with freebies, engage in ongoing dialogues, and keep them interested and excited about your offerings.

When introducing a new product and service, it is essential to inform your players and the community through a well-executed product launch. This principle applies equally to the establishment of an online store. To effectively announce the opening of your online store, follow these steps:

1. Initiate advertising efforts around the club approximately ninety days before the launch, aiming to generate anticipation and build excitement among your target audience.
2. At the sixty-day mark, release a teaser advertisement or announcement containing intriguing information about the upcoming online store. Provide glimpses of the products, exclusive offers, or unique features that will be available.
3. As the launch approaches within thirty days, maintain the momentum by unveiling further teasers or announcements. Highlight the specific benefits or advantages that customers can expect from the online store.
4. One week before the launch, publicize a noteworthy giveaway or promotional offer that will be accessible to all store visitors. This giveaway can range from a modest bag of logo tees to a more substantial raffle. Ensure that the offering resonates

with the interests of your golfers and remains within your financial means.
5. Host a launch party at your clubhouse to celebrate the opening of the online store. Utilize this occasion to engage with your players, foster a festive atmosphere, and generate enthusiasm for the new service you have introduced.

By orchestrating a well-planned product launch, you can effectively communicate the launch of your online store to your players and the community. This additional revenue source will contribute to the growth of your business while enhancing your overall service offerings.

**Marketing with No Downside**
Achieving golf marketing with no downside is indeed a possibility. At MMC®, we offer four no-risk/self-funding golfer acquisition campaigns that have been carefully crafted based on the principles of "no downside" golf marketing. Throughout my extensive career, my primary focus has been on minimizing the risks associated with golf course marketing while maximizing its potential rewards. I have always challenged those who make bold claims about their abilities by asking them to invest their own money and share in the success if they are truly confident. Over my forty-year career, I have found that only my own company, MMC®, is willing to assume all the financial risks involved. It is rare to find another company that is willing to shoulder the entirety of the risks, which is why I aim to teach you how to minimize the downsides on your own.

Most investments indeed carry some potential downside. There is a prevailing belief in society that significant returns can only be achieved by taking enormous risks. However, this belief is more of a myth than a reality. While it is important to be informed and make wise decisions, there are numerous ways to achieve substantial returns on investment by thinking creatively and stepping outside conventional boundaries. Moreover, it is not just the downside that should concern us; the upside is equally important. Often, investors talk about a 10 percent return, but the accompanying risk factor is disproportionately high in many cases. Unfortunately, most investment scenarios yield returns that hardly justify the time and capital invested.

Having made a significant investment in your golf course, it is crucial to ensure that it yields the desired dividends instead of becoming a drain on your physical, mental, emotional, and financial resources. It is time to demand a return on your investment. While it may not be possible to find completely risk-free approaches, you can certainly reduce potential downsides by conducting thorough market research and implementing soft launches to assess the risk-return ratio.

When it comes to advertising your golf course, it is advisable to select platforms that offer risk reversal options. However, it is important to note that these options are not always without risk, as failure to convert prospects can still result in expenses. The term "risk reversal" may sound appealing, but in reality, if your conversion rate is not favorable, the campaign can become costly. For instance, many online marketing companies promote pay-per-click programs with the claim that you only pay for customers who click on your link. They further assert that only consumers with an interest in your product and service will click. However, this representation is not entirely transparent. The truth is that a significant number of internet users spend their time browsing indiscriminately and will click on anything. Most of these individuals have no genuine interest in your product, making it unlikely that they will convert into paying customers.

While it is true that many platforms offer reasonable rates per click, it is important to ensure that the cost of reaching surfers is justified by the number of qualified prospects generated. To make the most of this approach, it is crucial to have a well-established sales system in place. Your ability to smoothly guide customers through the conversion process and prompt them to take immediate action is

# EGO: EDGING GOLF OUT

paramount. Therefore, careful planning of the conversion process is essential before considering a pay-per-click strategy.

The concept of pay-per-click originated from a traditional marketing approach in which manufacturers would negotiate contracts with various media outlets such as newspapers, radio, and magazines. The goal was to ensure that payment was based on the actual results achieved. While this approach may have been challenging, persistent marketing representatives could often find willing partners. However, it is important to consider the time invested versus the potential savings when evaluating this strategy.

Let us consider an example to illustrate how it can work effectively. Suppose you are a golf ball manufacturer who understands your product and your customers well. You know that most core and avid golfers have a preference for a specific brand of golf ball and tend to remain loyal to it. With the understanding that your customers typically purchase an average of 1000 balls over their lifetime, you can leverage this knowledge in your marketing efforts. As a manufacturer, you can seek out advertising mediums that are willing to accept a free sleeve of golf balls in exchange for customers providing their complete contact information.

In this scenario, the manufacturer offers a deal to ad companies where the company receives 100 percent of the sale price for each sleeve of golf balls sold through their advertisement. The manufacturer's primary objective is to obtain the customer's complete mailing address to fulfill the order by sending out the sleeve of golf balls.

You might wonder why newspapers, radio stations, or other entities would agree to such an arrangement. These types of ads are known as fillers, as they help these media outlets fill empty spaces in their publications or broadcasts. It creates a mutually beneficial situation. The ad company has the potential to sell a significant number of sleeves of golf balls, generating higher revenue than they would have obtained through selling the ad space alone. Meanwhile, the manufacturer acquires a large customer base at no direct cost, apart from providing free samples.

This approach leverages the concept of win-win partnerships and creative thinking to achieve marketing objectives with minimal downside risk. By exploring innovative strategies, it is possible to find opportunities for no-risk or low-risk marketing initiatives that can lead to substantial returns and business growth.

**The Six Reasons Why Golfers Buy**

In this section, I will present the top six reasons why core and avid golfers choose one golf property over another, based on extensive research conducted by MMC® since the late 1990s. While most marketers would typically begin with the sixth reason and count down to the most significant factor, I am going to reverse that order. I believe the least important reason may surprise you, and it is important to highlight the number one reason right from the start.

So, let us dive into the findings. The number one reason why core and avid golfers choose a specific golf property is trust. Trust is a critical factor that encompasses confidence in the brand, the operator, and the individuals representing the property and its offerings. Even if a golf course boasts exceptional facilities and pristine course conditions, it can still struggle to thrive if golfers lack trust in the operator, staff, or overall experience.

During my travels, I have come across operators who have created exquisite facilities but face challenges in sustaining their business. Upon interacting with the staff and operator for just a brief period, it becomes evident that golfers do not have confidence in them or the product they offer. However, the good news is that this problem can be easily resolved. Improving someone's experience and earning their trust does not require significant financial investments. It simply requires a commitment to enhance interactions and communication and consistently deliver on promises.

Renowned motivational speaker Zig Ziglar once wisely said, "If your thinking is stinking, you need a check-up from the neck up." This quote holds true when it comes to the perception of your golf course by your players. If your players are not feeling valued and appreciated, it is time to give everyone an attitude adjustment. Let your staff know that their conduct, lack of professionalism, and attitudes of noncommitment will not be tolerated. It is equally important to examine your own behavior and presentation, as the way you present yourself reflects how golfers perceive your brand. Building 100 percent confidence in your brand requires a collective effort and a commitment to excellence.

Moving on to the second reason on our list, course conditions play a pivotal role in the purchase decisions of core and avid golfers. They place significant emphasis on the quality and upkeep of the course. These golfers want assurance that the course is well-maintained, with neatly cut grass, properly maintained greens, clean bunkers, filled divots, and an overall pristine playing surface. This factor sets core and avid golfers apart from casual and non-golfers, who may prioritize price over course conditions. It is crucial not to underestimate the value of your memberships, green fees, and amenities for core and avid golfers. They seek the best golfing experience and are willing to invest in it.

Moving on to the third reason on our list, service plays a crucial role in both acquiring and retaining customers. While being a skilled salesperson and offering a great product are essential for initial customer engagement, providing exceptional service is what transforms a golfer into a lifelong customer. When customers visit your golf course, they expect to see evidence of attentive service. This includes having an ample and attentive staff, clean facilities, well-maintained golf carts, a tidy parking lot, and a welcoming atmosphere. It is important for customers to witness staff members who are genuinely enjoying their work and creating a positive experience for everyone.

Number four on our list is amenities. Consumers appreciate having a range of amenities, choices, and options available to them. Golf courses can offer a wide array of amenities and services, such as banquet facilities, full restaurant and bar services, driving ranges, car storage, locker rentals, club storage, social events, outings, leagues, and club tournaments, among others. When deciding which amenities to provide, it is essential to focus on what sells. Amenities should be considered profit centers and must contribute to the overall profitability of the golf course. If an amenity helps attract and retain customers, particularly for memberships, then it is worth keeping. However, if an amenity does not generate the desired results, it may need to be reevaluated or eliminated.

Moving on to the fifth most important factor for golfers, convenience and location play a significant role in their decision-making process. Golfers prefer courses that are within a reasonable drive time from their location. Typically, golf courses draw customers from a radius of about twenty to forty miles, with the drive time being a key consideration. Most golfers prefer not to drive more than forty to forty-five minutes regularly to play golf. However, there can be exceptions, such as when golfers want to try out a new course or when they are playing with friends. It is crucial to communicate to golfers that your course is the most convenient and superior option within your market, leaving no room for alternatives.

Now, brace yourself for a surprising revelation: the sixth and final factor on our list is price. Contrary to popular belief, price is not the primary driving factor for core and avid golfers when making purchase decisions. Their focus lies more on the quality of the product, the brand, amenities, trust, and convenience. It may come as a shock to some, but the success of core and avid golfer acquisition campaigns is not solely dependent on lowering prices. Merely copying price points without considering other important factors is foolishness and will inevitably result in damaging the business. Price alone does not guarantee long-term success in attracting and retaining this particular segment of golfers. It is vital to understand that core and avid golfers value the overall package and the experience rather than just the price.

In contrast to prevailing assumptions, simply lowering prices does not guarantee success when targeting core and avid golfers. These passionate golf enthusiasts prioritize factors beyond price when making their purchasing decisions. To effectively engage with these segments, it is crucial to possess the knowledge, data, and experience necessary to identify and appeal to their wants, needs, and desires instead of resorting to price reductions that may, and most likely will, undermine long-term success.

When focusing on core and avid golfers, it is essential to highlight what matters most to them: convenience, amenities, service, course conditions, and above all, trust. While price does come into consideration, it is not the primary driving factor for this particular audience. They seek a comprehensive golfing experience that goes beyond financial considerations. By understanding their needs and preferences, golf course operators can tailor their marketing efforts accordingly.

It is worth noting that core and avid golfers are not impervious to analyzing value and calculating costs. They still desire favorable deals, but it is the holistic experience that holds greater significance to them. Therefore, knowing the target audience, leveraging the strengths of the facility, and maintaining the brand's integrity are fundamental to attracting and retaining these valuable golfers.

**Design Good Ads, Not Bad Ads**

It is undeniable that the golf industry often suffers from a proliferation of poorly executed advertisements. Many operators tend to mimic their competitors' marketing campaigns instead of embracing innovation. This lack of originality leads to lackluster ads that fail to effectively capture the attention of their target audience. When advertising a golf course, it is crucial to recognize that the majority of viewers are core and avid golfers. Understanding your audience is paramount when designing a marketing campaign. You need to determine what will pique their curiosity and motivate them to delve further into your offering.

If you have familiarized yourself with the section on the "Six Reasons Why Golfers Buy," you are aware that price ranks sixth on the list of crucial factors influencing a golfer's choice of a property. Trust, confidence, course conditions, and amenities take precedence for core and avid golfers. Price plays a minimal role in their purchasing decisions. However, many operators mistakenly believe that price is the sole driving force and focus solely on price points. In reality, price holds a much lower position on the list of priorities.

If you aim to achieve better results with your advertisements, it is essential to design them to be distinct from anything the public has ever seen before. The pique technique, a marketing strategy, revolves around the concept of making your advertising stand out amid the clutter, noise, and, most importantly, your competitors' ads. You must create something so unusual and different that people are compelled to take notice instead of simply passing over it.

Imagine the familiar saying, "Been there, done that, got the T-shirt." This is how most advertising comes across to golfers. When they encounter generic advertising, their brains quickly register it as something they have already seen before, leading them to dismiss it and file it away as unimportant. Our brains are adept at rapidly processing and categorizing information, causing the golfer to disregard the ad without further consideration.

However, by applying the pique technique, you strive to create something truly extraordinary and unconventional. Your goal is to interrupt the golfer's thought process, much like scratching a CD and causing it to skip when played. The intention is to capture the golfer's attention, prompting them to pause for a few seconds and process the new and intriguing information presented in your advertisement.

An illustrative example of ineffective marketing campaigns is when operators rely on conventional methods such as placing ads in weekend newspapers or running Facebook ads highlighting discounts on green fees for weekends to attract more play on Saturdays and Sundays. However, come Monday morning, they find themselves puzzled by disappointing results and wonder why their ads failed to generate a better response. The answer is quite simple: their ads are all the same. Every golf course in the area is running similar ads with similar offers, causing them to blend and create a cluttered landscape.

Another common example of a bad ad is the two-for-one or buy-one-get-one-free promotion. While this offer can be a valuable marketing tool when used correctly, many people fail to understand its proper implementation. In the service industry, such as golf, the goal of this offer is to increase traffic, unlike in a retail setting where the objective is to sell products. When promoting golf, the aim is not to sell two products for the price of one but rather to sell an existing golfer something while encouraging them to bring a friend along to enjoy the complimentary offer.

In the golf industry, there is a multitude of examples showcasing ineffective ads, and the simplest way to avoid creating a bad ad is to refrain from copying others' advertisements. Your target audience comprises core and avid golfers, so it is crucial to design your ads based on their emotional and logical needs. Rather than fixating on price, emphasize the features, advantages, and benefits (FABs) of your business. Instead of engaging in a price war with competitors for cost-conscious golfers, concentrate on attracting players who seek the best experience and are willing to pay for it. "The best" is a subjective claim, but if you genuinely believe your product is superior, do not hesitate to proclaim it. Let the world know, shout it from the mountaintops, and above all, include it in your ad copy.

**Marketing Hooks and Taglines**

Golf courses heavily rely on golfers, and acquiring golfers requires well planned marketing campaigns. Even with limited or no budget, it is crucial to consistently think about growing your business and advancing your golf career. It is not the markets that underperform but the golf marketers themselves.

When designing your ad copy, a key starting point is crafting a compelling headline or "grab line." The opening statement should immediately capture the consumer's attention and convey why they should continue reading. Consumers are always seeking the highest benefits with the lowest drawbacks. A tagline can further emphasize your company's brand, delivering a clear and concise message that resonates with your target audience.

It is important to recognize that golfers do not simply purchase products; they seek a desired outcome and the corresponding emotions associated with it. For instance, when people engage with MMC®, they anticipate achieving financial freedom, while experiencing emotions such as success, growth, contribution, connection, security, excitement, and peace of mind. Focus on showcasing the end result and the positive feelings that golfers can expect from choosing your product and service.

Here is an example of a great ad to attract new players. This can be an inexpensive radio spot, email blast, SMS, and so on. "First 10 callers get FREE Golf Lessons!"

While it may not be feasible to offer free golf lessons all day, you can allocate a few hours each day to provide introductory lessons as a way to introduce golfers to the course and showcase the pro's teaching skills. For example, you can offer the first ten golfers a free thirty-minute lesson and provide a free fifteen-minute consolation prize to the remaining fifty or so golfers. By doing so, you can potentially acquire sixty new prospects. Even if you only convert 20 percent of those relationships into paying customers, you would still have twelve new golfers. Multiply that by your regular lesson fees, and the cost to acquire those new students would be minimal. If the numbers make sense from a business perspective, it is worth considering. If not, you can experiment with different offers until you find a compelling and financially viable option.

Effective marketing strategies often incorporate a hook, which serves as a sample or mental appetizer for your prospects. The hook should provide just enough of a taste to leave them wanting more. It captures their attention and resonates with their needs, making them think, "Yes! This is what I have been looking for." The marketing hook acts as a way to attract prospects and eventually convert them into customers by meeting their specific needs.

It is important to remember that this is just one of many marketing approaches you can take for your golf business. These small, incremental ideas help you grow your business over time and are not intended to make you rich overnight. Emphasize innovation and continuously come up with new hooks to keep your ads fresh. While the core message remains the same, finding different ways to convey it can help capture the interest of your target audience.

Marketing hooks can be best understood by drawing parallels to songwriting. In a song, the hook is the catchy and memorable part that sticks with you, often found in the chorus. Even if you cannot recall the rest of the lyrics, the hook is what you will likely remember and sing along to. It is what captivates the listener and draws them into the song. In fact, there is a saying in songwriting, especially in the pop genre, that goes, "Don't bore us, get to the chorus."

Similarly, when crafting marketing hooks and taglines for your business, you want to create something that grabs the attention of your audience and sticks with them. It should be memorable, engaging, and resonate with their needs or desires. The hook serves as a powerful tool to captivate your target market and draw them in to learn more about your offering.

In addition to creating effective hooks and taglines, it is crucial to have a unique approach to your golf marketing strategy. This involves developing a list of actionable steps that guide you through a systematic process when launching a campaign. It is important to carefully plan and outline your strategy before implementation. Marketing campaigns can be costly, so it is your responsibility to minimize wasteful spending and maximize returns.

As a golf course operator, your focus should be on retaining and acquiring golfers to ensure the success of the business. When you propose marketing campaigns and allocate your owner's investment, it is essential to be confident that the campaign will succeed and generate a ROI. By creating a list of action steps, options, and a checklist to keep you on track, you can strengthen the effectiveness of your campaign and feel assured of its success. This structured approach helps solidify your strategy and ensures you're making the most of your resources.

Being accountable for your actions is crucial in establishing yourself as a valued asset to the owner or organization you work for. When you consistently deliver on your promises and achieve a proven track record of success, you eliminate many obstacles when seeking approval for future campaigns. Each successful endeavor builds trust and confidence in your ideas, making it easier for owners to green-light your next initiative.

Maintaining good data and records is also essential. These data serve as a valuable tool for analyzing the outcomes of past campaigns, both successes and failures. By studying this information, you can uncover insights and patterns that inform the development of new taglines, hooks, and marketing strategies in the future. It is important to recognize that what works today may not work tomorrow, so continuous study, analysis, and innovation are necessary to stay ahead.

Marketing is an ongoing effort that requires consistent attention and adaptation. Whether you are a small business aiming to attract new customers, a large corporation striving to maintain your position as the market leader, or a significant organization responsible for shaping an entire industry, staying on top of your marketing efforts is essential. It is an ongoing process of staying informed, being proactive, and adapting to changes in the market to maintain your competitive edge.

To excel as a leader in your market, field, organization, or industry, it is essential to regularly sharpen your skills and abilities. As Abraham Lincoln once said, "If I only had an hour to chop down a tree, I would spend the first forty-five minutes sharpening my axe."

# 7

## DEVELOPING LEADERSHIP SKILLS

Will the industry recover or not? Basic physics provides a clear answer to this question. According to the principle of inertia, an object in motion will continue to stay in motion unless acted upon by an external force. Similarly, an industry that is in decline or experiencing setbacks will continue in that direction until an external force intervenes to reverse the trend. In 2019, the COVID-19 pandemic served as that external force. However, as COVID-19 lost its grip on society, it simultaneously loosened the tourniquet it had on stopping the golf industry's hemorrhaging of players, revenue, and golf facilities.

Any leader understands that when a business or industry stops growing, it is showing the initial signs of decline. In other words, stagnation can be a precursor to failure. Leaders in the golf industry must recognize the importance of continuous growth and innovation to ensure long-term success. Although external factors such as the COVID-19 pandemic caused a temporary pause on the downturn, it has now lost its grip on society, and as a result, it is losing its grip on the tourniquet that was once used to stop the bleeding in the golf industry.

In 2023, most revenue streams have experienced significant declines. However, it is uncommon to hear individuals openly acknowledge this without first highlighting that their business, their company, or the industry is reporting gains compared to the pre-COVID-19 years. The motivation behind this approach is understandable, as executives often strive to maintain a positive image and avoid delivering bad news. Shareholders, stockholders, donors, sponsors, and advertisers generally prefer to hear positive earnings reports. Consequently, there is a widespread fear of being the bearer of bad news. Personally, I find it difficult to comprehend how anyone can confidently compare their performance and boast about growth when the benchmark being used is the industry's worst years. Such a comparison can be likened to a touring pro boasting about a victory over a casual golfer, which is ethically questionable and lacks genuine merit.

The ironic aspect of this entire downturn is that the industry was granted a Mulligan by the heavens above, a second chance, absolutely free. It felt as if the industry was headed straight toward an iceberg, and everyone abandoned the ship in panic. Miraculously, the iceberg crumbled, offering a clear path, and everyone returned on board. However, in a bewildering turn of events, a significant number of passengers began disembarking out of frustration, leaving the captain and crew with an empty vessel. Even though the vessel was saved, a ship with no passengers will eventually sink to the bottom of the sea.

The pandemic compelled people to return to the golf courses, providing sufficient numbers to support the surviving facilities. Yet, closures continued to occur at an alarming rate. This raises important questions: Why is this happening? How can we reverse this trajectory? As someone who looks at numbers and values their significance over mere words, I believe in the power of data. Fortunately, the numbers are on our side, and if we unite our resources, we can completely transform the golf industry within a year.

By the end of 2024, we can proudly hold our heads up high and say, "I played my part, and today, the game of golf is more popular than ever." Despite being an optimist, I still rely on the evidence presented by the numbers, and they demonstrate that a turnaround is within our reach.

The path to a successful recovery in any industry begins with acknowledging and accepting that there is a problem. Everyone involved in the golf industry must recognize this crucial fact. While it may not be ideal to broadcast this news to the public, those responsible for the industry's growth must confront the reality to bring about change.

The data speaks for itself: Manufacturers and retailers have experienced a significant decline in revenue, with drops of up to 40 percent from 2006 through 2019. Similarly, 18-hole golf facilities have seen a decrease of as much as 33 percent during the same period. The number of lost golfers has reached the millions.

During the COVID Bump, there was a temporary increase in both play and sales. However, it is important to note that some of the revenue growth can be attributed to price increases rather than an actual increase in the number of items sold. The increase in revenue from the rounds played can also be partially attributed to the closure of thousands of golf facilities. It is important to acknowledge these facts as they form the basis of our current situation.

The discrepancy in the numbers regarding the total number of golfers and the average number of golfers per facility is puzzling. While it has been reported that there are approximately 30,000,000 golfers in the United States, this figure seems disproportionately high when divided among the 15,000 golf facilities. The average facility may have around 600 unique golfers at best, which raises questions about the accuracy of the reported numbers.

To gain a better understanding of how to grow a business and/or the industry, it is important to categorize golfers into four types: core, avid, casual, and non-golfer. Each type of golfer plays a specific number of rounds per year or season. When considering the non-golfer segment, the figure of 30,000,000 golfers may indeed be accurate and potentially even underestimated, as indicated by our research. This fact alone indicates that there is a substantial pool of consumers who have expressed interest, to some extent, in the game of golf.

The key question then becomes: Why are these individuals no longer actively participating in or purchasing golf-related products and services?

The disconnection and lack of engagement among potential customers are significant factors in the current state of the golf industry. It is comparable to seeing someone in a precarious situation, hanging on a ledge, where our instinct would be to offer them a lifeline. The same principle applies to potential customers in the golf industry.

In the realm of golf, there is a remarkable opportunity for every golf facility in the nation to invite 500–1,500 eagerly awaiting customers into their club and welcome them to the game. It is astonishing to realize that, even after two decades, over 20,000,000 individuals are aspiring to become golfers and are still awaiting that invitation. This situation calls for leadership at all levels to step forward and redefine the narrative surrounding golf.

Regrettably, the golf industry finds itself deeply rooted in a culture that upholds impractical norms through conformity. However, it is essential to recognize the significant impact that leadership can have in catalyzing cultural transformation within any industry, including golf. When leaders proactively seize the opportunity to advocate for and spearhead change, they not only establish the prevailing tone but also pave the path for the entire industry to embrace such transformation.

Leaders have the power to influence the attitudes, beliefs, and actions of those within their sphere of influence. When they actively promote and embrace a new cultural direction, it sends a clear message to others that change is not only necessary but also beneficial. This can break the inertia of conformity that often exists within an industry, encouraging individuals to question existing norms and adopt new behaviors.

In *Golf: The Untapped Market*, I highlighted how some individuals in the industry blindly follow the crowd, without questioning who is leading or where they are heading. As social beings, humans have an innate desire to belong, form connections, and gain the respect and approval of their peers. Throughout our evolutionary history, these inclinations have played a crucial role in our survival within tribal communities. Being isolated from the tribe, or worse, being cast out, meant certain peril. The act of collaborating and forming strong connections with others ensured not only safety but also facilitated access to vital resources. Consequently, the need to belong has become deeply ingrained in our core emotional needs, exerting a significant influence on our present-day behavior.

In our early stages of development, we mimic the behaviors of those around us, starting with our families. As we grow, we shape our behavior based on the influence of mentors, peers, and leaders in our respective fields—those whom we aspire to emulate. Each of these cultures and groups comes with its own set of expectations and standards, which often become the invisible rules guiding our daily behavior. Most of the time, we find ourselves adhering to social norms without questioning their validity, sometimes even being unaware of the underlying reasons. The tendency to conform to these norms arises from the inherent comfort and security that comes from going along with the group. Extensive research has been conducted on this phenomenon, revealing that even when individuals are aware that their choices may be unfavorable, they persist in following the crowd simply because everyone else is doing so. In moments of uncertainty, we instinctively seek guidance from the collective, constantly observing our surroundings and contemplating, "What is the prevailing behavior?" While there can be a sense of reassurance in numbers, it is important to acknowledge the potential drawbacks that accompany this conformity. As I always quote, "When you follow the herd blindly, you are bound to step in the manure of those ahead of you." I respect traditional rules but find it challenging to adhere to them when it comes to growing a business or the industry, particularly when those norms have been proven to be a major impediment to the growth of the game. Remember, what may have been thought as the best way to grow a business or industry ten years ago may, and probably is, antiquated thinking today.

In my previous book, I discussed how individuals within a tribe often exhibit similar dressing styles, speech patterns, thought processes, and even mannerisms to some extent. These behaviors serve as a way for them to communicate their membership and belonging to the tribe. This phenomenon is commonly observed in various contexts, such as school colors, uniforms, and other shared symbols. Both our physical and social environments have a profound impact on shaping our behavior.

We naturally acquire behaviors from the people in our proximity. We absorb the perceptions, attitudes, and beliefs of those around us, whether consciously or unconsciously. We tend to emulate the actions and approaches of our peers, coworkers, and even competitors to achieve similar results. Typically, the closer our relationship with someone, the greater the likelihood of us imitating specific elements of their behavior. Our friends, peers, and leaders possess an inherent ability to exert unseen peer pressure that impacts our choices and draws us toward their influence. It is critical to remember that the influence of peer pressure can be negative only if we are surrounded by detrimental influences.

We must understand that as humans, we possess an inherent drive to pursue power, prestige, and status. Seeking recognition, acknowledgment, and praise may appear self-centered, but in reality, it is a strategic inclination. Throughout history, those who have wielded greater power and attained higher status have enjoyed increased access to valuable resources and a reduced concern for survival.

Our innate desire for respect, approval, admiration, and status leads us to adopt behaviors that set us apart from the crowd. Once we have assimilated into a group, our focus shifts toward distinguishing ourselves and earning the admiration and praise of our peers and subordinates. The approval of our tribe becomes a paramount quest, prompting us to imitate those whom we envy.

Individuals with elevated status receive the validation, respect, and acclaim of others. Consequently, behaviors that garner approval, respect, and praise become particularly attractive to us. Simultaneously, we are motivated to avoid actions that might diminish our status. The perpetual question of "What will others think of me?" constantly lingers in our minds, shaping our behavior and leading us to make adjustments accordingly. As leaders, however, it is imperative that we transcend our egos and self-centered desires and prioritize the greater good of our subordinates and our business. True leadership lies in serving others, setting aside personal aspirations to empower and uplift those around us.

For a business or organization to thrive, its leaders must possess a certain willingness—a willingness to take calculated risks and make difficult decisions. This encompasses the courage to transform the existing culture when it no longer serves the best interests of the industry. Playing it safe and avoiding taking chances may seem like the path of least resistance, but it seldom leads to superior performance or remarkable achievements. Instead, the companies and institutions that rise to prominence are those led by leaders who possess the courage to step out of their comfort zones, challenge conventional thinking, and take educated risks.

If you want to be respected—operate from a position of strength. Not as an oppressive leader, but as a leader who operates and makes decisions fearlessly at all times. True leaders do what is right regardless of what their peers or subordinates think. That is why they are in the leadership role; to make the tough decisions and to do so without fear. The ego keeps people living in constant fear—fear of losing their status, their work, their passions, being ridiculed by their peers, and so forth. One thing is for sure, fear brought on by an inflated ego will render you crippled more quickly than any debilitating illness known to man. Leaders confront their fears and conquer them by prioritizing the needs of others before their own. For example, the jobs of the employees, the business, the community's open spaces, the wildlife, the plant life, the members, the guests, the suppliers, the retailers, the vendors, the manufacturers, the game, and even the industry rather than the imagined self-serving reward their ego may be seeking to satisfy.

Cultural change in golf requires us to confront a fundamental truth: change is often met with resistance when it challenges the established norms and beliefs of the golfing community. Within the tribe, there exists a natural inclination to adhere to tradition and resist anything that disrupts the familiar. Yet, if we truly desire progress and inclusivity in golf, we must recognize that change can be incredibly alluring when it aligns with the values and aspirations of the tribe.

In the dynamic landscape of today's business world, leaders must be proactive and adaptable. They cannot afford to merely react to circumstances or passively follow the status quo. True leaders have the audacity to envision a better future for their organization and take the necessary steps to bring that vision to life. They understand that to shape the company and/or the industry, they must be unafraid of being shaped by it. They have a deep sense of responsibility to their team members, shareholders, and stakeholders to create an atmosphere of excitement, progress, and continuous improvement.

When an organization starts to settle into a comfort zone or falls into a state of stagnation, it is the leader's duty to shake things up. They gather their executive team and encourage everyone to think outside the box, challenging the existing norms and brainstorming innovative strategies to propel the organization in the right direction. This infusion of fresh perspectives and the pursuit of new opportunities can breathe new life into the company, reinvigorating both its employees and its market presence.

Leaders are learners—they constantly strive to improve themselves, their team members, and the businesses they lead. Committed to personal development, they actively seek opportunities to grow, expand their knowledge, and refine their skills. Equally important, they invest time and effort in nurturing the growth and development of those under their leadership.

Furthermore, effective leaders are dedicated to the development and progress of the business they oversee. They embrace innovation, identify areas for improvement, and proactively work on optimizing processes and strategies. By combining their focus on personal development, team growth, and business success, leaders create a harmonious synergy that propels both their own growth and the prosperity of the organization as a whole. This dedication to continuous development enables leaders to lead with confidence and adapt effectively to the ever-evolving challenges of the business landscape.

The captivating story of Henry Ford and the creation of the V8 engine serves as a testament to the importance of determination and visionary leadership. In the face of skepticism and engineers insisting it was an impossible feat, Ford remained resolute. He firmly believed that the V8 engine could be achieved, and he refused to succumb to doubts or settle for mediocrity. Through unwavering commitment and relentless pursuit of the goal, the V8 engine became a reality under Ford's leadership. This extraordinary accomplishment not only revolutionized the automotive industry but also exemplified how anything can be achieved when a leader possesses the determination, conviction, and audacity to lead their organization toward a better future.

While smooth waters may appear safe, it is important to recognize that dangers can lurk beneath the surface, such as rocks or other obstacles. Simply playing it safe does not eliminate risk or guarantee success. Leaders, at times, can lose sight of their true goals and become engrossed in pursuing other more enjoyable objectives, inadvertently neglecting the core purpose of their business. This tendency is understandable as people naturally gravitate toward what is easy and enjoyable. However, it is crucial to acknowledge when our focus is misplaced on irrelevant information, tasks, or specific areas of the business or organization. We must acknowledge the primary reason for being in business and recognize when we are veering off track. Taking risks and embracing challenges can lead to growth and extraordinary achievements. True progress requires leaders who are unafraid to navigate uncharted waters and chart a course toward innovation, cultural change, and success.

Many individuals within the golf industry find themselves immobilized by the fear of ridicule and failure, causing them to resist making significant changes. However, it is important to realize that these concerns hold little significance in the grand scheme of things. What truly matters is the collective effort to grow the game, regardless of individual ego or the potential for ridicule. Shift your fear to curiosity. If you are afraid of launching MMC®'s golfer acquisition campaign or even the growth initiative, ask yourself why. Replace the fear with curiosity. Curiosity will better serve you, the business, the game, and the industry.

Transform your curiosity into "knowing." Knowing comes from experience. "Knowing" is not the same as "knowing about." Knowing about something is still a belief. You know something after you have experienced it firsthand. For instance, I have personally seen the outcomes of over 1,000 MMC® projects, therefore I am confident in the efficacy of this proposed growth initiative and these golfer acquisition campaigns.

Success comes from practice and doing, not just planning endlessly. Avoiding action out of fear of making mistakes is counterproductive. Making mistakes is an inevitable part of the journey, and it applies to everyone. Embracing this reality is crucial. While I personally make numerous mistakes, I also achieve a great deal by continuously progressing and implementing my ideas. I take action to test their effectiveness, and if they do not yield the desired results, I adapt and make necessary changes. By analyzing the outcomes and staying focused on the goal, I persistently adjust my approach and determine how to reach that desired destination. This dynamic process of continuous improvement enables me to accomplish more and move closer to my objectives. Take a chance, embrace the possibility of making mistakes, and learn from them. The saying "study long, study wrong" emphasizes the importance of taking action and gaining real-world experience.

The key lies in maintaining a forward momentum, always striving to make progress. Embracing a mindset of resilience and adaptability allows me to learn from my mistakes, leverage my experiences, and refine my strategies. Through this iterative process, I remain committed to achieving my goals and stay determined to find the most effective path forward.

In the journey of growth, both individuals and organizations must adhere to numerous essential conditions. At the core of these conditions lies the imperative of possessing a receptive mindset—an attitude characterized by open windows that eagerly welcome the invigorating winds of renewal in the form of fresh ideas and creative thinking. Regrettably, we often encounter individuals and organizations that operate as closed systems, who are convinced that they already possess all the necessary knowledge. Although some of these entities may boast substantial size and influence, they gradually diminish over time. Like a sealed container, a closed system is destined to dwindle and eventually perish if it resists the inflow of new insights. Similarly, individuals occupying management positions within any organization who staunchly oppose novel ideas or refrain from challenging their own beliefs unknowingly embark on a perilous path toward stagnation and decline.

Having an idea alone holds little value if it remains stagnant and there's inaction. The true worth of an idea lies in its execution and implementation. Merely possessing knowledge or concepts without taking action renders them futile and inconsequential. Many individuals often get caught up in seeking the perfect approach, preventing them from taking action. When it comes to transforming or expanding a particular field, what truly matters is taking risks. Occasionally, it is necessary to experiment and see what works. If an idea shows promise, it is crucial to continue pursuing it. Conversely, if it does not yield the desired outcome, it is essential to be open to changing directions. It is important to remember that not everything operates on a win-lose or all-or-nothing basis. Taking risks and exploring new avenues is not dangerous; it is leadership. Embracing this mindset allows for the opportunity to try innovative approaches and foster progress.

Sometimes, motion can create the illusion of progress without the risk of potential failure. It is important to distinguish between mere motion and true momentum. While motion initiates movement, it is the actions we take that truly drive significant change and yield results. Many individuals find themselves trapped in a perpetual state of motion, often driven by a fear of failure. In doing so, they inadvertently fulfill a self-fulfilling prophecy, ensuring their own failure. They become so preoccupied with avoiding failure that their constant movement becomes aimless, lacking any substantial achievements. Their ego often deceives them, whispering false reassurances that they are making progress and moving in the right direction. However, such claims are nothing but empty rhetoric. The truth is that mere busyness or superficial actions do not equate to meaningful progress. Allowing their ego to dictate their perception of success only perpetuates the illusion they have created for themselves. They become akin to a magician, distracting themselves by focusing on one hand while disregarding the other. This pattern arises from a deep-seated fear of failure, leading to a reluctance to take decisive action.

It is important to avoid disguising procrastination as preparation. Do not get caught in the trap of continuously preparing without taking action. Instead, embrace the need to let go and actually do what needs to be done. It is crucial to take the leap, launch your plans, and put them into motion. Rather than getting stuck in a loop of perpetual preparation, be willing to try something new and take calculated risks. Do not be afraid of potential failure or the possibility that things may not work out perfectly. Taking action, even if it does not yield the desired outcome, is far better than not taking any action at all.

Facilitating growth encompasses more than just embracing new ideas and taking action; it necessitates a readiness to challenge long-standing assumptions and conventional wisdom, ultimately driving a transformation in the prevailing culture. Those individuals and organizations that dare to question the status quo and critically evaluate commonly held beliefs are poised to break free from the limitations of mediocrity.

It is essential to emphasize that the pursuit of growth is not a solitary endeavor. Individuals and organizations must recognize the power of collaboration and collective wisdom in propelling them forward. By fostering a collaborative spirit, entities can tap into the diverse talents and expertise of their teams, creating a synergy that transcends the capabilities of any single individual.

The second condition influencing personal or organizational growth is the source of ideas. When our ideas are derived solely from individuals who mirror our lifestyles and perspectives, we inadvertently reinforce existing notions, limiting our capacity to explore new horizons and embrace fresh perspectives. This phenomenon holds true within the context of organizations as well.

An individual can be likened to an organization—a complex entity with its own dynamics, goals, and aspirations. Just as the success or failure of any business or organization hinges on effective management, an individual's success or failure depends on their ability to effectively self-manage. Each one of us is a unit of production, generating tangible outcomes, words, and attitudes that reflect our unique management style. The quality of our "total product"—the sum of our actions, ideas, and contributions—is intricately tied to the quality of our self-management.

To foster personal and organizational growth, it is vital to embrace diversity and actively seek out ideas and perspectives that differ from our own. By engaging with individuals from diverse backgrounds, cultures, and experiences, we expand our mental horizons, challenge our assumptions, and unlock new realms of creativity. This diversity of thought enriches our understanding, enhances problem-solving capabilities, and fuels innovation.

Within an organizational context, creating an inclusive and diverse environment becomes paramount. Organizations that promote diversity and actively seek input from individuals with varied perspectives benefit from a wider range of ideas and insights. This diversity of ideas stimulates creativity, encourages critical thinking, and enhances decision-making processes.

Similarly, on an individual level, seeking out diverse sources of inspiration and engaging in meaningful conversations with people from different walks of life broaden our mental horizons. They expose us to alternative viewpoints, challenge our assumptions, and enable us to develop a more comprehensive understanding of the world.

Creating an environment that fosters growth, both for individuals and organizations, requires a deliberate focus on certain key elements. First, it is crucial to foster individuality and create a space where each member feels valued and encouraged to express their unique perspectives and ideas. Recognizing and celebrating the diverse strengths and talents of individuals within the group cultivates a sense of belonging and empowerment, enabling them to contribute their best to the collective goals.

In this growth-oriented environment, self-criticism is not seen as a negative trait but rather as a constructive tool for personal and collective improvement. Encouraging individuals to engage in self-reflection and critically evaluate their own performance and ideas can lead to valuable insights and the identification of areas for growth.

An atmosphere where uncomfortable questions can be asked is essential for fostering growth. Encouraging open and honest dialogue, even when it challenges the status quo, enables individuals and organizations to identify blind spots, uncover hidden opportunities, and address underlying issues. By embracing discomfort and acknowledging that growth often requires stepping outside of comfort zones, individuals and organizations can foster a culture of curiosity, innovation, and adaptability.

The internal structure of the individual or organization should also promote fluidity and flexibility. By breaking down rigid jurisdictional boundaries and encouraging collaboration across different departments or teams, the flow of information and problem-solving can be enhanced. This fluid structure allows for a free exchange of ideas, enables cross-functional collaboration, and prevents isolated thinking. It also empowers individuals to take initiatives, contribute beyond their designated roles, and adapt to evolving circumstances.

Effective communication is essential, as it ensures the free flow of information and ideas. An individual and organization must also combat the tendency for procedures and rules to stifle innovation. While processes and guidelines are necessary for maintaining order and ensuring efficiency, they can inadvertently create rigid structures that hinder creativity and impede progress. To combat this, individuals and organizations must strike a balance between adhering to necessary protocols and fostering an environment that encourages flexibility, experimentation, and out-of-the-box thinking. By focusing on what they can become rather than dwelling on past accomplishments, they can break free from the constraints of routine and embrace the possibilities of growth and improvement.

Within any organization, managing vested interests is crucial for fostering continuous renewal and promoting growth. Whenever change occurs, it inevitably poses a threat to the privileges, the authority, or the status of certain individuals or groups. Addressing these vested interests requires skillful navigation and strategic decision-making to ensure that resistance or opposition does not impede progress.

Successfully managing vested interests involves creating a shared understanding of the need for change and the potential benefits it can bring. Leaders must effectively communicate the rationale behind the proposed changes, emphasizing how they align with the organization's vision and goals. By demonstrating the positive impact and opportunities that change can bring, individuals with vested interests are more likely to see the value in embracing it rather than resisting it.

Motivation, conviction, and morale are key drivers of an organization's capacity for self-renewal. When individuals within the organization feel that their efforts matter and will be recognized, they are more likely to actively engage in the change process. Leaders must foster a sense of purpose, ensuring that individuals understand how their contributions fit into the larger picture and how they can positively influence the organization's trajectory.

Creating a culture of collective commitment and engagement is essential for successful change implementation. It requires involving stakeholders at various levels, encouraging their participation, and soliciting their input and feedback. Building trust, fostering collaboration, and promoting a sense of ownership among team members are vital in creating a collective commitment to change.

Change cannot be achieved by apathetic individuals or by relying solely on top-down directives. It necessitates a shared responsibility and a genuine belief in the potential for improvement. Leaders must facilitate open dialogue, encourage collaboration, and provide opportunities for individuals to contribute their unique skills and perspectives.

The quality of our ideas is a crucial determinant of our overall management quality. Innovative and impactful ideas can drive growth, differentiation, and success in today's competitive landscape. By nurturing a receptive mindset, we create a fertile ground for the generation of new ideas.

Continuous self-challenge is also vital for personal and organizational growth. By regularly questioning our assumptions, beliefs, and approaches, we can uncover areas for improvement and push ourselves to reach higher levels of performance. This process of self-reflection and self-criticism helps us refine our ideas and strategies, identify gaps or weaknesses, and continuously evolve and adapt to changing circumstances.

By embracing a receptive mindset, fresh perspectives, and continuous self-challenge, we create a culture of learning, innovation, and growth. This culture becomes the foundation for sustained success as it fosters creativity, agility, and the ability to seize new opportunities. It encourages individuals and organizations to stay ahead of the curve, anticipate market shifts, and adapt to evolving customer needs.

The future of any organization and individuals hinges on its ability to continually renew itself, which, in turn, relies on the vitality and dedication of the individuals within it and the leaders who manage it. By embracing a growth mindset, nurturing talent, fostering individuality, encouraging self-criticism, maintaining fluidity, promoting effective communication, combating entrenched procedures, managing vested interests, and cultivating motivation and morale, an individual or an organization can position itself for sustained success and adaptability in an ever-evolving landscape.

The acceptance and adoption of new behaviors by the industry as a whole are greatly influenced by the actions and attitudes of its leaders. When leaders actively model the desired behaviors, it creates a ripple effect throughout the industry. Others observe and take cues from these leaders, realizing that change is not only necessary but also valued and rewarded.

When leaders green-light change, they create an environment where individuals feel empowered and supported to embrace innovation, challenge the status quo, and explore new possibilities. By fostering an inclusive and open-minded culture, leaders encourage diverse perspectives and ideas to flourish. This, in turn, leads to increased creativity, collaboration, and a willingness to experiment with different approaches. Furthermore, leadership's role in changing the industry culture extends beyond individual organizations. Collaborative efforts among industry leaders, associations, and governing bodies can have a profound impact on shaping industry-wide norms and practices.

An organization that can serve as a catalyst for this transformation is the PGA. Established over a century ago, the PGA is a highly respected institution with a rich history. As a leading organization in golf, it plays a critical role in promoting professionalism, developing players, and fostering the overall growth of the sport. The PGA's efforts extend beyond organizing prestigious tournaments; it actively fosters collaboration within the industry. Its primary objective is to promote professionalism by setting and upholding high standards of conduct, ethics, and expertise among golf professionals. This is achieved through certification programs, ongoing education, and professional development opportunities that equip PGA members with the necessary knowledge and skills to excel in their roles as golf instructors, club managers, and tournament administrators.

Recognizing the importance of nurturing talent and providing opportunities, the PGA offers player development programs for individuals of all ages and skill levels. From grassroots initiatives such as the PGA Junior League to specialized training programs for elite players, the PGA creates an environment that supports the growth and success of golfers at every stage of their journey. Additionally, the PGA organizes premier golf tournaments such as the PGA Championship, which not only entertain fans but also serve as platforms for professional golfers to showcase their skills, compete for prestigious titles, and contribute to the sport's legacy. These tournaments inspire and motivate future generations of golfers.

The PGA understands the value of forging alliances and partnerships with fellow golfing organizations to advance the sport. It actively collaborates with esteemed entities such as the United States Golf Association (USGA), PGA Tour, and international golf associations to establish uniformity in rules, regulations, and governance. This collective effort benefits players, fans, and the overall growth of golf on a global scale.

Diversity and inclusivity are pivotal pillars of the PGA. The organization is committed to making golf accessible to individuals from all backgrounds, regardless of gender, age, ethnicity, or physical abilities. It spearheads initiatives such as the Women's PGA Professional Championship and supports under-represented communities, aiming to dismantle barriers, challenge stereotypes, and foster a more inclusive golfing environment.

The objectives embraced by the PGA reflect its unwavering dedication to professionalism, player development, collaboration, diversity, and community engagement. Through its relentless pursuit of these goals, the PGA exerts a profound influence on the golf industry, propelling the sport to new heights and leaving an indelible impact on players, fans, and communities. With an unwavering commitment to excellence and progress, the PGA serves as an inspirational force, guiding the golf industry toward a radiant future.

Another organization that holds immense potential to empower change is LIV Golf. This esteemed organization, which has garnered significant attention from golf enthusiasts worldwide, stands as a testament to the transformative power of visionary leadership. Launched in 2021 under the visionary leadership of Greg Norman and supported by a Saudi investment fund, LIV Golf stands as a distinctive professional golf league that sets itself apart from the traditional landscape shaped by the PGA.

LIV Golf's unique identity arises from its approach to the game. The league showcases shorter events that eliminate cuts, placing a heightened emphasis on team play. This innovative format has garnered widespread acclaim and fascination. A key point of intrigue lies in the substantial bonuses offered to participating golfers, including renowned figures such as Phil Mickelson, as well as payouts that surpass those witnessed in the established PGA Tour.

The name "LIV" itself draws from the Roman numerals representing 54, an integral figure in the world of golf. This number carries immense significance, symbolizing the total number of holes played in LIV Golf events. Moreover, it aligns with the concept of perfection in golf. For instance, accomplishing a score of 54 would signify achieving a birdie on every hole of a par-72 course. This connection to perfection serves as a testament to the lofty aspirations and unwavering standards upheld by LIV Golf.

At its core, LIV Golf is driven by a primary mission: to breathe new life into the professional golfing realm by expanding opportunities for players and captivating fans on a deeper level. The organization strives to introduce innovative approaches that enhance the player experience, fuel fan engagement, and propel the sport toward a progressive future.

However, LIV Golf's aspirations extend beyond the immediate objectives. It embraces a holistic perspective, aiming to bolster the overall health and well-being of professional golf on a global scale. In doing so, LIV Golf seeks to unlock the untapped potential residing within the sport. This comprehensive approach encompasses various facets, including enhancing player experiences, fostering fan engagement, reimagining tournament structures, and driving the overall growth and development of the game. Through their concerted initiatives and unwavering endeavors, LIV Golf endeavors to effect positive transformation, elevating the sport to unprecedented heights.

Both the PGA and LIV Golf share a common objective of propelling the game of golf to new heights. While the PGA focuses on advancing the sport through its established platform and long-standing traditions, LIV Golf aims to modernize and supercharge the game by introducing innovative approaches and expanding opportunities for players and fans. Despite their different approaches, both organizations share a common goal of enhancing the overall experience of professional golf and driving its growth and success. Through their collective efforts, these two entities contribute to the continuous evolution and advancement of the game, bringing it to new levels of excellence and popularity.

While the PGA and LIV Golf may appear to be competing for attention, their collaboration can coexist harmoniously. We must set aside any differences, whether expressed or unexpressed, and prioritize the betterment of the game and the satisfaction of the fans. Our goal should solely revolve around what is best for the game, without being influenced by personal opinions or other considerations. Let us shift our focus entirely toward the shared objective and work collaboratively toward its achievement.

MMC® aligns closely with the shared vision of both the PGA and LIV Golf, which revolves around growing the game through increased participation and heightened awareness. These three entities share similar MVPs, all centered around prioritizing the players, the game itself, golf professionals' careers, and the fans.

According to pga.org:

- The PGA of America's Mission: To serve the member and grow the game.
- The PGA of America's Purpose: To elevate and advance the member, profession, and game.

According to livgolf.com:

- LIV Golf's Mission: To modernize and supercharge the game of professional golf through expanded opportunities for both players and fans alike.
- LIV Golf's Purpose: To holistically improve the health of professional golf on a global scale and unlock the sport's untapped potential.

For MMC®:

- MMC®'s Mission: To grow the game, industry careers, and golf facilities by acquiring players from all four segments of golfers, including core, avid, casual, and non-golfer.
- MMC®'s Vision: To make golf accessible for everyone and promote inclusivity.
- MMC®'s Purpose: To save and grow golf facilities, provide gainful employment and fair compensation, and ensure lifelong job and financial security for operators and golf professionals.

Leadership plays a pivotal role in spearheading the transformation of norms within the golf industry. It carries the weight of crucial missions that demand unwavering dedication to initiating change. From the grassroots to the executive levels, leaders are entrusted with the responsibility of actively seeking and championing progressive shifts. They must not only generate innovative ideas but also act upon them with conviction. By doing so, leaders create an environment that fosters openness and collaboration, bringing together all stakeholders in the golf industry with a shared purpose of nurturing and advancing the beloved game we all cherish. Through united efforts and a collective vision, these leaders can pave the way for a dynamic and promising future, where cultural change is embraced, and the growth and prosperity of golf are safeguarded.

As we turn the page to the next chapter, we embark on a transformative journey focused on the preservation and expansion of the game of golf. This pivotal chapter delves deep into the strategies and initiatives that can save golf from stagnation and propel it toward a future of growth and prosperity. We will unravel innovative approaches, industry-wide collaborations, and groundbreaking ideas that have the potential to breathe new life into the sport. From attracting new players to reinvigorating existing enthusiasts, we will explore the pathways that lead to a thriving and inclusive golf community. Prepare to discover the keys to saving and growing the game of golf, unlocking its limitless potential, and securing its enduring relevance in the modern era.

# 8

## SUSTAINABLE DEVELOPMENT

I want to begin this chapter by expressing my sincere gratitude to all of you who share the same passion for the game of golf and have chosen to embark on this educational journey with me. Your love for the sport is truly remarkable, and I appreciate your willingness to explore different perspectives on the industry.

In the pages that follow, I anticipate encountering strong opposition from individuals within the industry who are content with the status quo and hold a romanticized view of the industry's current state of health. This book, however, has been written specifically for individuals who seek factual information, eschewing filters, fluff, or fantasies. The recent closures of golf courses have inadvertently favored many of these individuals, making it easier for them to expand their businesses with less competition.

It is undeniable that having fewer competitors can simplify the process of growing a business. Some owners may take advantage of this situation by setting arbitrary prices for rounds, season passes, or memberships, adopting a dismissive attitude toward any objections raised. They might assert, "If you don't like it, tough luck! There are no other places for you to play."

It is disheartening to witness the act of cornering a market and charging exorbitant prices for a game that many typical players simply cannot afford. While it is only natural for there to be a range of courses catering to different budgets, it is essential to recognize that hindering the growth of the entire industry for the sake of self-gain is both unethical and detrimental.

As Americans, we embrace a diverse spectrum of golf courses, encompassing both high-end establishments and more affordable options, with everything in between. However, we must not allow personal interests to obstruct the progress and accessibility of the industry as a whole.

In this chapter, my primary objective is to emphasize the significance of promoting an inclusive and sustainable golf industry. By challenging the existing norms and practices, we have the potential to create a path toward exponential growth. Together, let us strive for an industry that experiences collective growth rather than focusing solely on individual gains.

Even though our efforts at MMC® have resulted in the direct recruitment of over a million new golfers through our campaigns with more than 500 golf facilities, and potentially a few million more through our innovative ideas, we still acknowledge that we have not achieved substantial growth in the game itself. Nevertheless, we remain dedicated to doing everything within our power to save jobs and preserve golf courses from closure. Despite our unwavering commitment, the sobering fact is that we are falling significantly short of our aspirations, and we need help. At the current pace, the industry is barely recovering the lost golfers and has done almost nothing to rebuild the facilities that have been forced to shut down. The expansion of the sport itself seems like a distant goal. It appears that many people are simply relying on the hope that the COVID Bump will endure indefinitely. However, hope alone is not a viable growth strategy.

These challenges only reinforce the urgency for collective action and a fresh approach to industry-wide growth. Merely relying on the COVID Bump, isolated efforts, or incremental progress is not sufficient. We must come together as a community, actively challenge the status quo, and explore new avenues for sustainable development.

Throughout this chapter, I will share insights and strategies that have the potential to transform our industry. By adopting a collaborative mindset and embracing innovative practices, we can move closer to our shared vision of a thriving and accessible golf industry.

We must acknowledge the reality that the golf industry is facing significant challenges. The game needs saving from the downward spiral it is currently in. We cannot rely on recycled golfers alone; we must attract new players, expand our demographic reach, promote new course development, boost merchandise sales, create more employment opportunities, attract new sponsors, engage more donors, and entice advertisers. Most importantly, we need to cultivate a larger fan base. By doing so, we can shift the narrative from golf being perceived as a "Rich man's sport" to it being embraced as "Everyone's game."

While the game is not in critical condition, it would be devastating if we chose to ignore the warning signs and vital indicators that the golf industry is presenting. If you believe that your golf facility is immune to the potential downturn, you would be dead wrong. Disregarding the warning signs and assuming invincibility can be detrimental to your business's health. Just as in medicine, a proactive approach to optimum care is crucial, with a strong emphasis on prevention rather than merely treating symptoms. It is imperative for owners and operators to take the initiative and implement preventive measures to ensure the overall health and well-being of their golf facility, the heart of the industry.

This growth initiative aims to achieve prevention by equipping owners and operators with the necessary tools and techniques for sustainable, long-term growth. Simultaneously, it offers therapeutic solutions for immediate intervention and assistance to facilities in need of urgent support. Similar to how people often delay action when it comes to serious health problems until they experience the urgency of riding in the back of an ambulance that rushes them to the hospital, some facility operators wait until the last moment to take action to save the business in their charge. Monitoring these vital signs allows us to assess the industry's internal health and take appropriate actions to ensure its growth and sustainability.

Let us take a closer look at the facts surrounding the development of the game. In 2005, there were approximately 15,000 18-hole golf facilities catering to a population of around 300,000,000 people. Fast-forward to today, and with a population of over 330,000,000, we now have around 10,000 18-hole golf facilities. This means that despite a population increase of more than 10 percent, the number of golf facilities has actually decreased by 33 percent. Clearly, these figures contradict the propagated notion of "growth" being promoted within the industry.

In 2005, we were at least able to keep up with the population's growth in terms of golf facilities. In the worst-case scenario, we should strive to bring the number of 18-hole facilities back to 15,000 as soon as possible. However, this can only happen when the demand for golf returns.

The bottom line is that the golf industry needs to recapture the gains it has lost. Every effort should be made to save every golf course, and we must equip owners, operators, and golf professionals with the necessary knowledge, tools, and resources to attract golfers from all four segments: core, avid, casual, and non-golfers. The goal is to establish long-term relationships between these new players and the facilities, allowing golf professionals ample time to develop and nurture these individuals as active participants in the game.

In 1970, the United States had a population of 203,392,031 people. Fast-forward to 2022, and the population has risen to 332,403,650. During this time, the number of 18-hole golf facilities increased from approximately 7,500 to around 10,000, representing a 25 percent growth. However, when we consider the population growth of 39 percent, it becomes apparent that there is a significant deficit of golf courses to cater to the existing golfers, let alone new players.

These figures reveal a pressing need to address the shortage of golf courses that can serve the growing interest in the game. It is particularly disheartening to see courses accessible to the working classes facing closure at an alarming rate. These are the facilities that require our attention and support. While high-end elite courses may have the financial backing to sustain themselves, it is the entry and mid-level courses that play a vital role in making golf accessible to a broader range of individuals.

To foster the growth of the game, we must prioritize the protection and revival of these entry and mid-level courses. By ensuring their preservation and providing the necessary resources and assistance, we can meet the needs of existing golfers and create opportunities for new players to embrace the game.

Today, there is more spin being put on the health of the golf industry than most professional golfers can put on a ball. The golf industry needs growth—not spin.

There must be a mistake in the stated number of golfers in the United States. The statistics just aren't supported by the evidence. These figures are greatly exaggerated because the current number of 18-hole facilities is insufficient to accommodate that many golfers. If they were, every golf course in the United States would be overflowing with activity; charge exorbitant membership, season pass, and greens fees; and have a mile-long waiting list. For the vast majority of golf facilities, this is undoubtedly not the case. Of course, there are a select few fortunate golf courses in top markets with minimal rivalry that are enjoying the "bump in play," but the majority of entry and mid-level facilities are still having trouble.

Here is an excerpt from an article published by the National Golf Foundation, "The Fight for Municipal Golf": In truth, since the beginning of the correction in golf supply that began in 2006, the number of municipal golf facilities has actually increased, not decreased. Only slightly mind you (about +5 percent) but a gain nonetheless in a market where the balance of facilities—comprised of daily fee courses and private clubs—has declined by 15 percent. The increase in municipal courses has come mainly through the acquisition of daily fee courses, rather than new construction. Seriously, any reduction in public golf supply in California, be it of the daily fee or municipal variety, will only exacerbate the undersupply situation there, making it even harder for existing golfers to find tee times, while at the same time increasing the barrier to entry for new golfers. This is not how we are going to grow golf participation and rounds played. Further, this sets a very dangerous precedent, arming golf oppositionists elsewhere with a legislative example we really don't want them to have. I was overjoyed to read this article, as it was the first piece I came across since the COVID Bump that truly supports what I have been trying to make everyone in the industry aware of. It highlights the lack of sufficient golf courses to cater to the existing golfers, let alone attract new players. True "growth" can only come from bringing in new golfers, and this article effectively presents the industry's realities, even if it focuses specifically on California. It reaffirms MMC®'s data and serves as a validation for naming this growth initiative "Save and Grow the Game."

Allow me to digress for a moment: whether you are the mayor, a member of a community development committee, a park and recreation director, or a manager or operator at a municipal golf course, this concept is ideal for your town. If you are in a position of community leadership, this program allows you to construct or acquire a golf facility for your residents without using any of your existing funds. If you want to build a golf course, we can start a presales program to generate the necessary revenue for the project. If you want to buy an existing facility, MMC® can launch a campaign for you to generate cash for the acquisition as well as the backend/operational revenue needed to sustain the business for long-term growth. It is important to note that MMC®'s most successful campaign to date was for a municipal course in the Midwest, where we raised $1,700,000 in immediate cash and substantially increased the backend/operational revenue.

Furthermore, we have observed some of the most absurd management agreements of municipal courses throughout the years, which must be remedied. We understand that managing a full town, city, or even state is difficult, and adding a golf facility to the mix is seen as simply another expense by most people. This is the most erroneous thought. The best investment someone, a business, municipality, city, or state can make is in land. The open green areas are enjoyed by everybody, and despite what some may say, the amenities are beneficial to both people's general health and the environment.

All that is required is for MMC®'s program to form a partnership with a skilled and driven operator who can effectively manage operations and execute the model's second, third, and fourth phases: customer/player development, player ambassadorship, and player retention. The municipality will own a lucrative parcel of land, a self-sustaining business, the community will enjoy beautiful open green spaces, the course will support plants and wildlife, and the course will represent the community by being affordable, diverse, and all-inclusive. Win-win.

Referring back to the industry, I introduced the term "COVID Bump" to describe a temporary upsurge in activity. It provided a momentary pause in the industry's decline, giving a false impression of growth. Unfortunately, this bump was misleadingly hailed as the turning point for the game's future. However, as I foresaw back in 2020, this bump is gradually diminishing, resembling more of a small nodule. If left unaddressed, it has the potential to become a cancerous cell, permanently hindering the growth of the game. We must take crucial action to prevent such a scenario from unfolding.

These so-called "new" players are actually former golfers who rediscovered the sport due to COVID's social distancing measures. Many individuals picked up golf again as they found themselves with extra time and limited options for outdoor activities. However, as anticipated, their interest is waning once more. Back in 2020, I predicted these returning golfers would gradually lose their enthusiasm and quit the sport once again.

It is important to recognize that the recent increase in sales for manufacturers and retailers in the golf industry is not primarily driven by new golfers. Rather, it stems from former golfers who have reengaged with the sport, and since most of them had either disposed of or outgrew their old equipment, they purchased new golf equipment. This familiarity with the brand prompts them to be more willing to invest in higher-priced products. The success of your business is closely intertwined with the growth of the game, just like any other entity in the industry. Without actively fostering growth, there is a risk of reverting to the pre-COVID era. Advertisement revenue, sponsorships, and donations significantly contribute to initiatives aimed at expanding the game. It is important for everyone to play their part by urging leadership to change their strategies and genuinely focus on growing the game. If they fail to do so, make it clear that you will withdraw your support.

Unfortunately, some people mistakenly pinned the industry's future solely on the presence of these reengaged players. It serves as a reminder that a temporary success can sometimes have unintended negative consequences. Such was the case with the COVID Bump.

The COVID Bump may have blessed your property with more play and some additional revenue, but it did not penetrate untapped markets, and it definitely is not sustainable. In the next paragraphs, I will share with you numerous ways you can capitalize off the COVID Bump and retain a lot of your new golfers.

In 2024, the focus for the golf industry must be on retention, retention, and more retention. It is a rare opportunity for an industry to have a chance to hit the reset button, and the golf industry was fortunate to experience that in 2020. Now, every owner, operator, and leadership of every organization must maximize this windfall by doing everything possible to retain these newfound golfers.

Many of the golfers who played in 2020 had prior experience with the game but did not stick with it. We have witnessed this scenario before at the turn of the century, and we cannot afford to repeat the same mistake twice. Therefore, all stakeholders in the industry need to focus on essential strategies and initiatives that encourage these golfers to stay engaged and committed to the game.

Whether it is enhancing the overall golfing experience, providing personalized coaching and support, or creating a welcoming and inclusive environment, every effort should be made to retain these golfers and prevent them from losing interest or drifting away. By prioritizing retention, the golf industry can capitalize on the opportunity presented in 2020 and ensure long-term growth and sustainability.

Just like any instrument (expensive or inexpensive), a business must get a tune-up from time to time. This tuning process can only be done by the business's staff. These new golfers must be engaged and developed as golfers as well as consumers. They must be conditioned to spend freely in the profit centers and be encouraged to support the course—their new golfing home. In short, when you engage your golfers, you are giving the business a tune-up, and by doing so, the business is bound to perform better. I often use the analogy of tuning my guitars. The better-crafted instruments tend to stay in tune longer but still need tuning from time to time. A business is no different. Once you have acquired the new golfers, you must keep them engaged.

After the first big push, whether it was from the COVID Bump, MMC®'s campaign, or a combination of both, future growth will inevitably be gradual, because the instant growth you experienced in the initial phase is less likely to be repeated, so the operators must implement a sales system and train the staff on the new system. I am not suggesting you turn your staff into used car salespeople; that would be unwise and completely unnecessary. Little things such as incorporating a few sentences and/or questions into your everyday conversations with golfers can drastically increase revenue, and it will feel completely natural to all parties. Your golfers will never notice the change in conversation, and the staff will just think the course has added some greatly needed new customer service. Neither party needs to know this has been done to increase revenue; it will come across as completely natural.

McDonald's is a great example of how just a couple of questions added to everyday customer service can dramatically increase sales. How many times have you gone into a McDonald's and, after placing your order, been asked, "Would you like fries with that?" How many times have you been asked by a McDonald's cashier, "Would you like to upsize that?" All the time, the staff member is making you feel special because they are reminding you to get fries, just in case you may have forgotten to add them to your order. You cannot imagine the positive effect these two simple questions had on McDonald's customer service and bottom line.

Take a moment to consider how these questions can be applied to other aspects of your business, such as food and beverage, car rentals, range, lessons, outings, leagues, bag storage, pull cart rentals, and more. These questions can be adapted and customized to fit any scenario and profit center within your operation. By making small adjustments and improvements to your existing operations manual, you can elevate your business above your competitors, regardless of whether you are considered the best or worst in town.

Let us once again consider McDonald's as an example. When it comes to hamburgers, many would argue that McDonald's does not offer the best burger in town. However, they are the most successful fast-food chain in the world. Why is that? The answer is simple—marketing and sales. McDonald's has mastered the art of marketing their products and driving sales, allowing them to create a massive presence and attract a large customer base.

Similarly, by focusing on effective marketing and sales strategies in your own business, you can achieve significant growth and success. It is about understanding your target audience, creating compelling offers, implementing innovative marketing campaigns, and delivering exceptional customer experiences. These principles can be applied across all profit centers within your business, helping you achieve remarkable results. Once owners and operators become aware of the numerous opportunities to enhance revenue, they will be empowered to take action. However, if they remain unaware that it is acceptable to step outside the boundaries of traditional teachings and conventional wisdom, they may continue to shut their bars and restaurants, mistakenly perceiving them as liabilities.

Business owners and operators must be fully informed, with complete transparency regarding the state of the industry and the available options. When presented with the unvarnished truth, along with the implicit encouragement to explore alternative approaches, owners and operators will seize the opportunity and strive for success. Conversely, if their leaders paint an overly rosy picture, claiming that everything is fantastic and golf courses are witnessing unprecedented surges in new players, struggling owners and operators may silently question what they are doing wrong, unable to understand why they are not experiencing the same level of success.

Unfortunately, a few business executives opted to highlight the increased play at a few golf courses as evidence of industry expansion, while disregarding the fact that thousands of courses had closed. Some people chose to stop being proactive in favor of resting on their laurels due to this false sense of achievement. Everyone in this group assumed that the game would be fine and maybe even better off with fewer facilities. This has turned out not to be the case.

There's an old saying that goes, "Only when a man reaches his destination is he allowed to throw away his maps." However, in the golf industry, we haven't yet reached our destination or achieved our goals. Therefore, it's crucial for us to keep looking at the maps daily to stay on the right track and continue progressing toward success.

Saving and growing the game cannot be done through passivity; it can only be accomplished through focused activity. A casual approach to growing the game will only result in more casualties. Too frequently in life, nothing happens and progress is seldom made until someone from the inner circle offers the essential critical input, putting the situation's true conditions into perspective and bringing them to light for everyone to see. It is only when things go wrong that most people take action. Now it is time to stop talking about growing the game and start taking action.

When you work in the trenches, as MMC® does, you witness the day-to-day hardships suffered by owners and/or operators. Your connection to the industry's reality is maintained by having boots on the ground. On the ground, in the field, the situation appears very different than it does from behind a desk, in an office, reading reports made out by devoted followers running upscale facilities, who are now prospering because the herd has been thinned out.

There are those in the industry who like the fact that there are fewer rivals and long for the days when everything was simpler. Sadly for them, those times are long gone, and if they do not join the effort to save and develop the game, it may very well be their employment and businesses that are the next to go.

Growing the game is easy, but changing the entrenched attitudes toward growing the game is the challenge. Millions of golfers and thousands of businesspeople are committed to maintaining the game's exclusivity and will stop at nothing to block outsiders from joining their exclusive club. This is the only logical conclusion that can be drawn in light of all the resistance and lack of effort by individuals inside the industry. MMC® has repeatedly shown how decreasing entrance barriers and broadening the game's demographic is a far superior business model than the traditional model when it comes to revenue, expansion, and long-term employment and financial security for golf professionals and their staff. Fortunately, many more people want golf to develop and embrace being more diverse and affordable, including golfers and industry leaders. We have noticed that the percentage is roughly 80:20—with 80 percent of players and leaders supporting the game's growth and expansion and only 20 percent actively trying to thwart it. Unfortunately, at the moment, the 20 percent have the greatest power, influence, and wealth.

Growing the game is as simple as putting a golf club in someone's hand. For those of us who golf, we know how accurate this statement is. This may very well be what terrifies the 20 percent. Everyone who has ever felt the rush of correctly swinging a golf club, striking a ball, and then watching it travel through the air slightly in the direction of the intended target becomes a lifelong golf fan. Even if they never pick up another club, they will always be enamored with the game. They will purchase clothing in the category, welcome the chance to gather with family and friends for dinner and drinks at the clubhouse, encourage their kids and/or friends to try the game, will not be as irritated by others watching the game even though it may not be their preferred program to watch on television, consider holding their events at the club, and welcome and support the open green spaces in their community.

Let us take a moment to acknowledge the reality. Golf is a demanding sport and can often be an expensive hobby. The truth is that many newcomers to the game will not continue playing in the long term. After giving it a few tries, they may not find it to be their passion and ultimately move on to other activities. This reality is not unique to golf but applies to various aspects of life. For instance, millions of guitars are sold each day, but many end up gathering dust in corners as people realize the dedication and practice required to master them.

The same can be said for golf clubs. However, even if individuals do not continue playing the game, we can still create lifelong fans by offering them the opportunity to try it. By providing a positive and inclusive experience, we can leave a lasting impression that will keep them engaged and supportive of the sport. While the retention of new golfers is a challenge, we can still cultivate a broader appreciation for the game by ensuring a welcoming and enjoyable introduction to it.

Golf has traditionally been perceived as a sport primarily enjoyed by the upper classes, and this perception has hindered its growth potential. For golf to expand its reach, this needs to change. Let us consider the popularity of sports such as basketball and soccer for a moment. These sports have a massive following and attract millions of fans worldwide. One of the main reasons for their widespread appeal is their accessibility. Almost anyone, regardless of their physical attributes, background, age, or financial status, can participate in these sports. The acceptance and affordability of these sports make them accessible to a diverse range of individuals. You can travel to any country and observe children playing basketball or soccer because these sports have low barriers to entry. Due to their inclusive nature, these sports have naturally developed and retained their popularity over time.

Some traditionalists may think that making the game "all-inclusive" is a really poor concept; however, this concern stems from misinformation. Let me explain; MMC®'s program is specifically designed to target casual and non-golfers, but it would be remiss to ignore the changes in perceptions and attitudes of the biggest generation ever—the Millennial, particularly because they represent the majority of casual and non-golfers today and during the ensuing decades.

Facts about Millennials you should be aware of include:

- Millennials know the power of words. They adore the word "disrupt," which to them is a synonym for change. By analyzing this generation, it becomes very evident that they are determined to alter or disrupt anything that does not conform to their worldview, including their vocabulary.
- Soccer moms and fathers have taught Millennials that everyone should be able to participate, no matter their circumstances or skill level. This is just one of the ways MMC®'s program appeals to Millennials because they think it is innovative and view it as being all-inclusive.
- Millennials have an affinity for instability. To give the employees enough time to develop the bond, it is crucial to lock up Millennials in long-term relationships with their local golf course.
- More than half of Millennials have an entrepreneurial spirit. We should begin interacting with this generation now and start adjusting our business strategy to meet their wants and needs considering that they will eventually lead our businesses.
- Millennials have grown up participating in teams where everyone benefits. This one simple truth makes it clear that this group wants everything to be "all-inclusive" in general.

- This generation will disregard, turn away from, abhor, boycott, and flatly refuse to participate in any enterprise, endeavor, or sport unless it is "all-inclusive."
- The first wave of Millennials, who are now in their early forties, are excellent golf prospects. Tomorrow will be too late if our industry does not alter its strategy now.
- Millennials live in fear of missing out (FOMO). The experience of a lifetime will be too good for Millennials to pass up once the game of golf has been properly introduced.
- Millennials are also recognized for being naturally uncommitted and preferring to be mobile with many options, but if you get to know them, you can coach and engage them. Owners and operators need to accept this reality and prepare for a considerably higher attrition rate than in the past. This is advantageous for the industry as a whole, even though these new players may decide to play the game without committing to a home course. This obstacle can be overcome though by immediately locking up these new golfers in long-term alliances and nurturing them as customers as well as players. Whether they like it or not, owners and/or operators will need to improve their marketing and sales abilities to keep up with the unavoidable attrition rate. MMC®'s second phase of the Save and Grow the Game program, the customer development phase, will become invaluable over the next several decades.
- Millennials value collaboration and want everyone to participate. When you look at a Millennial, you either see their face buried in a device or their fingers and thumbs moving at 90 miles per hour on their cell phone. I know this reality may be challenging for many of us Baby Boomers and Gen Xers to understand. We tend to overlook the fact that these Millennials stay in constant contact with their "friends." Despite the fact that their pals may be seated right next to them, Millennials are continuously conversing with them on their gadgets.

- Millennials call for all-inclusion. Keep in mind that when these young adults were younger, their Baby Boomer parents made them play on teams where the focus was on inclusiveness rather than winning. The "experience," not winning or losing, was what mattered most to the parents and children. This message echoes the one that the golf industry preaches, does it not? Is it not our intention to give the players the best experience possible?
- The good news is that Millennials are all about self-development and progress. If the game is appropriately presented, Millennials will actively contribute to the industry's expansion. Hence, it is the best sport for Millennials, but they are unaware of this because we have not explained to them why they should play; why it is the best game ever; why it is the best sport for the mind, body, and soul; and why, why, why. Because they are inquisitive, Millennials always want to know the why first before being told who, what, where, when, and how.
- They desire teamwork but yet want to be recognized as individuals. When you consider Millennials, it can seem a little counterintuitive since, while they value teamwork, they are also tremendously interested in self-development and self-improvement. They only aim to raise their personal performance; they do not want to compete with the team or their teammates. This is another reason why golf is a perfect fit for Millennials since, after all, most golfers are primarily concerned with improving their own game.
- Millennials desire leadership positions and careers in politics. They will be the corporate and political leaders of the future, and if the golf industry does not reform its mentality and become all-inclusive, it will miss out on a significant potential to expand the game. What's more, numerous politicians will have their eye on dismantling the industry.
- Millennials are overflowing with suggestions on how to alter the status quo, or how to upset it. They aim to improve things

# EGO: EDGING GOLF OUT

and shape the world in accordance with their all-inclusive worldview.
- Millennials love the environment and open green spaces. Everything about golf appeals to Millennials, yet the true nature of the game is not conveyed in the narrative or in the message that is being stated. The game is actually all about connecting with others and forming relationships—all the things that Millennials care about—but this is not being said or shown. As such, it is important to focus on these areas now and in the future. When advertising golf, we should also emphasize how beneficial golf courses are to the environment. Everyone can benefit from the beauty and peace of the golf course, and open green spaces are good for everyone's general health. The future of golf should be all about transformation. Offer Millennials a justification for why they can take pride in playing golf and promoting the golf industry. Let them take pride in the fact that by supporting the local golf course and preserving open green spaces, they are doing their part to protect the environment. They want to get behind the cause; they just need a valid reason why. When we market to Millennials, we need to instill the belief that by supporting our brand, they are changing either the world or themselves.
- Millennials want to know how much you care before they care how much you know. The meaning of this Theodore Roosevelt quotation ought to be incorporated into a slogan for the golf industry. For instance, just as baseball is known as "America's game," the slogan for golf could be "Golf is Everyone's Game!"

As you can see, every single one of these data points complements MMC®'s strategy for expanding the game perfectly. The only way this game will ever grow at an acceptable pace is if this knowledge of Millennials is combined with that of casual and non-golfers. As I said in the opening, "Growing the game is easy." The only question that remains is: Are you among the 20 percent who want to stifle the game's growth, or are you among the 80 percent who want to truly grow the game by making the game more affordable, more diverse, and all-inclusive?

At MMC®, our mission is to develop two websites that will serve as the drivers for this proposed growth initiative, one of which has already been launched in 2023, while the second is scheduled for release as soon as we garner support, partner with sponsor(s), and/or raise the necessary funding. These websites will cater to a wide range of individuals involved in the golf industry, including owners, operators and/or golf professionals, as well as enthusiasts worldwide. These platforms will provide a welcoming community that transcends the boundaries of the United States, welcoming individuals from all corners of the globe.

The first website, affordablegolfmemberships.com, has been successfully built and launched this year. It provides a free platform for all types of golfers, including core, avid, casual, and non-golfers, to discover exceptional membership opportunities offered by partnering golf courses. At MMC®, we firmly believe in prioritizing the needs of our customers, and this website reflects that commitment. It is solely dedicated to granting access to affordable golf memberships throughout the United States.

Our objective has always been to support the growth of businesses, careers, and the game itself. To achieve this, we are personally investing in creating a platform where golfers from across the country can connect with our partner facilities. These players are highly desirable customers as they often visit a specific area for business or vacation, resulting in increased spending and the potential to bring local guests who pay green fees. Additionally, destination golfers, regardless of their golfer type, tend to spend more liberally while traveling compared to their expenditures at their home courses. This arrangement creates a mutually beneficial outcome.

Our dedicated team works tirelessly to address the challenges faced by owners and operators, continually seeking innovative solutions and aligning our programs with their goals.

Our primary responsibility is to discover new golfers for our clients, especially those who play a few times each season but are enthusiastic spenders during their rounds. Our ultimate aim is for our clients' renewal programs to be exclusively offered to players acquired through MMC®. This approach allows us to elevate the number of core and avid players in diamond, platinum, and gold memberships to 50, 150, and 200 respectively, while filling the remaining tee sheet slots with casual and non-golfers as needed, thereby establishing a strong long-term customer base.

To ensure sustained success for golf courses, we constantly generate fresh ideas and enhance our offerings. This motivation led us to launch affordablegolfmemberships.com, enabling us to create a comprehensive database of golfers and players in every market. This resource empowers us to bring these individuals to our clients to eliminate introductory membership offers to core and avid golfers or diamond, platinum, and gold members by the second renewal cycle. Our introductory membership will exclusively cater to players acquired through MMC®.

We are relentless in our pursuit of enhancing the quality of our products and services. Offering affordable memberships is just one of the strategies we employ to contribute to the growth of the game while simultaneously providing exceptional value. It serves as an additional tool in our arsenal as we strive to save and grow the game.

We allocate a substantial amount of resources to initiatives that we believe will greatly benefit our clients' success. The purpose of this website serves a dual function. First, it offers a platform for golfers actively seeking additional playing opportunities. Second, it aims to support our clients in boosting their membership sales by reaching out to individuals from different states who may not have previously been aware of these opportunities. Even if these golfers fall within the core and avid segments, it poses no problem since destination golfers tend to spend generously while traveling. We continuously test new strategies and evaluate their effectiveness in supporting our clients. Thus far, we have successfully sold numerous out-of-state memberships, and we anticipate the popularity of this website to grow as word spreads.

The second website will serve industry professionals by providing them with a comprehensive range of tools, techniques, and resources to expand their businesses, and careers, and contribute to the growth of the game. Our entire system, comprising four fully integrated golfer acquisition campaigns, six mini-profit center campaigns, and two multimedia course curriculums, has been designed to seamlessly adapt to an online module for users.

The upcoming website designed for owners, operators, and/or golf professionals will follow a turnkey approach. By logging into their account on the website, users can customize a no-risk, self-funding, turnkey golfer acquisition campaign, from costs to content. We will offer full access to our preferred vendors and extend our negotiated preferred pricing, which has remained largely unchanged since 1990, spanning over three decades. Users of the website will have the option to utilize our vendors or choose their own. Additionally, all users will have the opportunity to rent mailing lists at wholesale pricing, based on specific criteria, utilizing MMC®'s proprietary consumer profile that effectively targets casual and non-golfers.

The entire process will be turnkey and worry-free. Above all, our primary objective is to gain industry-wide support to ensure that both websites are offered absolutely free of charge to users.

Here is how simple it will be for owners, operators, and/or golf professionals to design, launch, and manage a golfer acquisition campaign:

- Step 1: View the menu for Golfer Acquisition Campaigns and targeted audiences, that is, core, avid, casual, and non-golfer.
- Step 2: Click the Golfer Acquisition Campaign of choice.
  There will be two buttons:
    - Traditional Campaign
    - Customize Campaign

Under the Traditional Campaign option, you will find pre-filled templates for all campaign materials, except for the property-specific information. To get started, simply attach your course's logo and input details such as the name, address, phone number, and website URL. Once completed, you can email the materials to your preferred printer. This option saves you time and effort as the majority (99 percent) of the Facebook ads, newspaper ads, radio scripts, mail pieces, text messages, telemarketing scripts, voicemail scripts, presentation scripts, info call scripts, emails, and more are already complete. Just enter the relevant information, print the materials, train your staff, and launch your campaign.

On the other hand, the Customize Campaign option provides operators with the flexibility to personalize every aspect of the campaign, from the offer to the price point. This section offers various tools, templates, and a range of proven price points and variations. Operators can unleash their creativity while still aligning with market-tested strategies, tailoring the golfer acquisition campaign to their specific needs.

Additionally, there will be two courses available: "Locking up Golf Relationships" and "Low to No Cost Marketing Strategies." These courses were designed to be shared with operators over a four-month period, allowing them to view, study, and implement the information on a daily basis. Each curriculum is dedicated to sixty days of focused learning and application.

Users will have the freedom to download audio files, videos, and written materials according to their preferences. The possibilities are limitless, providing users with a wide array of options.

MMC®'s dedicated team will develop a comprehensive training video script that guides users through the process of designing, launching, and managing the four marketing campaigns. This script aims to eliminate any confusion or potential errors, ensuring a smooth and successful implementation.

In addition to the training materials, MMC® is committed to providing exceptional customer support for a minimum duration of five years. This extended support period ensures that users can rely on the expertise of MMC®'s team, gain confidence in their own campaign implementation, and address any queries or challenges along the way.

With the successful launch of the growth initiative, MMC® is highly optimistic about the prospect of witnessing the launch of at least 100 golfer acquisition campaigns within the very first year. Given that MMC® will typically acquire 1,200 new golfers per campaign, this equates to 120,000 new golfers, at least 100 golf professionals gaining a lifetime of employment and financial stability, 100 golf course owners forgetting about ever closing or selling their golf course to housing developers, and, at the very least, 500 industry workers securing a lifetime of gainful employment.

Once this takes off, these figures will undoubtedly double each subsequent year as word spreads and owners and operators begin to grasp the concept behind the campaign. The bottom line is that business owners want to deliver the finest product and customer experience while earning a respectable ROI. When it comes to consumer involvement, ROI, sustained organic growth, and value to the neighborhood and society at large, this program outperforms all other models.

## Growth Table

|        | Facilities | New Golfers | Golf Professionals | Industry Employees |
|--------|------------|-------------|--------------------|--------------------|
| Year 1 | 100        | 120,000     | 100                | 500                |
| Year 2 | 200        | 240,000     | 200                | 1,000              |
| Year 3 | 400        | 480,000     | 400                | 2,000              |
| Year 4 | 800        | 960,000     | 800                | 4,000              |
| Year 5 | 1,600      | 1,920,000   | 1,600              | 8,000              |
| Year 6 | 3,200      | 3,840,000   | 3,200              | 16,000             |
| Year 7 | 6,400      | 7,680,000   | 6,400              | 32,000             |
| Year 8 | 12,800     | 15,360,000  | 12,800             | 64,000             |
| Year 9 | 25,600     | 30,720,000  | 25,600             | 128,000            |

With MMC®'s growth initiative, the number of golfers in the United States could double in just 9 years, from the estimated 30 million to over 60 million, allowing for the development and/or reopening of about 7,500 golf facilities, including public, private, semiprivate, and municipal courses with 9, 18, 27, and 36 holes.

I want to clarify my stance regarding the expansion of golf facilities in the United States over the next decade. I am not advocating for a repeat of the 1990s, when numerous golf courses were developed in markets that could only sustain a smaller number. It is important to avoid overbuilding golf courses, as there should always be a sense of scarcity surrounding the availability of any product or service to maintain its desirability. This principle aligns with human nature.

Approximately 20 percent of the population has some level of interest in golf, whether it be the game itself, the associated lifestyle, clothing, electronic games, golf-related merchandise, reading material, and so on. All these individuals have the potential to become golfers, whether they are aware of it or not. This means that as long as a golf facility is situated within a twenty to forty-mile radius of 50,000 people, they can operate a highly successful facility with the right tools and attitude. In fact, a market of this size could easily support up to four facilities, each with 2,500 committed players, all of which have the potential to thrive. While this formula is simplistic, it can serve as a starting point for developers, as well as city and state officials who wish to bring a profitable and aesthetically pleasing golf course to their area for the benefit of their constituents.

It is highly encouraged for all individuals who rely on the golf industry for their livelihood or as part of their lifestyle to wholeheartedly support this growth initiative. In particular, the endorsement and support from the PGA of America would greatly accelerate the industry's expansion, considering its extensive presence in around 10,000 golf facilities nationwide. The PGA's abundant resources and network of 29,000 golf professionals and member presence in almost 75 percent of all golf facilities in the United States offer an incredible opportunity to introduce an educational program within the PGA. This program can become a standard and integral part of their curriculum, providing training to all PGA members on effectively working with new golfers, developing their skills, and attracting them to the sport. By gaining the PGA's endorsement and association, these programs will naturally generate interest and participation, creating a domino effect that inspires others to follow suit. This collective effort, starting from the top, working from the bottom, and meeting in the middle with open arms to welcome new players, will result in an elevated experience for golfers and a stronger, more inclusive golf community.

By providing training to all PGA members on how to effectively acquire new golfers from all four segments, educate them on how to engage these new golfers, develop them as customers and then as players, and elevate the skill sets of the golf professional in the areas of personal development, professional sales, and marketing, we can make a significant impact on the industry. Additionally, this added training and enhanced skill sets will elevate the status of the PGA professional in the minds of owners, resulting in more employment opportunities and lucrative management and operation agreements, which in turn will result in lifelong job and financial security.

We are eager to establish a partnership with the PGA. Their esteemed reputation, extensive membership, and rich tradition lend significant weight to any collaboration. Once they grant their official approval, symbolized by their prestigious stamp of sanction, the impact will be extraordinary and far-reaching. It is important to acknowledge that the program itself will be effective regardless of the PGA's involvement. However, with the PGA's esteemed stamp of approval, its potential for rapid acceleration becomes evident. The PGA has the power to initiate a significant turnaround in the industry simply by endorsing the program. Nevertheless, the collective support of all stakeholders is crucial for its tremendous success. Our aim is to rally everyone who genuinely desires to foster the growth of the game, going beyond mere rhetoric, and unite them behind this program and initiative.

# EGO: EDGING GOLF OUT

The only thing that can stand in the way of this enormous growth and expansion of the game is a lack of desire. I firmly believe that if we can conceive it, and we believe it, we can achieve it. This strategy offers benefits to all parties involved. Maximizing the earning potential through the sale of unused tee times to casual and non-golfers at existing facilities will reignite interest in course ownership. This, in turn, will help revive some of the lost properties and spur new developments driven by increased demand. People from diverse demographics will be encouraged to engage with the game and feel embraced and accepted. As this customer-centric approach becomes widespread, its positive impact will extend across the entire country. In the near future, in any city or town across the United States, the average person will be aware that they too can afford to indulge in a round of golf. There will be more than enough potential market share for all owners to sustain tremendous growth. Under MMC®'s model, businesses, careers, and the game will grow exponentially.

By launching the golfer acquisition campaign, the concerns and worries of owners, managers, and golf professionals will soon fade away, replaced by an abundance of golfers and a steady flow of revenue. The campaign will bring about a transformative shift, creating a thriving environment where the worries of the past are forgotten, and success becomes the new norm. With an influx of golfers and a flourishing financial situation, the future will be as sweet and satisfying as a fine wine.

However, these new golfers will only stay around if they are engaged. This is only a process that can be achieved by the course's staff. MMC®'s staff cannot run the day-to-day operations and implement all of the things necessary to keep the business on its upward trajectory. MMC® will do 99 percent of the work during the initial golfer acquisition campaign as well as during the EFT, Elite, and Ambassador Campaigns, but when it comes to everyday operations, the operators must take the helm and steer the ship in the right direction. MMC® will provide all of the training and materials, but the operator must implement and enforce them for the business to be successful and sustain growth.

Yes, the user can always design and launch another marketing campaign, but the first campaign *always* yields more customers than the succeeding campaigns. The correct approach is to follow the entire strategy and not just rest on your laurels once the first campaign comes to an end. Growing a business is not a one-and-done proposition. Growing a business is like farming; there is a season for planting, a season for maintenance, and a season for harvesting. Operators must be forward-thinking at all times.

The great thing is that we have done everything for the user. We truly have made it as simple as one, two, and three. Follow our program to grow the game and develop players to the letter. Do not try to reinvent the wheel and do not skip steps. We will lay out financial success on a platinum platter for the users, and all they have to do is click, copy, and paste.

There are two types of growth: organic and artificial. The COVID Bump was entirely artificial and, therefore, unsustainable. MMC®'s growth initiative is 100 percent organic, ensuring sustainability for the long term. After the acquisition of the golfers, you must be prepared to engage, lock up, and cultivate long-term relationships with these new players no matter how they were acquired. Lightning rarely strikes twice in the same spot. As powerful as MMC®'s campaigns are, they will rarely if ever produce the same number of golfers their second, third, and fourth time. You must go as deep as you can into the first campaign and immediately incorporate the consumer development strategies to keep the new golfers engaged. All additional campaigns launched after the first campaign must be viewed as support campaigns to compensate for the churn rate.

In many cases, the second campaign will produce as much or even more revenue, but rarely, if ever, will it produce more players. This is why I tell everyone I speak to, to partner today with MMC® because you always want to be the first one at the table in your market.

The MMC® golfer acquisition and retention system is a comprehensive solution designed to support the growth of the game, golf businesses, and golf careers. MMC® provides golf professionals with the tools and resources they need to expand their opportunities, secure gainful employment, negotiate lucrative contracts, and have lifelong job security in the industry they love. The by-products of focusing on the golf professional are that the game grows far beyond anyone's imagination, golf courses do not close, industry jobs and opportunities increase, and consumers get developed into players and super fans.

MMC®'s goal is to provide a website where anyone in the golf industry can access our designs and launch effective marketing campaigns to grow their business. Our dedicated staff will offer full-service customer support for five years, assisting golf courses with their marketing and sales training needs. It has been proven that any discipline can be mastered within five years. This service aims to support the growth of all 15,000 golf facilities and individuals interested in building new golf facilities and will have a sister site (www.affordablegolfmemberships.com) welcoming anyone looking for a golfing home to find a participating facility that is within their market.

Developers of golf facilities will find our platform to be a valuable industry support system, providing resources and tools to help them establish and expand their businesses. Every aspect of our campaigns will be fully customizable and tailored to the specific needs, wants, and culture of each facility. Rest assured that our service will not devalue or disrupt the natural flow or culture of any facility.

On average, our campaigns are expected to acquire 1,200 new golfers. Course operators have the flexibility to adjust their rates based on amenities, competitive pricing, and quantitative and qualitative data specific to their area. For example, a prime-time golf round may generate between $48 and $98 in revenue, while non-prime-time rounds could yield between $28 and $75 per golfer.

Realistically, considering the number of facilities and potential price adjustments, even if our results were reduced by half, we could still attract approximately 500–600 golfers per facility. With a nationwide release of this program within nine years, we could potentially double the number of active golfers, significantly expanding the market for golf participation and purchasing. We, in the industry, have a favorable advantage in terms of numbers. The majority of golf facilities operate at less than 40 percent capacity. This indicates that despite the industry's shortage of facilities, there is ample inventory available to accommodate a doubling of players, particularly from the casual and non-golfer segments. Once existing courses reach their capacity, developers can also explore reentry into the industry.

When we double the number of golfers, we will also double the opportunities for compensation. This is a direct application of the law of cause and effect. The results you achieve are directly proportional to the effort and resources you invest.

MMC® and its 500 partnering golf courses have only tapped into a fraction of the game's growth potential. With over a million golfers currently participating across these 500 courses, the scope for expansion is immense. By scaling this model to ten times the number of courses, we are looking at a staggering 10 million new golfers entering the industry. Even if certain courses opt to significantly raise prices, leading to a reduced acquisition rate of 500 golfers per facility, we can still expect the game to grow by 10 million individuals. This increase in players is a highly realistic projection.

However, the growth potential becomes even more explosive when we consider the endorsement and support of the PGA. If the PGA not only blesses this program but also integrates it into its operations, the impact will be tremendous.

The PGA along with LIV Golf could be enormously valuable partners in this growth initiative due to their alignment with our shared goals of growing and diversifying the game of golf and making it more inclusive. Overall, MMC®'s alignment with the PGA and LIV Golf stems from a shared vision of advancing the sport of golf, enhancing player opportunities, and delivering exceptional experiences to fans and enthusiasts. Through our collective efforts, we can propel the

# EGO: EDGING GOLF OUT

game to new heights and ensure its continued success in the ever-evolving landscape of sports and entertainment.

With a large and engaged audience, both entities can thrive and be more productive than ever before. Furthermore, it is important to note that LIV Golf and the PGA have distinct focuses within the golf industry. While the PGA has various facets and influences across the industry, LIV Golf is perceived to primarily focus on its tour. However, LIV Golf makes its mission very clear by expressing its intent: "To modernize and supercharge the game of professional golf through expanded opportunities for both players and fans alike." In my personal interpretation, the term "players" encompasses a wide range of individuals engaged in golf, including, but not limited to, touring professionals, golf professionals, as well as the various categories of players mentioned in this book: core, avid, casual, and non-golfers. In essence, all these individuals are considered "players" within the golf industry. Involving LIV Golf in programs aimed at supporting golf professionals and fans will provide additional opportunities for growth and engagement.

LIV Golf has the opportunity to make a significant investment by allocating a minuscule portion of its current budget for this growth initiative. LIV Golf can positively impact the lives of tens of thousands of golf professionals for a fraction of what it pays to contract one touring professional, while benefiting over 15,000 businesses and creating tens of thousands of jobs. This strategic move has the potential to generate a substantial increase in fans and goodwill, surpassing the impact that could be achieved through ten seasons of traditional tours. With a single decision, LIV Golf can make a profound and lasting difference in the golf industry.

Both the PGA and LIV Golf organize professional golf tours that heavily rely on attracting a dedicated fan base. The success of these tours is contingent on securing sponsorships, donations, and advertisers. Understanding the impact of growing the game on their financial bottom line is crucial. By collaborating with us, LIV Golf can reap numerous benefits. Not only will they align with their own mission of enhancing the professional golf experience through modernization and expanded opportunities for players and fans alike, but they will also attract a larger fan base. This increased fan base will subsequently attract more advertisers, sponsors, and donors.

The PGA Tour reaps numerous advantages, with an additional bonus for the PGA's association arm. This particular benefit will have an immediate and significant impact on over 15,000 or more of their members, comprising both currently employed professionals in golf facilities and those who have struggled to secure gainful employment within their beloved industry.

Similarly, apparel companies will witness a surge in clothing sales, while equipment manufacturers will experience higher demand for their products. Golf car companies, in particular, will be significant beneficiaries, as they provide owners with the means to update and maintain their fleets.

Increasing the number of golfers will have a positive ripple effect throughout the industry. It will not only double the viewership but also lead to increased sales for merchandisers, manufacturers, and retailers. The growth of the industry will create ample opportunities for everyone involved to achieve their financial goals and exceed previous benchmarks.

Empowering golf fans with more opportunities to play the sport is a significant way to support golf professionals and foster the overall growth of the game. MMC®'s team is committed to doing the work on the ground level to ensure the growth comes to fruition. After twenty years of on-the-ground experience, it is crystal clear that the only way to grow the game is to begin at the ground level starting with assisting golf professionals, operators, and owners in acquiring new players and teaching them how to get their communities enthusiastic about golf. This approach reflects the proverbial adage of teaching a man to fish instead of giving him a fish, ensuring long-term expertise in growing the business and the game itself.

In five years, with concerted efforts and the right support, professionals in the golf industry can become experts in driving business growth and expanding the game. The by-product of this endeavor would be their careers skyrocketing to new levels of success.

Together with the support of the PGA, LIV Golf, manufacturers, retailers, sponsors, donors, and golf enthusiasts can effectively save and grow the game by starting from the foundation and working our way up. It begins with equipping those responsible for acquiring golfers with the necessary skills to attract and engage new customers. It is crucial to teach them how to create a welcoming environment and nurture relationships, ultimately turning players into valued customers, members, or season pass holders.

Industry leadership must essentially support and endorse our approach. They need to communicate that adopting these strategies is optional but encouraged, presenting them as valuable tools in everyone's arsenal. With nationwide implementation, we can provide customizable solutions that would empower businesses to thrive. By effectively presenting, identifying, engaging, and nurturing relationships, we can attract individuals within various demographics and maximize utilization during non-prime-time slots.

The key to thriving in these difficult times is to embrace growth by reaching new consumer segments. Sticking to outdated business practices is no longer sustainable, and innovation is the key to staying relevant. Just as there are multiple generations to cater to, there are also different types of golfers: core, avid, casual, and non-golfers. Unfortunately, the industry "experts" think of golfers only as a single group—golfers. It is this oversight that has made it difficult for most courses to bounce back.

The call to "Save and Grow the Game" is more important than ever. By recognizing the challenges we face, embracing innovation, and fostering inclusivity, we can pave the way for a thriving and accessible golf industry. Let us break free from traditional barriers, engage with new generations, and cultivate a sense of community and excitement around the sport. Together, we can ensure that golf evolves, adapts, and continues to captivate players of all ages and backgrounds. The future of the game lies in our hands, and with concerted efforts, we can secure a bright and sustainable future for golf. This is a call to action, a rallying cry for all who share our passion, to unite and unleash a tidal wave of change that will reverberate throughout the industry and make golf "Everyone's Game!"

Show your support today!

www.saveandgrowthegame.com

# 9

## HEALTHY EGOS AND NEW OPPORTUNITIES

As we reach the final chapter, I would like to express my gratitude for your support and engagement throughout this book. I hope that by now, I have successfully conveyed the value and potential of the golf industry, inspiring you to consider getting involved. In this concluding section, I aim to make the proposition even more compelling by presenting a practical pathway toward owning your very own golf course. Brace yourself for a profound exploration of the possibilities that lie ahead, as we delve into the intricacies of acquiring a golf course with limited financial resources. Through meticulous planning, unwavering determination, and a belief in your own abilities—in other words, a healthy ego—you will uncover the secrets to securing this coveted investment without substantial upfront capital. This book will serve as your trusted guide, unveiling the path to entrepreneurial triumph and proving that with the right mindset, anything is attainable. So, immerse yourself in these transformative pages and let the journey toward owning your own golf course commence.

The current landscape presents an ideal time to consider purchasing your very own golf course. The golf industry offers unprecedented opportunities to acquire golf courses at significantly reduced prices compared to the past. Despite the numerous closures witnessed over the last two decades, there are still numerous properties available for acquisition and a vast number of dormant properties awaiting revitalization.

I spend the better part of my day engaging in conversations with both owners and operators in the business. Operators express their frustration with owners who are reluctant to invest in new equipment, additional staff, and other items on their wish lists. On the other hand, owners feel frustrated with operators who consistently seek additional expenditures without effectively increasing revenue. Operators tend to remain in their positions because they fear unemployment more than the daily frustrations, while owners hesitate to impose stricter performance demands out of concern for losing their operators and impacting their financial well-being. This creates a challenging dilemma where both parties reluctantly accept the unacceptable to make it through each day.

The primary goal of buying or building a business is to generate a profit. Every business, regardless of its nature, sells something—be it a product, service, emotion, idea, or opportunity. However, for a business to survive, let alone thrive, it must successfully sell its offering to the public. Niche products and services present additional difficulties as there is a smaller pool of potential customers. Thus, if an owner has an operator who lacks enthusiasm for selling and marketing and is resistant to seeking external assistance due to their ego, coupled with selling a niche product or service to a niche market, the likelihood of success is significantly diminished.

Enormous opportunities await in the golf industry, and one area where these opportunities arise is when owners express their desire to sell their business due to the burden of self-funding. However, if the right person with a healthy ego approaches these owners, there is potential to negotiate a lucrative management contract or, even better, a lease-to-own agreement. It is crucial to emphasize the right kind of individual with the right characteristics to find and put this kind of deal together: someone who exudes ability, confidence, and leadership, rather than arrogance, cockiness, or dictatorial tendencies. Above all, this person should be focused on the goal of growing the business.

In my conversations, I have been frequently asked to open a division exclusively for property management. However, as property management is outside my realm of expertise, it would be a disservice to owners if I were to accept that responsibility. Fortunately, there are highly qualified individuals and companies already operating in this space, with room for more to enter and make a positive impact.

Recently, an owner reached out to me, seeking assistance. As part of our standard protocol, we conduct a needs analysis that involves a series of questions to better understand the owner's motivations and identify areas where they may have fallen short of revenue goals. In this particular case, the owner and her husband wanted to sell their 9-hole facility but had received minimal interest thus far. They hoped that we could make the numbers more attractive to potential buyers. Naturally, this was a straightforward situation since our campaigns focus on increasing cash flow, backend receivables, and traffic, all of which greatly enhance the financial statement and make the facility more appealing to prospective buyers.

The response to the second question provided a striking revelation. The owner highlighted the usual suspects for insufficient growth: inadequate marketing efforts, a disengaged team, a manager with a negative attitude, limited market size, challenges in reaching potential customers, and the perception that women slow down play, leading to a predominantly male membership. Notably, the owner herself is a woman. This revelation raised two significant red flags.

First, it became clear that the "old grump" manager needed either an attitude adjustment or a replacement. Second, expanding the course's demographic by actively engaging women and diversifying the membership should have been a priority. These insights were quite apparent and offered a clear path for immediate improvement.

However, the owner seemed hesitant to address the issue with the old grump as he had been with the course for decades, and the few existing members had grown accustomed to his demeanor. Additionally, the owner and her husband were no longer able to manage the course due to health issues. Although the course thrived when they were actively involved, the current situation reflected a common occurrence in many properties. Owners who can no longer manage their business must rely on inadequate management until they can sell the property. Their primary concern is relieving themselves of the burden; even if they wish for the property to remain a golf course, they will sacrifice the business and hope they can make up the lost revenue on the property.

Operators like the old grump seem unaware of the detrimental impact they have on people's lives. These individuals, who struggle with embracing progressive ideas, fail to recognize that their actions not only harm their own business prospects but also jeopardize the livelihoods of their employees. It's disheartening to think about the potential opportunities this facility had missed in terms of game growth, diversifying play, and engaging the entire community. Most importantly, it was a missed opportunity for the old grump himself to finally contribute meaningfully and be of service in his life.

I came across a profound insight stating that the essence of life lies in the act of serving others. It suggests that each of us has been bestowed upon this Earth to extend our support to fellow beings. Embracing this perspective can dramatically transform our lives, blessing us with an abundance that transcends material wealth alone. It encompasses love, opportunities, joy, health, strong familial connections, and all the other wondrous elements that make our journey through life miraculous.

This unfortunate scenario was the result of human error and had little to do with the viability of the business, the property, or the market. An ambitious prospective owner could engage in negotiations with this couple and potentially secure an incredibly favorable acquisition contract. The couple was in distress and seeking relief, as they were more afraid of parting ways with the old grump than they were of him running the business into the ground. They had essentially given up on the business and shifted their focus to selling the land.

The golf industry requires proactive individuals, "Go Getters," rather than being stuck in the mindset of "Old Grumps." For those with a healthy ego, the right education, a strong determination to succeed, and the ability to think innovatively, immense opportunities are awaiting them in the greatest industry in the world. The example discussed earlier is just one instance among hundreds that I am personally aware of. It is staggering to consider how many others may be silently enduring similar situations, perhaps burdened by unwarranted embarrassment or shame.

As I am writing this, the golf industry is witnessing a remarkable resurgence, building upon the hope instilled during the 2020 season. It was a year that brought renewed optimism as golf courses experienced a significant upturn in revenue, surpassing pre-COVID figures. Many establishments were blessed with a remarkable surge, reporting up to a remarkable 20 percent increase in the rounds played compared to previous years. However, not all properties benefited equally from this surge, and even those that did saw setbacks in ancillary revenue streams such as food and beverage and car rentals. Furthermore, many missed the opportunity to establish long-term relationships with the newfound influx of golfers. While 2020 injected vitality into the industry, there are still numerous properties available for purchase or lease with little to no money down, provided the right entrepreneur comes forward. As the saying goes, "A man with money meets a man with experience, the man with experience walks away with the money, while the man with money walks away with experience."

Uncertain economic climates often present the best opportunities for starting a new business. History has shown that more millionaires are made during downturns than in prosperous times. Successful individuals are forward thinkers who recognize that the recent global pandemic and its economic repercussions have left an indelible mark on the United States and the world. The massive debt and incessant printing of money without sufficient backing are worrisome signs of a potential disaster. Fortunately, for astute entrepreneurs, an abundance of opportunities will arise.

Starting your own business requires three essential characteristics: a willingness to work hard, a drive for self-education, and unwavering dedication. In an unpredictable economic climate, one must be prepared and equipped with these qualities.

The most practical, cost-effective, and straightforward approach to owning a golf course is by purchasing an existing one. The course's condition, bankruptcy status, or even its closure do not matter in most cases. Properties such as these can often be acquired for a fraction of their market value. Mentioning the purchase of real estate for a significantly reduced price may elicit incredulous reactions from most individuals. However, such transactions occur every minute of the day. Many owners, even those who have recently gone out of business, desire their property to remain a golf course. This situation is particularly prevalent with properties that were built for housing developments and municipal courses. Banks are also excellent sources for acquiring repossessed properties at a low cost. Typically, banks have a requirement of a 2:1 ratio of collateral to the loan amount. In the event of a foreclosure, banks aim to recover their investment from the collateral and often offer the asset at a significant discount to expedite its removal from their books. It's important to remember that banks prioritize their involvement in the financial sector rather than the real estate business. This arrangement presents a win-win situation for both the bank and the investor, allowing for favorable opportunities to be seized. It would be impossible to list down in this chapter all the ways and scenarios in which golf courses can be obtained for negligible amounts or even no money. Rest assured, the methods available are as diverse as the means of acquiring any other asset.

To illustrate this concept, let me share an example from my personal experience. Prior to the pandemic, during the peak of the housing market and economic boom, my wife and I purchased a home. The property's market value was $600,000, but I made an offer of $450,000. Although the initial offer was promptly rejected, the owner eventually responded with a counteroffer. After a thorough investigation and due diligence, I stood firm at $450,000. Everyone, including my wife, children, and real estate agent, thought I was being unrealistic and unreasonable, believing that the owner would never accept such a low offer. The home was located in a desirable gated community, and properties in that area typically sold for their full market value within a short period.

I was able to successfully purchase a property at a significant discount by employing a strategic approach. I did my homework, and I discovered that the house I was interested in had been on the market for a longer period compared to other homes in the community. It had also been listed and delisted on the Multiple Listing Service (MLS) multiple times. However, I conducted a thorough inspection of the property and found no issues with it. I deduced that the previous buyers must have faced financing problems rather than problems with the actual home. Armed with this knowledge, I decided to make a move.

To demonstrate my seriousness as a buyer, I provided a letter from my bank, confirming my preapproved financing. I also included a significant earnest payment and guaranteed a closing within thirty days. Despite some negotiations and pushback, I stood firm and held my ground. Eventually, the seller accepted my offer. It was a surprising outcome that left everyone astonished. While others doubted the possibility, my unwavering confidence and lack of hesitation in making the offer set me apart from the rest of the group. Not only did I secure a home in the location my family wanted, but I also managed to save a significant amount of money. My negotiations resulted in a remarkable $150,000 (25 percent) reduction from the original purchase price.

The seller, on the other hand, found satisfaction in the deal as well. Having downsized and relocated to the beach, the seller had grown weary of dealing with the property and simply wanted to move on. My assessment of the situation turned out to be accurate, as the seller had encountered multiple failed attempts from previous buyers due to various financial issues. In the end, the outcome was mutually beneficial, leading to a win-win situation. I secured my family's dream home while saving a substantial amount of money, and the seller achieved their goal of parting ways with the property. Both parties involved were content and satisfied with the transaction.

My approach to buying properties involved making low-ball offers and conducting thorough research on each property. I emphasized the importance of having knowledge and confidence when negotiating deals, even in challenging market conditions. If a property has been on the market for an extended period, surrounded by other properties in a slow-moving market, and economic factors such as hyperinflation, recession, or depression come into play, it becomes even more feasible for someone with knowledge and determination to craft a win-win proposal and purchase the property at a fraction of its value, potentially with low or no money down. My example suggests that with the right preparation and determination, it is possible to acquire properties at substantial savings.

When it comes to buying a golf course, my advice is to consider the real estate value as the most valuable aspect. I recommend evaluating the market appraisal, analyzing the true cost of building a golf course, and assessing the guaranteed income from the property. It is crucial to gather accurate financial information and not solely rely on profit and loss statements, as they can be misleading. I also emphasize the importance of understanding the local market and demographics when selecting a golf course.

Negotiating the purchase of a golf course should be approached as a business decision, not a personal or emotional one. I suggest being respectful and considerate of the seller's feelings, especially if it is a family business. Understanding the seller's goals and motivations can help in structuring a mutually beneficial deal. Leveraging pain and pleasure as negotiation tools can also be effective, as most decisions are driven by these factors. Sellers motivated to sell quickly, such as those experiencing financial difficulties, can be more flexible in their terms. By leveraging these factors and understanding the seller's motivations, buyers can negotiate advantageous deals.

It is crucial to understand that utilizing this information does not involve taking advantage of the seller. On the contrary, by being aware of the true situation, you may be offering a way out for someone trapped in a financial burden that is draining them. By assuming the debt and providing a solution, you have the potential to safeguard their financial future. In this scenario, it becomes a win-win situation for both parties involved.

Ultimately, I believe that with proper research, preparation, and negotiation skills, anyone can successfully purchase a golf course or any other business. It requires commitment, flexibility, and the ability to blend family life with business responsibilities. By following these principles, individuals can achieve their goals and create a thriving business in the golf industry.

Buying a business can be easier than growing one, and the skills you have acquired for business growth can be applied to purchasing your own golf course. Begin by conducting thorough research and identifying geographical areas where you and your family would be happy living. Prepare in advance so that when an opportunity arises, you are fully prepared to seize it. Review chapter 2 to refresh your knowledge and follow the same steps during your due diligence process. Since the initial steps remain the same, there is no need to rehash them in this chapter. I will provide you with new information to further assist you.

Before embarking on this venture, it is crucial to be realistic about the responsibilities of being a business owner. If you are reading this book, chances are you are not a trust fund beneficiary or a wealthy individual seeking tax shelter. Instead, you likely possess determination and resilience, even if you lack significant financial resources. Without deep pockets, you must be prepared to invest everything else you have. Sacrifices will need to be made, and during the initial five years of owning your business, holidays, weekends, and evenings off may not be realistic luxuries. Entrepreneurs bear the weight of their family's future and success, which necessitates finding a balance between work and quality family time. This could entail involving your family in the business, spending time at the golf course together, dining at the club restaurant, or combining work tasks with family activities. It is essential to address these considerations before diving in and ensure that your entire family is committed to the journey ahead.

While some may argue that incorporating family life into a business is impossible, the reality is quite different for many families starting their own ventures. It is indeed possible to strike a balance between business and family, allowing children to grow up healthy, emotionally stable, and exceptionally happy due to the abundance of quality time spent with their parents. Furthermore, these children have the opportunity to learn valuable life lessons that will benefit them throughout their entire lives.

For a golf professional, buying a golf course presents a unique advantage. With your background, education, experience, passion for the game, and interest in the industry, you already possess a solid foundation. Unlike starting a business from scratch or requiring further education, the golf course industry is already established, eliminating the need to reinvent the wheel or go back to school. The key is to find a golf course where you are confident, without a doubt, that you can immediately grow the business. During your research, identify areas where the business is lacking or falling short, and if you are fully confident in your ability to enhance those areas, you have found a promising prospect.

When purchasing your own golf course, remember that the real estate itself holds the most significant value, while the business component is often the least valuable. If possible, determine whether the business itself is a viable investment. You may consider approaching the deal as a straightforward real estate purchase. However, in many cases, the business and real estate are bundled together, leaving you no choice but to acquire both as a package deal.

As you embark on your journey to buy a golf course, it is crucial to explore various deal structures that align with your goals. One viable option is to attempt purchasing the business first while securing an option on the real estate. However, if there is any possibility of acquiring both the business and the real estate together, that should be your preferred route. After all, real estate holds the true investment value in this context.

When seeking potential golf course owners to collaborate with, it is essential to find someone who exhibits flexibility. Look for owners who demonstrate flexibility in their thinking, terms and conditions, and overall approach. Pay attention to advertisements containing phrases such as "rush sale," "owner financing," or "motivated seller"— these indications suggest that the owner is open to negotiation.

It is often possible to encounter owners who have become disillusioned with their real estate agents' inability to attract qualified buyers, leading them to list the property independently. Collaborating with such owners can be advantageous since there are no middlemen involved, granting you direct access to the decision-maker. Additionally, many owners aim to circumvent the substantial commissions paid to real estate agents, making them more receptive to direct negotiations.

During the crucial stage of due diligence, it is imperative to consider the following key points:

- Ensure there are no liens on the property when making the purchase.
- Thoroughly study all zoning laws relevant to the property to ascertain its future possibilities.
- Gain a comprehensive understanding of the total debt associated with both the property and the business.
- Determine whether the debt will transfer to the new ownership.
- Evaluate existing commitments to members and assess if they will continue under the new ownership.
- Calculate the actual hard costs of running the property, avoiding exaggerated or underestimated estimates.

- Assess the expenses required to repair equipment, grounds, and the clubhouse accurately.
- Scrutinize all relevant numbers—leave no stone unturned in understanding the financial aspects involved.

These numbers are vital pieces of information that you must possess before proceeding to the next step of the purchase. They provide the foundation for making informed decisions and ensuring you have a clear understanding of the financial implications associated with owning a golf course.

When venturing into the realm of buying a golf course, it is essential to be aware of common challenges such as underestimating construction costs and the time required for completion. The unpredictable nature of construction means that until walls are opened, hidden issues and necessary repairs will remain unknown. Prepare yourself for the possibility of your contractor informing you that the costs will exceed your initial expectations. Remember, the money you spend on construction is your own, whether paid today or in the future. Dedicate time to thorough research and due diligence to avoid costly surprises.

Furthermore, it is crucial to exercise caution when evaluating membership-based businesses. Many such businesses have been sold to unsuspecting buyers, lured by inflated membership numbers. These inflated figures are often supported by member logs, creating a misleading perception of the business's performance. However, upon assuming ownership, buyers discover that these numbers were vastly exaggerated, including inactive members who stopped paying dues, canceled contracts, and even deceased members who are still listed as active. To avoid falling into this trap, take the initiative to call every member on the roster and conduct spot-checks on other membership lists before entering negotiations. Armed with accurate information, you gain a significant advantage and can potentially save hundreds of thousands of dollars. Remember, the person with the most information tends to win the negotiation.

When considering multiple properties across different states, it is vital to understand that purchasing a golf course means investing in and committing to a community for the long term. Choose a stable area that exhibits growth potential, maximizing the opportunities for success. Avoid the mistake of purchasing a high-end golf facility in a low-income housing neighborhood with the expectation of changing the demographic through marketing efforts. Golfers who can afford memberships and green fees at prestigious courses are unlikely to traverse to a low-income area to play. The demographic of an area typically cannot be improved solely by offering an exceptional course and amenities. Your success will heavily depend on the local market, so it is crucial to align your course with the demographic and economic realities of the area. Placing a high-priced golf course in an area that can only support significantly lower fees will inevitably lead to challenges.

It is not uncommon to witness scenarios where beautiful golf courses are created amid low-income housing or inappropriate locations. Subsequently, these courses struggle to attract golfers willing to pay top dollar for rounds. Remember, location plays a pivotal role, and the age-old adage of "location, location, location" rings true. Take heed of this important factor when selecting a golf course to purchase.

In the world of golf course acquisitions, it is crucial to address the issue of owner expectations. In many cases, the golf course itself and its demographic are not the problem. Rather, it is the unrealistic expectations of the owner that hinder success. Numbers are fundamental, and if they align favorably, any golf course, regardless of location or demographic, can thrive. In fact, it can be argued that middle to lower-end golf courses have a higher chance of success compared to their higher-end counterparts.

During your analysis, there are three key factors to consider:

- **Market Appraisal:** Determine the market value of the property. Explore other golf courses in the same category offering similar amenities and assess their selling prices in the area.

Comprehensive research is essential to gain a holistic understanding of the market dynamics.
- **Construction Cost:** Calculate the actual cost of building a golf course in today's market. Accurate knowledge of the true expenses involved is crucial for making informed decisions.
- **Guaranteed Income (ROI):** Evaluate the projected income you will receive from the property. However, it is important not to solely rely on the provided profit and loss statement (P&L). P&Ls are often prone to exaggeration and misrepresentation. Utilize the techniques mentioned earlier to assess the value of the golf property, which will allow you to determine whether the purchase is financially viable.

When approaching negotiations, aim to purchase the business at a discount of at least 10–20 percent below the asking price. As a skilled negotiator, it is wise to begin with an initial offer that is 70–75 percent the asking price. Keep in mind that while the seller has their desired asking price, they are likely aware that it is negotiable and may not expect to receive the full amount. Frequently, during negotiations, you will find a middle ground between the asking price and your initial 70–75 percent offer, ultimately resulting in savings of approximately 10–20 percent of the purchase price.

It is important not to shy away from negotiating. The only individuals who avoid negotiations are those who lack financial means and fear being perceived as inexperienced investors. Their ego tells them not to negotiate for fear of the seller realizing their limited financial resources. However, it is crucial to understand that most significant deals involve minimal cash changing hands at the time of sale. This is due to various factors, such as individuals lacking immediate access to substantial funds. While they may appear financially stable on paper, it is often an illusion. Moreover, astute businesspeople with financial resources prefer spreading out payments over time for tax purposes. Nevertheless, some sellers desire to sell the entire asset to take advantage of the capital gains tax rate, which is typically lower than earned income taxes. The key takeaway is that there are numerous valid reasons to engage in negotiations, and it is essential not to let your ego hinder you from doing so.

Maintain a professional and objective approach during negotiations, focusing on the business aspect of the transaction. Show respect and kindness throughout the process, being mindful of the seller's emotions, especially if the property holds sentimental value as a family business. Understand their underlying goals and aspirations before initiating negotiations. This knowledge allows you to tailor your offers and approach accordingly, fostering a more effective negotiation process.

I firmly believe that achieving one's desires in life is possible by understanding how to fulfill the desires of others first. This principle applies to various scenarios, including acquiring golf course properties. For instance, many property owners are primarily concerned with ensuring that the property remains a golf course. In such cases, a favorable deal can be structured where no up-front cash is required, provided a certain percentage of revenue is committed to capital improvements.

I have encountered situations where individuals purchased properties out of bankruptcy but lacked the knowledge or energy to effectively operate the golf course. In these instances, the board often faces significant financial challenges, leading to substantial losses for the members. Their primary goal is to halt the financial bleeding. When confronted with a monthly deficit, the board becomes highly motivated to strike any deal that can immediately address the issue.

Leverage is an invaluable tool to bring to any negotiation. In essence, a lever is a mechanism used to advance or move something or someone. The most influential leverage tools in business are pain and pleasure, as I have always emphasized. To gain a more comprehensive understanding, it is recommended to revisit the material on this subject. However, for the purpose of this chapter, I will provide a brief overview.

The pain and pleasure principle underlies almost all decisions we make. The car we drive, the clothes we wear, the house we live in, and the life we lead are all products of decisions driven by either the pleasure we gain or the pain we avoid. Regardless of budget limitations, there are alternatives available to accommodate various preferences. Clothing styles, housing options, and car choices offer diverse selections within different price ranges. Lifestyle choices are also abundant. Ultimately, the decisions we make are motivated by the pursuit of pleasure or the avoidance of pain.

Understanding the motivations behind individuals' decisions and utilizing leverage effectively can greatly enhance your negotiation strategies. By aligning your proposal with the desires and needs of the other party, you increase the likelihood of reaching a mutually beneficial agreement.

The clothes we wear serve as a form of communication, signaling our belonging to a particular group or tribe. They convey acceptance, fitting in, and various other positive attributes that make us feel good. Similarly, the car we drive can evoke feelings of pleasure or security, providing a sense of dependability and alleviating the fear of breaking down in unfavorable circumstances. Our homes contribute to a relaxed and secure environment. Our lifestyle is shaped by decisions that bring us pleasure or help us avoid pain.

Every person involved in selling a golf property is driven by these motivating factors. Whether they represent a bank or a bankruptcy court, act as a trustee, serve on a board, or are a grieving family letting go of a cherished family farm, understanding what moves the seller is crucial on the path to acquiring a golf course with minimal up-front investment.

Attempting to purchase a golf course without prior experience in its operation is ill-advised. Success in this endeavor requires a comprehensive knowledge of the product. The most accomplished individuals in the industry possess an intimate understanding of every aspect of the business, both inside and out. Ideally, you would have spent a few years working for someone else in the industry, learning the trade on someone else's dime. This experience allows you to familiarize yourself with every department and the roles of each team member.

You don't need to perform every job better than your staff, but rather, you need to have a general understanding of the positions and their responsibilities. This knowledge is vital when it comes to staffing your own golf course. You should hire individuals who excel in areas where you are lacking and possess the necessary skill sets. Familiarity with all positions within the business offers numerous benefits. In the event of an employee's absence or resignation, you must be capable of stepping in and managing the responsibilities until a replacement is found. Furthermore, if you are operating with a limited budget, you may need to undertake the initial training yourself.

Having a comprehensive understanding of all aspects of the golf course business empowers you to make informed decisions, troubleshoot issues effectively, and ensure the smooth operation of the course. It positions you as a knowledgeable leader and enhances your ability to adapt to various circumstances that may arise.

When considering purchasing a golf course, it is crucial to prioritize education and learning from other people's mistakes (OPM) rather than making avoidable errors as a novice owner. Buying a golf course without sufficient knowledge indicates a surplus of financial resources but a deficit in education. As I aptly state, "You will pay one way or the other." Mistakes can either be paid for while gaining experience working for someone else or with your own money as a new owner. I strongly advise spending a minimum of five years or at the very minimum have someone on your team who has at least five years operational experience before taking on the ownership of a golf course. Building a successful track record in running or operating a golf course will provide a significant advantage when owning and operating your own property.

Before making any offers on a property, it is essential to run your own credit report. The three major credit reporting companies are Equifax, Experian, and TransUnion. Lenders usually merge the credit reports from these companies to determine your average credit score, which is used to assess your creditworthiness. It is advisable to have a high credit score when buying a golf course through conventional means, especially if there is an existing mortgage on the property or if you plan to take out a loan. Therefore, it is crucial to be aware of your credit score. Obtaining a free copy of your credit report can be done by simply requesting one from each of the three credit bureaus. Most negative items on a credit report can be addressed with a well-crafted letter, particularly if the blemish has been on the report for an extended period. It is wise to start working on improving your credit now, as the process of resolving any derogatory information may take several months.

Maintaining a strong credit profile not only enhances your chances of securing financing for a golf course purchase but also demonstrates your responsibility and reliability as a business owner. A positive credit history is an asset that can open doors to favorable lending terms and opportunities for future business endeavors.

If there are negative or derogatory items on your credit report, it is important to address them proactively. When requesting your credit report, consider asking the credit bureau to attach an explanation letter to provide a comprehensive view of your credit history. This allows the person or company pulling your report to understand the context behind any negative information. While the bank or lender will consider the credit report as part of their decision-making process, it is not the sole determining factor. Having a few blemishes on your credit report should not cause panic. Focus on strengthening other areas to outweigh any weaknesses and present a strong overall profile.

Commercial loans for purchasing a golf course are generally more challenging and come with higher interest rates compared to personal loans. It is essential to evaluate both options and determine which loan type is a better fit for your specific needs before committing to a loan agreement.

Even if your credit score is less than ideal, there are alternative ways to acquire a golf course without relying solely on conventional financing. One option is a lease option to buy with owner financing, which allows for a gradual transition to ownership while securing financing from the current owner. Another approach is to bring in partners who can provide the necessary financing. In this case, your equity in the purchase can be based on your contribution of "sweat equity," which refers to the work you put into finding and structuring the deal. If you choose this route, it is advisable to obtain letters of intent from potential partners before initiating purchase negotiations. Having preapproved financing from partners gives you more leverage during the negotiation process.

Exploring alternative financing options requires creativity and resourcefulness. It is recommended to consult with professionals in the field, such as financial advisors or business consultants, to determine the most suitable approach based on your circumstances and goals. These experts can provide valuable insights and guidance to help you navigate the financing process successfully.

When entering negotiations to purchase a golf course, it is crucial to come prepared with all the necessary paperwork and documentation. This includes your credit report, business plan, balance sheet, and marketing strategy. Having these materials readily available demonstrates your seriousness as a buyer and your preparedness to take on the challenges of golf course ownership.

It is important to reiterate that banks often shift the majority of risks on to the buyer when it comes to financing. They typically require collateral, such as the property itself, and aim for a 2:1 ratio of equity to borrowed funds. Banks prefer to see immediate equity in the property or a combination of equity and cash investment. This risk reversal approach makes conventional loans less attractive to many entrepreneurs, particularly those who are just starting out.

During the negotiation process, it is essential to uncover and list every problem or issue the golf course has, regardless of its size or significance. From minor issues such as golf cart dings to major concerns such as the irrigation system, documenting all problems will strengthen your negotiation position. The more information you have, the better equipped you will be to demonstrate why the asking price is too high.

A comprehensive marketing strategy and business plan are crucial components to have in place before negotiating a deal. Banks, partners, and sellers will want to see how you intend to grow the business and increase revenue. If you choose to partner with MMC® (a company with extensive experience in golf course marketing), we can provide you with a detailed financial proforma and marketing plan that showcases your ability to attract new golfers, including casual and non-golfers, without any up-front costs. This campaign, backed by MMC®'s track record, can carry significant weight in your negotiations.

While a hybrid version of MMC®'s campaigns have been proposed to be available online as part of the growth initiative, we anticipate that there will be numerous owners and/or operators who will still prefer the MMC®'s conventional approach to launching the campaign(s)—a comprehensive service where MMC® does 99% of the work, conducts a market analysis, an in-depth competitive overview, and custom designs the campaign to ensure it is tailored to the specific needs of the property. There will always be a group of owners and/or operators, such as those who have been working with us for many years, who will value the convenience and expertise provided by MMC®. Those partner facilities will undoubtedly want to rely on our team to spearhead, manage, and provide continued support throughout each phase of the campaign to safeguard its success, while also maintaining the exclusive rights to our premier services within their market. MMC® will continue to prioritize and protect the needs of our current and future clients just as we have done since 1991.

Alternatively, if you decide not to partner with MMC®, it is important to have your own marketing strategy and business plan readily available. These documents should outline your approach to attracting new golfers and increasing overall revenue. Being well-prepared in this regard will further strengthen your position as a serious buyer and demonstrate your commitment to the success of the golf course.

Remember, whether partnering with MMC® or developing your own marketing strategy, having a clear plan in place will greatly enhance your negotiating power and increase the likelihood of securing a favorable deal.

As an aspiring golf course owner, it is essential to adopt a critical mindset during the purchasing process. Playing the role of the devil's advocate allows you to identify the reasons behind a golf course's lack of success or profitability. Conduct a thorough investigation to unearth any underlying issues. These could range from poor management, a disliked owner, a damaged brand reputation, inadequate course upkeep, or subpar customer service. The key is to dig deep and uncover the root cause of the problem.

Once you have identified the challenges, evaluate whether you possess the skills and resources needed to address and rectify them. It is important to be honest with yourself about your capabilities and determine if you are equipped to turn the situation around. If you feel confident in your ability to overcome the identified issues, you can proceed to the next steps of the purchasing process.

My message is one of optimism and encouragement, emphasizing that buying your own golf course with little to no money down is indeed possible. I want to highlight the importance of believing in yourself, leveraging your skills and determination, and acquiring the necessary education to navigate the process successfully.

While the information shared in this chapter provides a foundation for the buying process, it is important to note that it is just one part of the overall journey. Buying a golf course involves various considerations such as financial arrangements, negotiation skills, market analysis, sales and marketing, and operational expertise.

My statement about acquiring assets with little to no money down applies to various types of investments, including businesses, homes, and cars. However, it is important to recognize that specific strategies and approaches may vary depending on the asset and the individual circumstances.

Ultimately, achieving your dream of owning a golf course requires dedication, thorough research, and a well-rounded understanding of the industry. It is recommended to seek professional advice and guidance, conduct thorough due diligence, and carefully evaluate the financial implications before making any significant investment.

If for any reason you find that owning a business is not feasible for you, leasing the business and/or management contracts could be a viable option. In the golf industry, there are countless opportunities for growth and success. For instance, in the past two decades, more than 5,000 18-hole golf facilities have closed, presenting a wealth of openings for ambitious individuals. By contributing our part, we can collectively foster the growth of the sport, and perhaps owning a golf course could be your unique way of doing so.

We have successfully executed campaigns to assist owners in selling their golf properties, making the business more appealing. If we are informed about a property's sale, we can support the transition by helping the new owners cultivate new players as customers and ensure their loyalty as members.

A few years ago, I had a conversation with a manager of a 9-hole facility. He expressed great enthusiasm for our golfer acquisition campaign. However, when his owner vetoed the project, he approached me with an unusual question. He asked if I believed we could achieve similar results at another 9-hole facility located nearby. Perplexed, I responded, "If it's within the same market, I am confident we can." Curious, I inquired further. He explained that there was a property for sale near his current facility, and he had been eager to purchase it but struggled to secure financing. Nevertheless, he believed he could acquire the necessary funds if he could guarantee repayment within a year. When he disclosed the amount he required, I assured him that raising the funds would not be a problem. We initiated the campaign, and as a result, he transitioned from a managerial role to becoming an owner practically overnight, without any financial burden.

Municipalities have a significant opportunity to acquire golf courses that have unfortunately closed down in their areas. Their representatives should proactively approach banks and developers to negotiate favorable acquisitions on these properties immediately. By swiftly taking action and submitting bids, they can expedite the process of revitalizing these courses and getting them operational once again. Ultimately, I believe that states, cities, and towns should all be heavily involved in providing the product required to expand the game, particularly from the bottom up. Every politician who asserts that they support diversity, equality, and inclusivity in all aspects of life, can lead by dedicating resources to fulfill their commitment to serve the entire community. Creating opportunities and providing a hand up the ladder of success seems to be the narrative but as I said, people, just like the industry need far more than mere words. If only these public officials would just take into account the enormous benefits that a community receives by having a golf course in their area including opportunities for business and employment (not just for those who work at the facility, but all of those employees who serve the golf industry as a whole).

From a revenue growth standpoint, the cost of all real estate—commercial and residential—is rising, which in turn boosts tax revenue. Most golf properties draw from a twenty to thirty mile radius around the course encompassing a diverse population. Nature lovers and environmentalists can rejoice in the preservation of large open green spaces within the community. Enthusiasts of the game gain an additional golfing option, and since the courses are publicly owned, they become accessible to people of all demographics. This inclusivity ensures that everyone can enjoy the facilities and participate in the sport. Moreover, municipal ownership of golf courses brings significant advantages beyond recreational opportunities. Local taxpayers can take pride in their investment, knowing that it not only serves their community but also generates profits. Owning at least one golf course becomes essential for every city and town, which serves the community at large.

The resources for entry-level golf courses should be provided by cities, municipalities, and states; nevertheless, this does not exclude the possibility of a lucrative market for private sector investment. As I previously mentioned, there should be several different golf facility levels with diverse price points and about four membership tiers. One thing owners, operators, and industry leaders may want to plan for is how to compete with non-profit entities in the future as more community leaders realize the enormous asset a golf course can be. Having to compete with the local YMCA was one of the main grievances I heard from owners and general managers in the health club industry. Upon the approval of a YMCA in an area, immediately, their non-profit organization acquired or built a massive facility and added ten times the amenities dwarfing the size of most health clubs and their services in the area. The YMCA was able to offer highly competitive pricing and make large investments in the business since it was a non-profit, which ultimately resulted in numerous mom-and-pop closures. Personally, I think every municipality should have a golf facility as well, provided they offer several programs that support diversity and inclusivity by making certain non-prime times affordable. The private sector can always outperform government-run institutions and/or non-profit organizations because they are not saddled with all of the bureaucracy, hence, they are able to make quick decisions which is often the differentiating factor as to the success or failure of most businesses. So, instead of worrying, be prepared. As my favorite proverb puts it, "Luck is when preparedness meets opportunity."

*Warning: Government officials and/or non-profit board members, however, will set the standard for the industry in each market in which they are well-represented if they do move forward on a project in the community. Remember, our most successful campaign was launched for a municipal course, and we generated 1.7 million dollars in immediate cash in just a few weeks, their backend revenue also increased by millions more.

No one in the industry denies that the impact of the COVID pandemic slowed down the industry's decline. Many attribute any increases in sales or rounds at their facilities or products solely to the COVID Bump. Everyone acknowledges that even modest gains are considered better than the pre-COVID period. In essence, without the pandemic, the state of the golf industry would be far worse today than it was just four years ago. However, we have the opportunity to correct our mistakes and change the industry's trajectory within a year if we can manage our egos; develop new skill sets; and shift our attitudes, perceptions, and beliefs. By presenting the game as affordable as it truly is, we can foster greater diversity and showcase golf as an all-inclusive sport.

The reality is that very few owners would ever consider closing or selling their cherished golf course if it were consistently profitable. Similarly, the same sentiment holds true even if the business at least covered its expenses. The issues at hand do not lie with the game itself, the alleged overbuilding of the industry, or the size of the markets. In some cases, the problems stem from overinflated egos, selfishness, outdated perspectives, and fear of embracing change. These factors can hinder progress and prevent the necessary adaptations required for sustained success in the golf industry.

Beyond the issue of closures, many golf facilities are facing another challenge with their operating capacities ranging from 20 to 50 percent. On most weekdays, particularly Mondays through Thursdays, as well as during a significant portion of Fridays, Saturdays, Sundays, and the facility's off-season, the golf courses often appear deserted, resembling ghost towns. To address this, our focus should be on aiding these facilities in growing their business by attracting more players during these nonpeak times. The key lies in filling the tee sheet with "new" golfers who are more flexible with their schedules. Instead of persistently offering these tee times to core and avid golfers who have consistently declined them, we need to target casual and non-golfers who are more willing to play during these off-peak hours.

Owners and operators have a straightforward solution at hand if they are willing to break away from conventional thinking. By recognizing the untapped potential in off-peak tee times that are currently not selling, they have the opportunity to double their income—boosting both cash on hand and operational revenue. The key lies in reimagining and repackaging this product, presenting it to a new audience in a way that resonates with their specific needs.

A simple shift in attitudes, perceptions, and beliefs can trigger an explosive growth in the game of golf, without the necessity of adding even one new facility to the existing 15,000 establishments. The reopening of closed facilities and the development of new courses in emerging markets would be an added bonus, providing more options and accessibility for all players.

Implementing this simple hack has the incredible potential to double the number of golf enthusiasts without the need to open a single new facility. Alongside this surge in interest, it will lead to increased revenue for the owners, providing a pathway for enhanced compensation for operators. Furthermore, it will create opportunities for new hires and generate additional revenue for vendors, advertisers, and other stakeholders involved in the golf industry.

Until this transformative step is taken, all parties involved, including owners, operators, vendors, advertisers, sponsors, donors, manufacturers, retailers, and more, will continue to operate their businesses at only a fraction of their true potential—mirroring that of most golf facilities, somewhere between 20 and 50 percent of what is achievable.

The groundwork for change always begins at the grassroots level, and this initiative is no exception. The sooner we equip owners and operators with the necessary tools, techniques, and resources to grow their businesses, the faster the game can expand. While I am urging you to learn new skills and adjust your strategies for the betterment of the game, it is important to note that your efforts will not go unrewarded. Owners can expect a potential doubling of their revenue, and operators or golf professionals will bring added value to their business, resulting in increased compensation. Sponsors, donors, and advertisers will enjoy heightened brand awareness, while touring professionals and their affiliations will cultivate a larger and more devoted fan base, elevating their value in the industry. Manufacturers and retailers will experience an upsurge in product sales, and the leaders of the industry will be remembered as part of the most remarkable team to ever hold positions in their esteemed organizations. Most importantly, the players will experience significant improvements in the quality of the game and the services provided. This enhanced experience will benefit all players, particularly casual players who may only participate a few times a year. However, it is the core and avid golfers who will truly reap the greatest advantages. They will enjoy a superior product, enhanced services, increased opportunities, and greater access to play at various facilities. The expansion of the game will provide them with more playing options and a wider range of opportunities. It is worth noting that these new players will primarily be playing during nonpeak times, ensuring that the core and avid golfers can maximize their playing slots without any inconvenience. By taking their leadership roles seriously and driving the industry toward unprecedented profitability, they will leave a lasting legacy, surpassing even the inspiring achievements of the 1990s.

However, we are aware of the industry's culture, and unless there is a green light from the top, the herd will never step out of line. Leadership must play its role by endorsing and supporting this growth initiative. Municipalities, manufacturers, retailers, touring professionals, sponsors, donors, advertisers, and even golfers themselves must rally behind this initiative, setting aside their individual needs momentarily and focusing on the greater good of the game. We possess the knowledge, resources, and manpower needed. All that remains is the desire and determination to make a positive change.

When individuals in the golf industry possess a positive and healthy ego, it creates a fertile ground for promoting change and driving progress. A positive ego encourages individuals in the golf industry to think creatively and explore innovative solutions. When professionals believe in their abilities and have confidence in their ideas, they are more likely to push the boundaries of traditional practices and seek out new approaches. This can lead to advancements in coaching techniques, player development strategies, equipment design, and overall industry practices.

The golf industry is continually evolving, and a healthy ego enables individuals to adapt and embrace new trends. Professionals with a positive ego are open to learning, willing to acquire new skills, and are proactive in staying updated with the latest developments in the sport. This adaptability allows them to respond effectively to changing demographics, player preferences, and market demands, keeping the golf industry relevant and appealing. It also fosters a collaborative mindset among individuals in the golf industry. Rather than viewing others as competitors, professionals with a healthy ego recognize the value of working together to achieve common goals. They willingly share their knowledge, insights, and experiences with others, creating a culture of continuous learning and improvement.

Individuals with a positive and healthy ego are more likely to become advocates for positive change within the golf industry. They have the confidence to voice their opinions, challenge outdated practices, and advocate for policies and initiatives that promote fairness, inclusivity, and sustainability. Their influence can extend beyond their immediate sphere of influence, impacting industry organizations, governing bodies, and decision-makers, thus shaping the broader landscape of the golf industry.

In conclusion, a positive and healthy ego among individuals in the golf industry is a powerful catalyst for change and progress. It fuels innovation, promotes collaboration, enhances player experiences, and amplifies the industry's voice. By embracing a constructive ego, golf professionals, administrators, coaches, and enthusiasts can contribute to a dynamic and thriving golf industry that continues to evolve, adapt, and inspire. Ultimately, a positive ego contributes to the overall satisfaction and growth of golfers, encouraging them to continue their involvement in the sport.

Let us unite in our mission to transform golf into a game that transcends boundaries and belongs to everyone. With unwavering determination, let us champion its accessibility, ignite its popularity, and pave the way for a brighter future. Together, we have the power to break down barriers, inspire new generations, and create a legacy that will resonate for years to come. As we embark on this journey, let us leave no stone unturned, no challenge unconquered. The time is now. Let us write a new chapter for golf, one that celebrates inclusivity, passion, and limitless possibilities.

As you reach the conclusion of this book, I want to be up front and acknowledge that it has served as a persuasive sales presentation. Throughout its contents, I have aimed to convince you of the importance of managing your ego, fostering career development and personal growth, acquiring new skill sets, advancing business endeavors, nurturing leadership qualities, and driving the growth of the golf industry. Above all, I have strived to persuade you to do everything within your power to help revive and expand the game of golf.

Over the past three decades, the golf industry has experienced significant impacts from two extraordinary events—the Tiger Woods phenomenon and the devastating pandemic. Unfortunately, even with the help of these two extraordinary events, the industry has yet to capitalize on the windfall. To ensure the industry's stability and prosperity, what it truly needs is a well-defined set of goals accompanied by a clear roadmap. By prioritizing consistent organic growth, we can steer the industry toward a more resilient and predictable future. While external factors may continue to influence us, a strong focus on our outlined objectives will provide the stability and direction needed to thrive.

Having a well-defined destination is paramount, even more so than possessing a detailed map of how to get there. A clear and concrete goal acts as a guiding compass, providing direction and purpose to our actions.

Regrettably, many executives tend to lose sight of their ultimate objective amid excessive planning and strategizing. They become entangled in the minutiae, attempting to camouflage the lack of a clear vision. It's akin to setting sail with a map in hand but no distinct port to reach.

To achieve success, we must emphasize the significance of setting a strong and meaningful goal before delving into intricate planning. With a defined destination, the strategies and actions can align purposefully, propelling us toward success without getting lost in the sea of uncertainty.

At MMC®, our ambitious goal is to double the number of golfers and golf facilities within the next nine years. This growth initiative serves as our well-defined roadmap, guiding us toward that goal while achieving measurable and sustainable gains in the industry along the way.

I am acutely aware of the very real and justifiable fears that some in the industry may have when considering rolling out such a progressive initiative. Understandably, caution is required to be exercised in moving forward slowly. However, it is essential to highlight that this initiative has been meticulously designed over the past thirty years and has seen over 1,000 tremendously successful acquisition campaigns. The trial-and-error phase is behind us; the initiative has been amply proven to work.

The need for baby steps to test the waters has already been surpassed, and the overwhelming success of the previous endeavors speaks for itself. Now, what lies ahead is the critical phase of implementation on a mass scale, tailor-made to suit the specific needs of each owner and operator. With a strong commitment from owners and operators to follow through with the second, third, and fourth phases of this initiative, the industry as a whole is poised for unimagined success, growth, and prosperity.

With a clear-cut destination in mind, we are determined to propel the golfing sector to new heights while staying focused on our purpose and direction. Through strategic planning and purposeful actions, we are committed to making this vision a reality without losing ourselves in unnecessary minutiae or uncertainties. Together, we will drive toward success, creating a thriving golfing community and expanding the reach of this beloved sport.

It is crucial for all stakeholders, including the PGA, LIV Golf, manufacturers, retailers, owners, operators, golf professionals, superintendents, and even golfers and non-golfers, to contribute in whatever way they can, regardless of the magnitude of their involvement. Together, we can embark on an initiative that breathes new life into the golf industry, moving beyond the temporary boost provided by the COVID Bump. With the pandemic now behind us, golf must rely on sustainable and organic growth that emanates from within, rather than relying on artificial stimulation.

To clarify, I want to emphasize that I am not a pessimist or a doomsayer in any way. In fact, I firmly believe that we have the potential to save and expand the game of golf beyond our wildest imaginations by drawing lessons from the past and capitalizing on the surge of golfers that the COVID Bump brought us. While some facilities may currently appear successful, it's more likely that their prosperity stems largely from the closure of 33 percent or more of other facilities in their area rather than from the COVID Bump. However, I agree that there has been an increase in new players taking up the game over the past few years, which can be attributed to the COVID Bump. Nevertheless, this number pales in comparison to the number of players who have left the game.

The purpose of this book is to alert everyone to how dangerously close we, as an industry, came to collapsing due to our failure to respond to the warning signs that the golf industry displayed at the turn of the century. Repeating the mistakes of the past could cause irreparable damage to the industry. COVID-19 gave us a Mulligan, an opportunity to rectify our approach. My goal is to rally the industry around a growth initiative that not only encompasses four fully integrated player acquisition campaigns but also includes personal development, customer/player development, player retention, and player ambassador programs. By implementing this comprehensive strategy, we aim to establish sustainable and organic growth that will endure for decades to come. This growth initiative is a global endeavor aimed at catalyzing the growth of the game of golf, advancing careers, and propelling the entire industry to new heights across the globe.

Our collective efforts can propel the industry forward, filling existing tee sheets and reestablishing closed facilities. By doubling the number of golfers, we can double the revenue across the board. This growth will yield numerous benefits, including increased fan bases for tours, greater enrollment in golf schools, a larger customer base for manufacturers and retailers, heightened interest from advertisers, increased support from donors and sponsors, flourishing careers, and ample resources to enhance the golfing experience. With a fresh approach to marketing and a shift in attitudes, perceptions, and beliefs, we can make golf more affordable, diverse, and inclusive. Our ultimate goal is to transform golf into "Everyone's Game!"

If you genuinely want to make a difference in preserving and expanding the game of golf, I encourage you to visit www.saveandgrowthegame.com and demonstrate your support. Regardless of the scale or nature of your contribution, whether it is personal or on behalf of your company, your actions will carry more weight than mere words. All contributions will be kept anonymous unless contributors request otherwise. By taking this step, you will exhibit genuine leadership qualities and dedication to advance the game of golf. Let us stand resolute, unwavering in our commitment to preserving this cherished sport. Together, we can save and grow the game by making it Everyone's Game!

Don't delay.<br>
Show your support today!

Save and grow the game dot com operates on a crowdfunding model to drive the expansion of the game we all love—golf! We understand the power of collective action, and that's why we've opted to employ this unique model to harness the support of golf enthusiasts and industry professionals such as the PGA, LIV Golf, touring pros, manufacturers, retailers, players of all levels, and anyone passionate about making a positive impact. We firmly believe in the potential of this growth strategy, and we invite you to become a part of this exciting journey.

The growth initiative I propose presents an exciting opportunity for every business including those that may think there is a conflict of interest such as third-party tee time vendors. Executives representing companies such as GolfNow and ForeUp should be enthusiastic about this chance as it allows them to offer their customers a product with long-term benefits. By becoming partners, sponsors, and donors for this initiative, they can benefit greatly; even when the acquisition campaign surpasses all benchmarks in attracting new golfers, there will always be a significant portion of tee sheet openings available for green fee play.

The collaboration with these vendors complements and enhances the existing industry offerings, rather than competing with them. Moreover, many of MMC®'s partnering clients already utilize a third-party tee time vendor, proving the potential for successful partnerships in this venture. It's a win-win situation for all involved, and this initiative is set to make a positive impact on the golf industry. We possess the knowledge, resources, and manpower needed. All that remains is the desire and determination to make a positive change.

MMC® welcomes partners, supporters, and funding from individuals, companies, and associations who genuinely care about the industry's growth and are willing to back their words with their wallets, whether they are currently active in the golf industry or not. By supporting us through this crowdfunding effort, you will be helping not only the game itself but also the professionals and workers in the golf industry. Let's come together and support this innovative initiative to shape the future of golf and make it more vibrant, diverse, and accessible than ever before.

We are committed to revolutionizing and expanding the game of golf from its core to reach new heights. Our focus will be on several key initiatives:

1. **Rejuvenating Closed Facilities:** We aim to breathe new life into dormant golf facilities, transforming them into thriving destinations that cater to all types of golfers.
2. **Developing New Golf Facilities:** By identifying markets with untapped potential and limited golfing options, we will advocate for building new golf facilities strategically placed to attract new players.
3. **Inclusivity, Diversity, and Accessibility:** We will strongly advocate for city and state officials to lead the way in the development of golf courses that cater to people from all walks of life, regardless of their socioeconomic background. We encourage both public and private sectors to invest in this lucrative opportunity.
4. **Continuous Education:** We will offer comprehensive education programs to golf professionals, course owners, and all industry employees to enhance their skills and knowledge, ensuring a top-notch experience for all golfers.
5. **Engaging Offers:** Special promotions will be introduced to entice both new and existing golfers, fostering a deeper connection with the game and their home golf facilities.
6. **Cultivating Relationships:** Through extensive research and understanding, we will engage with individuals showing even the slightest interest in golf, nurturing those relationships to create a new wave of passionate golfers.
7. **Powerful Marketing Support:** Owners and operators of golf courses will receive ongoing marketing support to spread the word and warmly welcome new players into the golfing community.

8. **Player Platform:** A platform (www.affordablegolfmemberships.com) will be provided where golfers of all levels can go to find affordable golfing options throughout the entire United States and eventually the world.
9. **Global Promotion:** With a relentless focus on promoting golf on a worldwide scale, we aim to generate a tsunami of loyal, committed, golf fans and enthusiasts across the globe.
10. **"Golf is Everyone's Game" Branding:** We will rebrand golf as "Golf is Everyone's Game," emphasizing its inclusivity and appeal to people of all backgrounds, making it a sport that everyone can enjoy.

Our growth initiative is designed to demonstrate to developers, investors, advertisers, donors, sponsors, industry leaders, owners, and operators that they can achieve both financial success and fulfill their social and civic responsibilities. We believe in a win-win philosophy, where doing the right thing for the community can go hand in hand with making a profit. It's not a zero-sum game, that is, an all-or-nothing approach; this initiative strikes a perfect balance.

We understand the importance of avoiding overbuilt markets with an excessive number of facilities, as that wouldn't benefit anyone—neither owners nor the game itself. We understand the valid concern about new players potentially impacting the pace of play. That's why our programs are thoughtfully designed to attract traffic to the facility during nonpeak times, days, and seasons. Our goal is not to devalue golf but to emphasize the affordable aspect of the sport, making it accessible to aspiring golfers from all socioeconomic backgrounds. Everyone should have the opportunity to take up the game, regardless of their financial status.

We fully respect the traditional dress code and code of conduct in golf, as it adds to the allure and prestige of the sport. Just as basketball players don't wear collared shirts on the court, we would never condone wearing tank tops on a golf course. Similarly, we believe players should support the facility by purchasing food and drinks on-site, embracing the complete experience provided by the course. We prioritize being mindful of the facility's culture, and that's why our team goes the extra mile to ensure that our offer is tailored to the specific needs of each owner and operator. In essence, our programs are 100 percent facility-friendly, ensuring a seamless integration that respects the uniqueness of each establishment.

The undeniable truth is that the game of golf is currently facing minuscule growth, and this "growth" is only relative to the pre-COVID years, which were the absolute worst for the industry. Personally, I am unwilling to sit back and passively witness the potential withering away of this beloved sport. We cannot afford to take a casual approach to this issue, as it will only lead to more unnecessary casualties. Simple changes that have been neglected for far too long can make a significant difference. Together, we have the power to revitalize the game, the industry, and careers in golf by transforming our attitudes, perceptions, and beliefs.

Affordability, diversity, and inclusivity have always been inherent to the game's DNA, though often overlooked. Our growth initiative is not as radical as some might think; rather, it brings to the forefront the reality of the game. Golf professionals are not hackers; they are consummate professionals in every aspect of their work, and I know most are frustrated with the progress, or lack thereof, that the industry has experienced. We all must rise to the occasion and champion the game with the dedication and expertise that true professionals possess.

Golf facilities serve as the lifeblood of the golf industry, providing the foundation for all its aspects to thrive. Associations, touring pros, tournaments, events, fundraisers, fans, and customers all depend on the existence and well-being of these facilities. Neglecting them would lead to a catastrophic impact on the entire industry, leaving many of us searching for new career paths.

Recognizing the significance of golf facilities is paramount. Saving existing ones and developing new ones are vital to sustaining the health of the industry. It is crucial not to underestimate the direct impact these facilities have on our lives and careers. Consumers only become players when they step onto a golf course, and players become fans after experiencing the game. Without customers, players, and fans, none of us would have a career in the golf industry.

Golfers and enthusiasts should understand the direct connection between facility availability and their enjoyment of the sport. The decline in the number of golf properties would limit options and lead to higher costs to enjoy a round. The frustrations of limited access could even discourage people from playing the game they love, resulting in further closures and perpetuating a negative cycle that could erode the essence of "golf."

While there will always be facilities for those who can afford big ticket items, we must ask ourselves if we belong to that top 4 percent who will be able to afford to play golf no matter how much it costs. We all share a collective responsibility to preserve the accessibility and affordability of golf for the broader population. Ensuring the health and vitality of golf facilities is essential not only for the industry but also for the enjoyment and growth of the sport we cherish.

LIV Golf's philosophy of emphasizing the team over individual players holds great wisdom. Golf needs stability and should not rely on calamities or the next Tiger Woods to save it. It's our collective responsibility to save and grow the game. We are all part of the same team, including the PGA, LIV Golf, touring pros, owners, operators, manufacturers, retailers, golfers, advertisers, donors, sponsors, and enthusiasts. We must unite with a single goal: Save and Grow the Game!

Don't Delay
Show your Support Today!

www.saveandgrowthegame.com

In closing, I would like to leave you with two quotes:

"The only difference between ordinary and extraordinary is extra."

—Jimmy Johnson

"With just a little effort, anyone can go from nowhere to now there."

—Chuck Thompson

A quick recap of the primary golfer acquisition campaign:

- MMC®'s program is not DISCOUNTING!"
- The program does not GIVE GOLF AWAY!
- MMC® can tailor the campaign from cost to content of the offer specifically to the facility's needs and wants.
- These new players do not SLOW DOWN THE PACE OF PLAY, because they are playing during the times and seasons when the core and avid golfers don't play.
- "OVERCROWDING" is highly unlikely when a course is operating at a mere 20%, 30%, 40%, or even 50% of capacity; which is where most facilities operate.
- MMC®'s golfer acquisition campaign is designed exclusively for CASUAL and NON-GOLFERS. These are new customers, not recycled golfers from other facilities.
- Casual and non-golfers spend, on average, far more per round than core and avid golfers. This is not hyperbole; this is a fact!
- There is absolutely no risk.

It's time to pay it forward and pass on the game and the unforgettable experiences to the upcoming generations of golfers. Let's ensure that we leave the game in a much better state than when we received it. I urge you to wholeheartedly support this cause, as your contribution will reflect your deep affection for the sport and the joy it has brought you. Every contribution, regardless of its size, holds immense value and is genuinely appreciated.

Together, let's work diligently to infuse new energy into the cherished game of golf and secure a prosperous future for it. Your support can create a meaningful impact, so I invite you to join us in this shared endeavor to make a real difference in the world of golf.

Show your support now!

Go To: www.saveandgrowthegame.com

Made in the USA
Middletown, DE
09 April 2024

52745394R00166